INSIDERS' GUIDE® TO

BATON ROUGE

HELP US KEEP THIS GUIDE UP-TO-DATE

We would love to hear from you concerning your experiences with this guide and how you feel it could be improved and kept up-to-date. Please send your comments and suggestions to:

editorial@GlobePequot.com

Thanks for your input, and happy travels!

INSIDERS' GUIDE® TO

BATON ROUGE

CYNTHIA V. CAMPBELL

INSIDERS' GUIDE

GUILFORD, CONNECTICUT
AN IMPRINT OF GLOBE PEQUOT PRESS

All the information in this guidebook is subject to change. We recommend that you call ahead to obtain current information before traveling.

INSIDERS' GUIDE ®

Assistant Acquisitions Editor: Kevin Sirois
Project Editor: Ellen Urban
Layout artist: Kevin Mak
Text design: Sheryl Kober
Maps by XNR Productions Inc. © Morris Book Publishing, LLC

ISBN: 978-0-7627-5671-1

Printed in the United States of America
10 9 8 7 6 5 4 3 2 1

CONTENTS

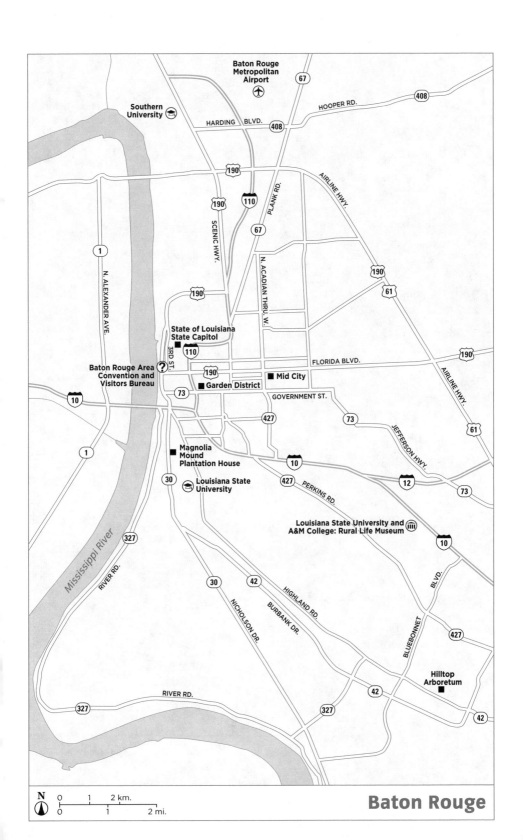

Baton Rouge

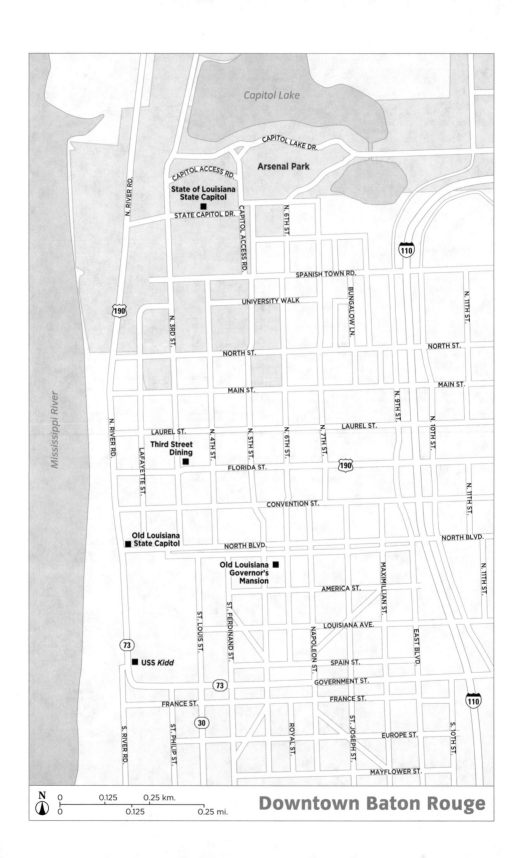

Capitol Lake

CAPITOL LAKE DR.

Arsenal Park

CAPITOL ACCESS RD.

State of Louisiana
State Capitol ■

N. RIVER RD.

STATE CAPITOL DR.

CAPITOL ACCESS RD.

N. 6TH ST.

110

SPANISH TOWN RD.

190

UNIVERSITY WALK

BUNGALOW LN.

N. 11TH ST.

NORTH ST.

N. 3RD ST.

NORTH ST.

MAIN ST.

MAIN ST.

N. 9TH ST.

N. 10TH ST.

LAUREL ST.

LAUREL ST.

Third Street
Dining ■

N. 4TH ST.

N. 5TH ST.

N. 6TH ST.

N. 7TH ST.

Mississippi River

N. RIVER RD.

LAFAYETTE ST.

FLORIDA ST.

190

N. 11TH ST.

CONVENTION ST.

Old Louisiana
■ State Capitol

NORTH BLVD.

NORTH BLVD.

N. 11TH ST.

Old Louisiana
Governor's ■
Mansion

MAXIMILLIAN ST.

AMERICA ST.

73

ST. LOUIS ST.

ST. FERDINAND ST.

LOUISIANA AVE.

NAPOLEON ST.

EAST BLVD.

■ USS Kidd

SPAIN ST.

GOVERNMENT ST.

73

FRANCE ST.

FRANCE ST.

110

FRANCE ST.

S. RIVER RD.

ST. PHILIP ST.

30

ROYAL ST.

ST. JOSEPH ST.

EUROPE ST.

S. 10TH ST.

MAYFLOWER ST.

N

0   0.125   0.25 km.

0   0.125   0.25 mi.

Downtown Baton Rouge

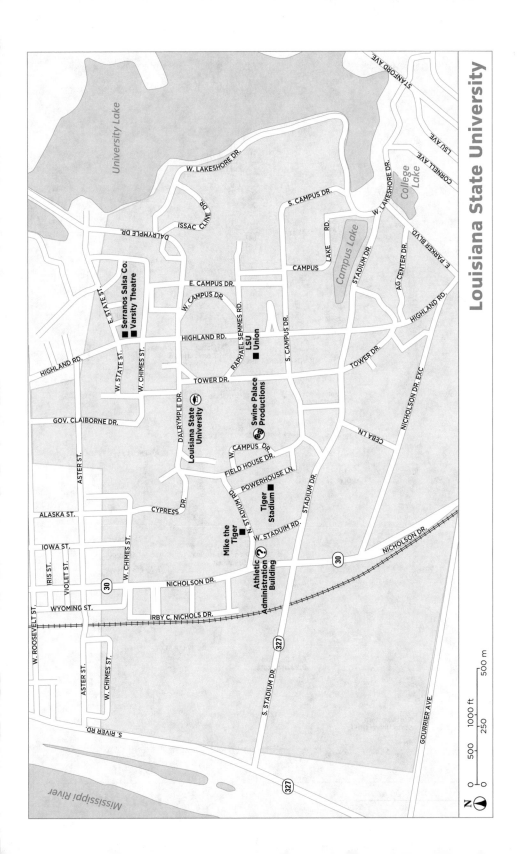

Louisiana State University

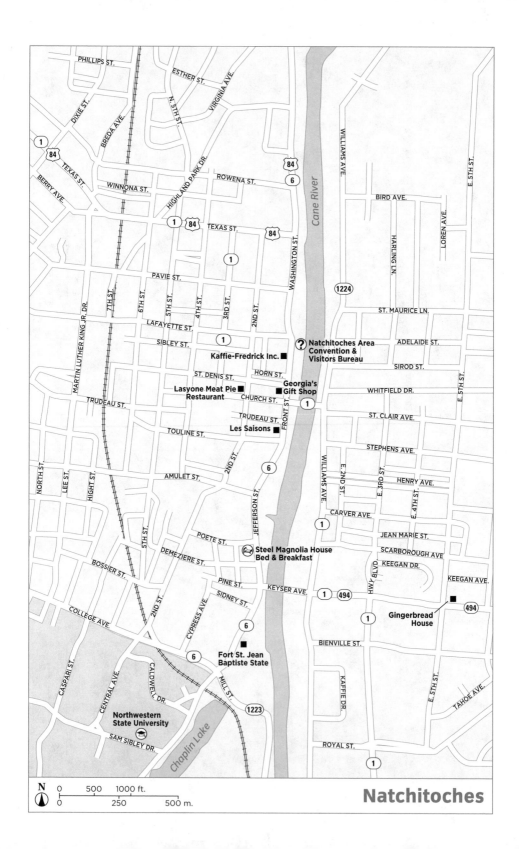

Natchitoches

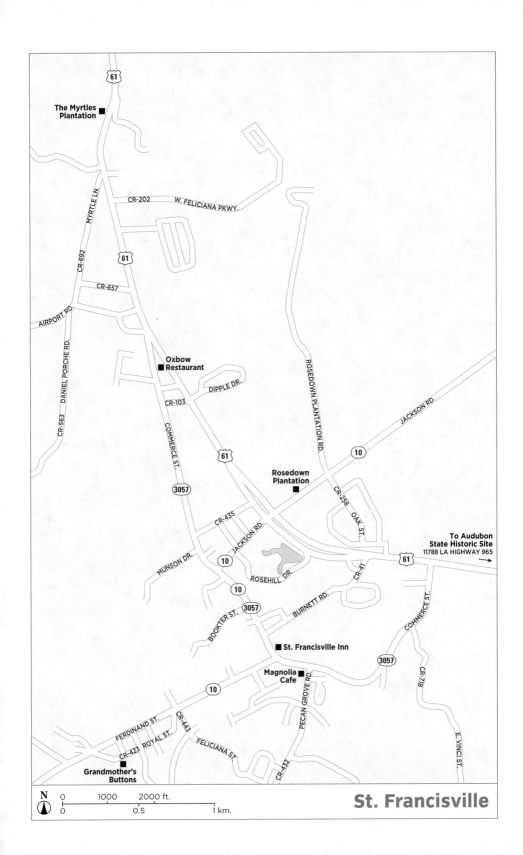

The Myrtles Plantation ■

61

CR-202 — W. FELICIANA PKWY.

MYRTLE LN.

CR-692

61

CR-657

AIRPORT RD.

DANIEL PORCHE RD.

CR-563

Oxbow Restaurant ■

DIPPLE DR.

CR-103

COMMERCE ST.

3057

61

CR-435

ROSEDOWN PLANTATION RD.

JACKSON RD.

10

Rosedown Plantation ■

CR-258

OAK ST.

To Audubon State Historic Site
11788 LA HIGHWAY 965
→

61

MUNSON DR.

JACKSON RD.

10

ROSEHILL DR.

CR-47

10

BOOKTER ST.

3057

BURNETT RD.

COMMERCE ST.

■ **St. Francisville Inn**

3057

CR-718

10

Magnolia Cafe ■

PECAN GROVE RD.

FERDINAND ST.

CR-443

ROYAL ST.

FELICIANA ST.

CR-432

E. VINCI ST.

CR-423

Grandmother's Buttons ■

N

0   1000   2000 ft.
0   0.5   1 km.

St. Francisville

ABOUT THE AUTHOR

Cynthia V. Campbell is an editor and writer with more than 30 years experience with the *Advocate* in Baton Rouge, Louisiana. She was founder and editor of the newspaper's travel pages. She planned content and wrote stories on every region of Louisiana as well as stories on other U.S. states and foreign countries. She created the Louisiana Travels column, covering all aspects of the Pelican State from lush swamps to sophisticated jazz spots. An avid cook, she also wrote restaurant reviews. Cynthia graduated with a journalism degree from the University of Texas at Austin. Prior to moving to Baton Rouge, she was the home and garden editor for the *San Antonio Express-News*. In 2008, she received the Baton Rouge Women in Media Excellence in Print Editorial award. Cynthia is a member of the Society of American Travel Writers, Baton Rouge Women in Media, Louisiana Youth Orchestra board of directors, and Baton Rouge Art League. With her husband, Larry B. Campbell, Louisiana State University music professor emeritus, she continues to travel, seeking out interesting places, good food, and warm-hearted people.

ACKNOWLEDGMENTS

Baton Rouge steals your heart. A historic city with towering trees and flowers year-round, it welcomes people with genuine hospitality. To write about the city and its people, I sought the advice of natives whose families have lived in the area for generations as well as newcomers still learning about traditions that reflect the dynamic mix of many cultures. I also talked with travelers whose curiosity helped me look at the city with a fresh perspective.

First, I must thank Mayor Melvin L. "Kip" Holden for his support and his enthusiasm about Baton Rouge and its future. I could not have attempted to write this book without guidance from Paul J. Arrigo, president and CEO of the Baton Rouge Convention and Visitors Bureau, and especially Theresa Overby, the bureau's communications director, for her assistance with information on Baton Rouge's many attractions. Jerry Stovall, president and CEO of the Baton Rouge Sports Foundation, provided a comprehensive perspective on collegiate sports and sports venues available to Baton Rouge residents and visitors.

For background and historical research, I owe a great deal to Judith D. Smith, head of the Louisiana Collection at the Louisiana State Library, who headed me in the right direction. John Sykes, education manager at Louisiana State Museum at Baton Rouge, went out of his way to provide a historical perspective on Spanish Town and old South Baton Rouge. Librarians at the Baton Rouge Public Library got on their hands and knees in the Louisiana section to help me find outstanding material on the region.

Visiting historic sites, attractions, restaurants, and parks, I talked to chefs, hoteliers, shopkeepers, and park directors about their establishments. I also depended on the people who make tourism in Baton Rouge and Louisiana work so well. Of particular assistance were Debra Credeur, Kristian Sonnier, Grace Wilson, Doobie Judice, Iris Harper, Katie Harrington, and Tarah Holland. For updates on some of my favorite out-of-state weekend trips, I thank Lindsey Brown of Houston, Kim Chapman of Gulf Shores/Orange Beach, Mississippi, and Janice Jones of Gulfport/Biloxi.

To my friends and family goes appreciation for putting up with my long hours, my many questions, and my passion for the beauty and hospitality of Baton Rouge and Louisiana. Special thanks goes to longtime friend Kathy B. Coon, who helped research education and child care in Baton Rouge, and to Cheramie Sonnier and Tommy Simmons for their support and tips on Louisiana cuisine.

Kudos go to Amy Lyons, Kevin Sirois, and Ellen Urban of Globe Pequot Press for their excellent suggestions and for keeping me on track.

Most of all I thank my husband, Larry B. Campbell, musician and educator, who spent a lot of time driving me to attractions, checking facts and figures, and putting up with my late night writing sessions.

PREFACE

Welcome to Baton Rouge, site of Louisiana's state capitol and political center. Whether you've chosen the city as a destination for a holiday or as a new home, you'll find the town a surprise. Wrapped in layers of lush green trees, the town unfolds its south Louisiana heritage as you walk in the footsteps of heroes and scoundrels, dine in quaint neighborhoods, take in exciting festivals, scream out at sporting events, or contemplate a sunset along the Mississippi River levee.

While the city has a French name, thanks to early explorers, the greater Baton Rouge area enjoys a rich multicultural mix. You won't find people speaking French here. But you will hear a smattering of French, Spanish, or African patois when walking through a mall or enjoying a meal in a local restaurant.

Hugging the east bank of the Mississippi River, the city is one of America's great river towns, constantly attracting new visitors and residents of all nationalities. The first European settlers left a legacy of antebellum homes and a sense of graciousness. New arrivals are constantly bringing fresh ideas and vibrancy. Louisiana natives often put down roots after attending major universities here. Others, from as far away as Norway or India, come for a short visit and decide to relocate here.

Baton Rouge is Louisiana's center for higher education, with Louisiana State University and Southern University attracting more than 40,000 students. The area's petrochemical industries and the Port of Baton Rouge put the city in an excellent position to compete in global markets. Baton Rouge's strong economy creates an energy that can be felt as you tour the city.

Exploring all aspects of the city, I've learned to cherish its beauty and diversity. Writing this guide has given me the chance to take a closer look at the place I call home. Along with my family and friends, I've revisited my favorite attractions and sought out exciting new places to explore.

As you follow this guide, you will discover Baton Rouge has many things to offer. You'll find world-class restaurants, music venues that set you humming, memorable museums, and drama-laden historic sites. Many will become special places you will want to see over and over again.

The lifeblood of Baton Rouge is the Mississippi River, which is about a mile across from bank to bank. Where a young steamboat pilot named Samuel Clemens glided past en route to New Orleans, massive barges and ocean-going vessels still stop at the Port of Baton Rouge in West Baton Rouge Parish. This is not a place to dip your toes in the muddy Mississippi. Instead the scenic view from the landscaped walk on the east bank levee is awe-inspiring.

Early in the morning breathe in the aroma of coffee beans roasting at the Community Coffee facility on the river's west side. At dusk, listen to jazz musicians perform at Lafayette Park on the east side. Stop for a bowl of gumbo or a catfish po'boy at a Third Street eatery.

Just a few blocks from the river, the pace picks up when you visit the towering State Capitol and nearby state office buildings. Legislators, lobbyists, powerbrokers, and state employees dominate the scene when the legislature is in session. A bit further away, the campuses of Louisiana State University and Southern University are like mini towns filled with energetic students pursing 21st-century dreams.

Short drives will take you to Magnolia Mound and the LSU Rural Life Museum, where you step back several centuries and learn the reality of life experienced by Louisiana residents in the early 1800s. Then join locals at a sports bar near one of the universities or take in a gospel concert.

HOW TO USE THIS BOOK

Wake up on a sunny morning listening to cardinals and mockingbirds beckoning you to get outdoors and stretch your legs. Spend a few days following the trails of explorers, trappers, soldiers, and pirates who forged trails through dense woods and bayous filled with alligators. Extend your late-night spree jammed knee-to-knee with friends over steaming cups of aromatic cafe au lait and hot beignets drenched in sweet powdered sugar. This book is planned to help you find the "real" Baton Rouge.

The book is for vacationers and conventioneers—people looking for an exceptional dining experience, a great night's sleep, a nifty shop, and exciting entertainment in the heart of historic Louisiana. It's also designed for those who have recently made Baton Rouge their home and for longtime residents who want to rediscover their city and show it off to family and friends. Keep it handy as a reference for a spur-of-the-moment outing. It is not meant as an all-encompassing guide, but rather one that takes you to the places that make Baton Rouge such a friendly and beautiful place to live.

You'll find the guide divided by types of activities and interests. Driving from nearby towns or on a cross-country excursion? Flying in from a national or international hub? Then check out the Getting Here, Getting Around chapter for information on rental cars, shuttles, and taxis. Discover how the Mississippi River defines the shape of the city and learn the importance of the I-10 bridge connecting East Baton Rouge Parish with West Baton Rouge Parish. You'll learn how I-10 and I-12 traverse through the center of the city. The highways and major streets leading from downtown outward define how far a restaurant is from your hotel or how many attractions you can see in a day.

When planning to book a hotel room, the Accommodations chapter covers all locales and all price ranges. If you are visiting for business or a political rally, you may want to stay downtown near the State Capitol. If you want to schedule your stay during a special event or festival, then check out the Annual Events and Festivals chapter. Sports fans often book rooms a year in advance for football and other major athletic events at the universities. The city also welcomes families with children participating in regional and national tournaments, including soccer, tennis, baseball, basketball, and track. A number of local hotels are accommodating and very friendly to sports-loving families.

The Restaurants chapter focuses on extremely popular dining spots operated by famed chefs as well as quaint eateries known for outstanding regional specialties. Eating out is a favorite pastime of south Louisiana residents. People think nothing of driving across town to enjoy their favorite bowl of gumbo. Some even plan an entire day's trip to a nearby town just to dine on exquisitely prepared crawfish étouffée or trout almondine.

Once you're settled, the guide will lead you to attractions, such as the dramatic Louisiana State Capitol, the tallest in the nation at 34 stories and 450 feet high. Children love exploring or even spending a night on the USS *Kidd*. The restored World War II Fletcher-class destroyer rests in its special cradle in the Mississippi River. The adjoining museum includes the largest model ship collection in the South and a fascinating exhibit of the USS *Constitution* gun deck. Gardeners will love walking through the LSU Hilltop Arboretum where they can view hundreds of Louisiana native trees and shrubs. In the center of the city, just off I-10, stop by the LSU Rural Life Museum to learn what daily life was like for the majority of families living in the rural South in the years before the mid-1940s.

This guide also will help you find many of America's earliest plantation homes, which have survived outbreaks of yellow fever, floods, hurricanes, and war. Those built in the late 1700s tell the story of early colonists and their lifestyle. The spectacular Greek Revival mansions constructed in the era prior to the Civil War exemplify the lavish display of wealth expected of their owners. The historic homes, both upriver and downriver from Baton Rouge, are the reason the region is known as Plantation Country.

The Kidstuff chapter spotlights cool stuff that will entertain the entire family. The Parks and Recreation chapter details hiking and biking trails, golf, and fishing in the Baton Rouge area. Nightlife explores the latest craze in wine bars, popular college hangouts, and jazz and blues clubs.

In the Culture and the Arts chapter, you'll discover that the city has a thriving creative community. World-renowned professors in art, design, theater, and music at Louisiana State University and Southern University participate and encourage citywide programs. The well-organized Baton Rouge Arts Council spurs and helps find funding for innovative projects that have wide appeal. Regional theater companies offer live drama and musicals year-round. The Baton Rouge Symphony Orchestra and the Baton Rouge Sinfonietta perform both classical and contemporary works and showcase famed artists such as Yo-Yo Ma and Chris Botti. Dance companies explore innovative modern dance as well as classical ballet. The Louisiana Arts and Science Museum and Planetarium showcases major exhibits, and local art galleries are especially known for their support of southern and regional artists. In recent years Baton Rouge has developed as a center for a budding film industry.

As you explore Baton Rouge, you will find the city's character is linked to Louisiana's colorful past. The book includes a brief history, from colonial rule by France, Britain, and Spain through the Civil War and the Huey Long era to the present. You'll learn about the changes from an 1800s plantation economy to the current move to build for the future.

Sprinkled through the guide are "Close-up" stories aimed at providing insight into things that set Baton Rouge apart. Insiders' tips (indicated by **i**) discuss things that are distinctly different.

No guide can provide every detail of a city. Use your own good judgment in making plans and exploring new places. Keep in mind your limits, and make plans accordingly. Be aware of conditions around you. Be prepared to stay flexible and make changes on a moment's notice. For example Baton Rouge is often hot and sultry in summer. Afternoon thunderstorms are not unusual. If you run into a late downpour, spend time lingering in a coffee shop, shopping indoors, or browsing a cool, air-conditioned museum.

Your visit to south Louisiana may take you down a path you didn't plan. For example, if your downtown visit coincides with Baton Rouge's carnival season, you may find an attraction closed or traffic moving at a snail's pace. Join the fun. You may find yourself in a crowd of people wearing strange hats and T-shirts covered with pink flamingos (the symbol of Spanish Town Mardi Gras). Chat with a local resident, and jump for beads being tossed from floats. You may be standing next to a local TV celebrity, a riverboat pilot, or a college basketball star. You will become part of what makes Baton Rouge special.

As you travel through Baton Rouge, keep in mind that the city is growing. Downtown is undergoing many changes, including the addition of an entertainment district. Streets are being reconfigured to meet traffic demands. New subdivisions are expanding the boundaries. Living in Baton Rouge affords residents many happy travel adventures. Often visitors comment about the city's beauty and its friendly people. While we cannot guarantee that every visitor will enjoy the same things, the following pages will put you on the right path.

Moving to Baton Rouge or already live here? Be sure to check out the blue-tabbed pages at the back of the book, where you will find the **Living Here** appendix that offers sections on relocation, real estate, health care, and media.

AREA OVERVIEW

The Mississippi River defines the topography of Baton Rouge (Red Stick). Along with bluffs and levees, the city is situated on the east side of the river. The high land with meadows and woods protected Native Americans and early Europeans from floods. Today, where plantations once flourished, there's a bustling city. Ancient oak trees draped with Spanish moss, azaleas, magnolias, and other semitropical plants create a lush parklike setting in neighborhoods throughout the region. Well-planned community parks tucked in distinctive subdivisions offer a variety of recreation and special-interest programs. Starting from downtown on the Mississippi, the city spreads out like a giant fan. Asked what makes Baton Rouge so appealing, Mayor-President Melvin L. "Kip" Holden said, "The people and their spirit. We never meet a stranger, and we have a knack for putting things together that highlight what we are all about."

Towering above the downtown skyline is the State Capitol, which was completed in 1932. The Art Deco structure and state governmental buildings anchor the north side of town, while within a short walking distance, city government structures guard the south side. Two historic neighborhoods, Spanish Town and Beauregard Town, feature a variety of architectural styles, ranging from antebellum to bungalow. Preservation groups support efforts to retain the character of these areas, where some residents can easily walk to work.

Baton Rouge has a parishwide system of government. In 1949 the city adopted a consolidated city-parish government, one of the first in the United States. Administered by a mayor-president and a city council, the town has been able to adapt well to economic and technological changes.

Baton Rouge's blend of diverse people adds spice to the city's quality of life. The influence of European, African, and Asian cultures may be found in the food, music, art, architecture, and growing businesses. Because of Hurricane Katrina in 2005, the city's population swelled by thousands overnight. Population estimates used here are based on the most recent U.S. census, which was in 2000. African Americans make up about 50 percent of the population and whites about 46 percent. The area's population also is made up of Native Americans, Asians, Native Hawaiians and other Pacific Islanders, and Hispanics or Latinos.

The link between the African-American community and Baton Rouge dates from the early 1700s when enslaved Africans were brought to southeast Louisiana by early planters. By the early 1800s many of their descendants were freed. Soon the population began to intermarry with Native Americans, Spanish, and French. The developing Creole population added to the rich cultural gumbo that makes up Louisiana. Today the U.S. Census Bureau estimates East Baton Rouge Parish's population at 428,360. The city population is estimated at 229,553. The metro Baton Rouge region estimates a total of 700,000 to 800,000 people living in East Baton Rouge, West Baton Rouge, Ascension, Livingston, Iberville, East Feliciana, West Feliciana, Pointe Coupee, and St. Helena parishes.

For the most part Baton Rouge was relatively immune to the economic recession of 2009. Much of that was the result of hurricanes Katrina and Ike in 2005. The storms turned Baton Rouge into a boomtown overnight when thousands of evacuees found shelter in the city. Many chose to stay and work in the area. Another hurricane, Gustav, hit the town September 1, 2008, causing enormous damage, but residents were in the streets the next day with chain saws and hammers clearing out debris. Rebuilding efforts combined with the flood of new residents provided the city-parish government surplus revenues, mostly from sales taxes. In early 2009 sales tax revenues were up by 5.3 percent. The city-parish's $690 million Green Light plan is designed to improve traffic flow on key surface roads. New neighborhoods provide a welcome retreat from bustling city streets. The new city economic and planning initiatives offer hope for a bright future.

With the Mississippi River serving as a major transportation link to the world, much of the area's economy has revolved around the petrochemical plants. Dow Chemical on the west side of the river near Plaquemine is the largest petrochemical facility in Louisiana. ExxonMobil, one of the world's largest refineries, just north of the State Capitol, is one of the area's major employers. Fortune 500 member the Shaw Group, Inc.; Albemarle, a Fortune 1000 member; and Turner Industries are among the leading industries.

The Port of Baton Rouge in Port Allen on the west side of the Mississippi ranks among the country's top 10 ports in tonnage. Adjacent to I-10, the port is situated at the convergence of the Mississippi River and the U.S. Gulf Intracoastal Waterway. The port is the head of deepwater navigation on the Mississippi and is capable of handling a wide range of products from agribusiness to general cargo. Oceangoing commercial vessels and huge barges can easily be viewed by walking along the downtown levee.

Social life is never dull in Red Stick. Numerous social and civic organizations sponsor major charitable events drawing large crowds. These benefit museums, performing arts groups, medical facilities, and many others. Among the many groups recognized for their efforts are the Rotary, Lions, Kiwanis, Masons, 100 Black Men, Fortune 35, Junior League, Symphony League, Baton Rouge Art League, The Links, and Quota Club. Other gatherings are strictly for fun, especially Mardi Gras balls and parades, as well as debutante pre-

sentations. On an informal scale, neighborhood block parties often spring up spontaneously, bringing people together on a moment's notice.

Baton Rouge's push to join the world as a first-class city is seldom outdone by its desire to have a good time. When things get tough, people in Baton Rouge work hard to recover. When work is done, residents follow the Cajun expression—"Laissez les bon temps roulez" (let the good times roll). Visitors are encouraged to join in the fun, especially for Mardi Gras, St. Patrick's Day, Christmas, and Fourth of July. Festivals incorporate food, dancing, music, and neighborly goodwill.

If you want to dance to a Cajun band, hear a gospel choir in an African-American church, walk beneath an alley of ancient oaks, or just read a really good book in a comfy lounge chair, someone will help you find the right spot.

DOWNTOWN

Baton Rouge downtown is the city's historical and political core. Here's where the town first formed with Florida Street starting at the river and running east. Walk along Third Street and view a variety of commercial architectural styles—structures housing retail, office, and residential sites. Pop into the Convention and Visitors Bureau office to pick up brochures and maps. During the day it's the place to see and be seen for those working in the area. Lunch spots are filled with legislators, lawyers, and office clerks ordering po'boy sandwiches or light salads. Stretch those tired muscles on state-of-the-art equipment at the gym in the Charles W. Lamar YMCA gym. At night newly created wine pubs, cafes, and music venues attract young professionals. Two nearby historic districts, Spanish Town and Beauregard Town, will give you a glimpse of bohemian residents in small cottages, while lawyers and clients stay busy in well-preserved homes turned into offices.

EASTWARD BOUND

Stretching eastward along the Florida Boulevard/Government Street corridors are some of the city's cherished suburbs, including the Garden District, the city's first subdivision staked out in 1911, and Old Goodwood, a haven for some of the city's oldest families. Prominent schools here include Baton Rouge High Magnet School and Sacred Heart Academy. Continuing eastward, businesses, churches, and grocery stores serve neighborhoods such as Walnut Hill, Westdale, and Goodwood. Webb Golf Course and Independence Park, featuring a city auditorium and garden center, are part of the mix. A major interchange at Florida and Airline Highway (U.S. 61) serves as a pivotal landmark. Here you'll find the Cortana Mall Complex. Beyond that point are additional major suburbs—Broadmoor, Sherwood Forest, and numerous other subdivisions.

LSU ENVIRONS

The Louisiana State University main campus, situated between the Mississippi River and University Lake, forms a hub for busy shopping areas and neighborhoods, including Lake Crest, Zee Zee Gardens, University Gardens, Southdowns, University Hills, Stanford Place, and Plantation Trace. Just north of the campus, the area is enjoying a revival with newly built apartment complexes and condos. Popular eateries, including Louie's, Chimes, and Serrano's, attract students, professors, alumni, and visitors. Retail stores here cater to academic needs. University Lake is a great green space. It's a perfect spot for walking, jogging, and biking. You're likely to see a fellow with a fishing rod and bucket at one bend and a mom with kids feeding visiting ducks at another spot. Nearby along Perkins Road, shopping areas include grocery stores, popular restaurants, nightspots, convenience stores, and service stations. Numerous apartment complexes and additional shopping/dining areas are situated south of the campus along Nicholson (La. 30) and Burbank Drive. Just off Highland Road, drive through College Town, with streets named after U.S. colleges, and University Acres to see beautifully landscaped homes built by university faculty and staff members in the 1920s and '30s.

MID CITY

Tucked between downtown and the growing eastern subdivisions, Mid City was carved out of forested oak trees. The area is bounded by I-110 on the west, College Drive and North Foster on the east, Choctaw to the north, and I-10 on the south. Socially and economically diverse, Mid City is enjoying a renaissance with mom-and-pop retail businesses and large commercial buildings on Florida Boulevard. From turn-of-the-20th-century row houses in Eden Park to elegant homes in the Garden District, the area is reminiscent of Baton Rouge in the 1930s and '40s. Locals shop here for antiques, folk and pop art, and whimsical accessories. Visit the Baton Rouge National Cemetery, 220 North 19th St. Officially established in 1867, it's one of the city's important landmarks. Stop by Baton Rouge Community College, 201 Community College Dr., to see one of the fastest growing community colleges in the nation.

NORTH BATON ROUGE

Just north of the Louisiana State Capitol, scenic Capitol Lake borders the Louisiana Governor's Mansion and the Old Arsenal museum. It serves as a natural barrier between the city and the major industrial area dominated by the Exxon Chemical Industrial Complex. A number of middle class neighborhoods in the north section of the city were established in the 1920s and early 1930s, just after Standard Oil established its refinery in Baton Rouge. Just above Exxon is Southern University, one of America's most distinguished black universities. Also in this area is the Baton Rouge Metropolitan Airport. Situated on Thomas Road is Clark Park Golf Course and BREC's Baton Rouge Zoo, a fully accredited zoo that both entertains and participates in renowned animal conservation projects. Follow La. 19 and Plank Rd. further north to visit the growing towns of Baker, Zachary, and Central.

Vital Statistics

Governor: Bobby Jindal

Mayor-president: Melvin L. "Kip" Holden

Population (estimate): Parish: 428,360; city: 229,553; greater metro: 774,000

Area (square miles): 455

Average temperatures (degrees Fahrenheit): Average summer: 81.3; average winter: 52.5

Normal annual rainfall: 55 inches

City founded: Discovered and named by French-Canadian explorers in 1699.

Major universities and colleges: Louisiana State University, Southern University, Baton Rouge Community College, Our Lady of the Lake College.

Major employers: Turner Industries Group, Louisiana State University, ExxonMobil Corporation, The Shaw Group Inc., Our Lady of the Lake Regional Medical Center, Baton Rouge General Medical Center, Dow Chemical Company, Ochsner Clinic Foundation, Woman's Hospital, Southern University and A&M College, H&E Equipment Services, BASF, Cajun Constructors Inc., Blue Cross and Blue Shield of Louisiana, ISC Group LLC, Aegis Lending Corporation, Ecolab Inc., James Construction Group LLC, Hollywood Casino Baton Rouge, Convergys Corporation, Georgia-Pacific, Syngenta Crop Protection Inc., Lamar Advertising Company, and Rubicon.

Native celebrities: Singer/songwriter Governor Jimmie Davis, "You Are My Sunshine"; actresses Donna Douglas and Lynn Whitfield; singers Percy Sledge and Johnny Rivers; band Better than Ezra; bluesmen Buddy Guy and Tabby Thomas; director Steven Soderberg; Scott Innis, the voice of Scooby Doo; athletes Billy Cannon, Doug Williams, Pistol Pete Maravich, Bob Petit, and Shaquille O'Neal.

Major airport: Baton Rouge Metropolitan Airport.

Major interstates: I-10, I-12, and Extension 110 provide access into and across the city.

Public transportation: Capital Area Transportation (CATS) serves the Baton Rouge area. Call (225) 389-8282

Driving laws: Right turn on red permitted. Headlights must be on when wipers are in constant use. Seat belts must be worn in both front and rear seats. Left lane in multilane highways is for passing only. Speed limit on highways is 70 mph on interstates. Speed limit varies in town as posted.

Alcohol laws: Legal drinking age is 21; blood alcohol content of .08 percent or higher is considered operating under the influence in Louisiana.

Sales tax: 9 percent.

Resources and Visitors Centers
Baton Rouge Convention and Visitors Bureau
359 Third St.
Baton Rouge, 70801
(225) 383-1825
(800) LA ROUGE (527-6843)
www.visitbatonrouge.com

State Capitol Welcome Center
State Capitol Drive at Third Street
P.O. Box 94291
Baton Rouge, LA 70804-9291
(225) 342-7317
statecapitolwc@crt.state.la.us
Open 8 a.m. to 4:30 p.m.

Capitol Park Welcome Center
702 River Rd.
Baton Rouge
(225) 219-1200
capitolpark@crt.state.la.us
Open 8 a.m. to 4:30 p.m.

SOUTH BY SOUTHEAST

Because the Mississippi River curves snakelike through the Baton Rouge area, major highways heading south of town actually run south by southeast. One of the oldest neighborhoods, Old South Baton Rouge, which started developing in the 1890s, became predominantly African American in the 1920s and '30s. Community leaders were descendants of people who worked the trades, including carpentry, cabinet making, and barbering, as well as doctors, nurses, lawyers, and teachers. Old McKinley High School located here had the first African-American graduates from a Louisiana state–approved high school in 1916. Among notable McKinley graduates are educator and coach Eddie Robinson, the "most winningest coach" in football history; opera singer and Grammy winner Donnie Ray Albert; and Randy Jackson, entertainer and judge on television's *American Idol*. Traveling further southeast past LSU, a number of roadways, including I-10 and I-12, Highland Road, Jefferson Highway, and Coursey Boulevard, serve as busy corridors to middle class and upscale subdivisions, parks, and commercial areas. Just off I-10 at Essen Lane, you'll find the LSU Rural Life Museum, focusing on life in the rural South. Shop or dine at the Mall of Louisiana, Towne Center, or along the Siegen corridor. Test your skills at Santa Maria Golf Club. In warm months take the family to Blue Bayou Water Park/Dixie Landing.

REGIONAL SUBURBS

The Greater Baton Rouge region includes several incorporated towns. Located on the edges of rural areas, they offer families more opportunities for less expensive housing, lower city taxes, and smaller school districts. They have small-town-America appeal. Social gatherings often center around church, school, and civic group activities. Many homeowners are descended from Louisiana's earliest settlers and share a deep sense of pride in their towns. As the area's population grows, these communities are transforming from country towns to popular suburbs.

Baker/Zachary/Central

Baker, situated north of Baton Rouge on La. 19, was established in 1812 and named for plantation owner Josephus Baker. Attractions include the BREC's Baton Rouge Zoo, Jefferson Park, Baker Park, Harding Park, Heritage Museum, and Baker Regional Shopping Center. Zachary, also on La. 19, was named for a farmer who owned land that became the present city in 1889. The Zachary school district became independent from the East Baton Rouge Parish school district in 2004. Notable residents include Jack Breaux, the first Republican mayor since Reconstruction; Donna Douglas, the actress famous for playing Elly May Clampett on *The Beverly Hillbillies* situation comedy in the 1960s; Roderick Mullen, NFL cornerback; and Doug Williams, former NFL quarterback for the Washington Redskins and MVP of Super Bowl XXII. Incorporated in 2005, Central is situated east of Baker and Zachary. A farming community in the 1800s, it became the site of the Greenwell Springs Resort and Spa in 1853. Following the Civil War, people dismantled the hotel and cabins to use wood to rebuild their destroyed homes. Life changed with the construction of Standard Oil in 1909. Farmers became plant workers, and Central became an extension of Baton Rouge. In 2005, Governor Kathleen Blanco approved the town's incorporation. In 2006, the Central Community School District was created and is considered one of the fastest growing school systems in Louisiana. Information is available for Baker at www.cityof bakerla.us, (225) 778-0300; for Central at www .centralgov.com, (225) 262-5000; and for Zachary at www.cityofzachary.com, (225) 654-0287.

Denham Springs

Denham Springs, just east of Baton Rouge, is the largest town in Livingston Parish. The parish landscape varies from slash pine and hardwood forests in the northern part to cypress forests and marshes bordering Lake Maurepas and the Amite River in the southern end. Denham Springs, situated on the Amite, is at the intersections of U.S. 190, I-12, and La. 16. In 1827, William Denham settled here and discovered a number of mineral springs. The town is named after Denham, and at Spring Park, you can follow a walking path from one of the springs to the Amite River. The city is also located on the Illinois Central Gulf Railroad. Antique Village, on Range Avenue at the railroad, has fine antiques and collectibles from more than 100 dealers. There are restaurants and a coffee shop in the village and several more within walking distance. There's an additional variety of local

and chain restaurants in the area. With more than 600 waterway miles in the parish, fishing sites are plentiful. More than 67,712 acres are available to hunters on the Maurepas Swamp Wildlife Management area. Fishing, hunting, and boating are popular in the area, and the new Bass Pro Shop just off I-12 has become a major attraction. Denham Springs is part of the Livingston Parish School System, which draws young families to the area. Also in Livingston Parish is one of only two worldwide Laser Interferometer Gravitational Wave Observatory sites, a National Science Foundation research station devoted to the detection and study of gravitational waves from outer space. Popular festivals include Springfest and Octoberfest held in the Main Street antiques district. A Mardi Gras parade takes place two Saturdays prior to Ash Wednesday, and the Chamber of Commerce Christmas Parade tops off December activities. For more information, visit www .livingstoneparish.com.

Gonzales

Just south of Baton Rouge on I-10 and U.S. 61, Gonzales and Ascension Parish is booming. Handsome new residential districts and one of the top 10 public school systems in the state attract people seeking a short commute to Baton Rouge. Early European inhabitants were, for the most part, squatters of Spanish and French ancestry settling amid the Houma Indians. Homesteading was granted to settlers in the mid-1880s, and in 1886 the settlement elected "Big" Joseph Gonzales as sheriff. In 1887, Joseph's son, "Tee Joe," opened a general store and post office. Eventually the village became known as Gonzales. The town is famed as the Jambalaya Capital of the World. Held the last weekend in May, the jambalaya festival draws thousands with championship cooks dishing out plates of spicy jambalaya and round-the-clock bands entertaining crowds. Major attractions just off I-10 include the Tanger Outlet Center, a sprawling shopping destination, and Cabela's, world-famous outfitter of hunting, fishing, and outdoor gear. Several of the country's most stunning antebellum plantation homes on the Mississippi River, along with specialty shops and regional restaurants, keep people returning time and again. More information can be found at www.gonzalesla.com and www.ascensiontourism.com.

Port Allen/Plaquemine

Port Allen is opposite Baton Rouge in West Baton Rouge Parish. Once a hub for sugar planters, the small town is a convenient commute from downtown Baton Rouge. More than 20 new subdivisions have developed in the past few years. The area's first settlement, named St. Michael, was laid out in 1809 by a French doctor, Michael Mahier of Nantes. But it was lost to the river. Port Allen acquired its present name in 1878. The terminus of a railroad delivering goods and produce from the Grosse Tete community to the Mississippi River "port," the town was named after Henry Watkins Allen, a planter and the Civil War governor of Louisiana. Major attractions include the Port of Greater Baton Rouge, serving barges and oceangoing vessels with international import and export facilities for all types of cargo. Nearby the Port Allen Lock connects the Mississippi River to the Intracoastal Waterway, an east-west inland waterway shortcut connecting Florida and Texas. Other attractions include the West Baton Rouge Museum with a 1904 22-foot working sugar mill model and an important collection of early Louisiana houses and worker's cabins. The Port Allen Railroad Depot Museum captures the life of railroad workers in the 1940s, and Scott's Cemetery, dating from the 1850s, is a historical burial place of African Americans. Brian's is *the* place to shop for outstanding cast-iron garden furniture and sculptured pieces.

Plaquemine, another west bank river town, is a 15-minute drive from Baton Rouge. The town sits on tranquil Bayou Plaquemine. Just off La. 1 is Plaquemine Lock State Historic Site, location of a lock constructed between 1895 and 1905 that served as a vital waterway from the Mississippi River to the interior of Louisiana. It was designed by Colonel George W. Goethals who was later the chief engineer on the design and construction of the Panama Canal. The site is free and open daily. Visit the city's new waterfront park and drive through town to view historic buildings and homes dating from the 19th and early 20th centuries. For recreation, the Island Country Club on La. 77 is a par-72 golf course, and is one of only six courses named among the initial members of Louisiana's signature Audubon Golf Trail. The parish also offers access to the Atchafalaya Basin, where birds, fish, and other wildlife abound. Information can be found at www.plaquemine.org and www.ibervilleparish.com.

GETTING HERE, GETTING AROUND

Getting to Baton Rouge is relatively easy. Two major interstates, I-10 and I-12, run through the town. Other highways, including U.S. 190 and U.S 61, are major thoroughfares. The Baton Rouge Metropolitan Airport connects with major hubs, including Dallas, Houston, Atlanta, and Memphis. There is no rail passenger service to the city. However, Amtrak has service to Hammond, Louisiana, and New Orleans. Three railways provide commercial service to the greater Baton Rouge area, including Canadian National, Union Pacific Railroad, and Kansas City Southern Railway Company. Boating is not an option, since the Mississippi River here is 1 mile across and is extremely busy with major shipping. However, river cruise ships and historic vessels can make short stops at the city's downtown dock. While downtown is very walkable, you'll need a vehicle to reach the area's many attractions. Driving can be confusing because most downtown streets are one-way. Also many city streets follow ancient trails leading away from the river and bayous. In some cases, a street will stop at a bayou where there is no bridge; then it will pick up on the other side in a different subdivision. We recommend picking up a map at local and state welcome centers downtown and on the first floor of the Louisiana State Capitol.

MAJOR HIGHWAYS

Interstate 10: East-West

One of America's busiest highways, I-10, running from Florida to California, cuts through the center of Baton Rouge, serving as a major freeway for locals as well as for interstate traffic. The I-10 bridge crosses the Mississippi River, connecting East Baton Rouge with West Baton Rouge, the Port of Baton Rouge, and other nearby towns. During rush hours, traffic can slow to a snail's pace. If there's a stalled vehicle on or near the bridge, traffic can come to a halt for miles. Loop 110 travels north from downtown. Major I-110 exits include the Baton Rouge Metro Airport, Southern University, and U.S. 61 north. The I-110 extension also provides an alternate route to U.S. 190 that crosses the old Mississippi River Bridge north of town. Heading west, U.S. 190 still serves as a main east-west route through southern Louisiana.

When in Baton Rouge you'll hear people refer to the I-10 bridge crossing the Mississippi River as the "New Bridge." It is the younger of two bridges that cross the Mississippi at Baton Rouge. Its actual name is the Horace Wilkinson Bridge, and it is named for three generations of Horace Wilkinsons who served a total of 54 years in the Louisiana legislature. Upriver, you'll find the "Old Bridge," opened in 1940 and named for Huey P. Long. It carries U.S. 190 (Airline Highway) and one rail line across the river.

Interstate 12: Eastern Shortcut

Located entirely within Louisiana, I-12 starts in Baton Rouge at the 10-12 split. In 1993 the state legislature named the highway the Republic of West Florida Parkway to highlight the history of Louisiana's Florida parishes. The highway travels through Denham Springs and along the north shore of Lake Pontchartrain before merging with

I-10 and I-59 near Slidell. Heavily used, I-12 serves as a bypass to New Orleans and provides fast access to subdivisions in east Baton Rouge and Denham Springs. Major exits lead to shopping and dining at Airline Highway (U.S. 61 south), Sherwood Forest Boulevard, and O'Neal Lane. Travel this route to Denham Springs to reach the 163,000-square-foot Bass Pro Shops Outdoor World and the Antiques Village on Range Avenue.

U.S. Highway 61: Airline Highway

U.S 61 runs 1,400 miles from New Orleans to the town of Wyoming, Minnesota. It cuts through Baton Rouge, then north along the course of the Mississippi River toward Canada. Local residents use the highway frequently. Travel north to visit Port Hudson State Historic Site and St. Francisville, as well as Natchez and Vicksburg, Mississippi. The roadway is also called Airline Highway since it is an alternative route between the Baton Rouge and New Orleans airports. Along the highway are commercial buildings, restaurants, and shopping centers, including Cortana Mall and Hammond Aire, as well as Woman's Hospital. Local residents often use U.S. 61 as an alternate route to New Orleans when there is heavy congestion or an accident tie-up on I-10.

i When driving in Baton Rouge, check a city map and determine your exact location and the exact name of the subdivision that will be your destination. Keep in mind that some streets have similar names, such as North Street and North Boulevard. Also some streets have several name changes, such as Acadian Thruway, which changes to Stanford then to LSU Avenue.

U.S. 190: Florida Boulevard

Starting at the Mississippi River downtown, Florida Boulevard is the main east-west thoroughfare through Baton Rouge. Once on Florida, you can connect with I-10 and major north-south cross streets. Ask for directions, and residents will most likely pinpoint your destination north or south of Florida. Along the road, you'll find banks, commercial establishments, shopping malls, and parks. Major sites along Florida include the main U.S. Post Office, U.S. Federal Courthouse, Greyhound Bus Station, Baton Rouge General Medical Center, and Baton Rouge Community College. Crossing Airline Highway, Florida also becomes U.S. Hwy 190 east.

BATON ROUGE METRO AIRPORT

About 7 miles from the center of town, the Baton Rouge Metropolitan Airport (9430 Jackie Cochran Drive, 225-355-9430, www.flybtr.com) is where air travelers begin their visit to the city. Originating as Harding Field in 1941, the facility operated four years as a training base for fighter pilots during World War II. In 1948 it became a public airport and in 1954 was named Ryan Field after Captain William Joseph Ryan. In 1981 the airport officially became the Baton Rouge Metropolitan Airport, Ryan Field.

The airport offers travelers a clean, attractive terminal with a wide range of amenities. The centerpiece is a three-story, landscaped rotunda featuring lush semi-tropical plants and a view of the airfield. The area includes a gift shop and small food court. Other amenities include an arcade, ATM, business center, courtesy phones, flight notification, hotel phone board, kids' room, nondenominational chapel, nursing room, reading room, pay phones, and a long distance phone card machine.

Major airlines operating all-jet service with nonstop flights to Atlanta, Dallas–Fort Worth, Houston, and Memphis include: American Airlines, (800) 433-7300; Continental Airlines, (800) 523-3273; Delta Air Lines–Delta Connections, (800) 221-1212; and Northwest Airlines, (800) 225-2525.

Boarding passes are required for access beyond security screening. Boarding passes may be obtained at your airline's ticket counter, self-service kiosk, or Web site. Curbside service is available with baggage check-in only. For additional check-in information, contact your airline.

Services include lost and found, security "mail it back" program if your item cannot go through security, parking shuttle, security escort to parking garage, smart carts, sky caps, travel insurance, and wheelchair services. Parking is available in a covered parking garage and an outdoor economy lot. Taxis and airport shuttles are available. Taxi rates are somewhat complicated. For details check ahead at www.flybtr.com and clicking on "Ground Transportation" for details.

GROUND TRANSPORTATION

Greyhound Bus Lines

BATON ROUGE GREYHOUND STATION
1253 Florida Blvd.
(225) 383-3811 (main); (225) 383-3761 (baggage)
www.greyhound.com
Greyhound serves cities throughout the United States. The Baton Rouge Station, a clean and simple facility, is 12 blocks from downtown. There's daily bus service to the Greyhound Station in downtown New Orleans. Greyhound does not stop at Louis Armstrong Airport in New Orleans. The Baton Rouge ticket office is open from 7 a.m. to 1 a.m. daily. The station is open 24 hours. The facility has a small shop offering packaged snacks and drinks as well as fried chicken, hot dogs, and sandwiches. There are no cafes or accommodations nearby, and there are no hotels nearby. No reservations required. Hours of operation are subject to change. Call to verify hours before making travel arrangements.

Public Transportation

CAPITOL AREA TRANSIT SYSTEM
2250 Florida Blvd.
(225) 389-8282
www.brcats.com
Baton Rouge's public transportation is provided by Capitol Area Transit System (CATS), with bus routes throughout the city. Bus stop signs are located at many street corners along each route. Wait for the bus at the stop sign. When the bus approaches, signal the driver so the bus will stop for you. Fares on city routes are $1.75 for adults; free for children under five. Seniors (age 62 and over), people with disabilities who show CATS ID card, anyone showing a Medicare card, and students up through high school with an ID pay 35 cents. You can transfer between bus routes, sometimes at the Florida and 22nd Street terminal. A transfer slip costs 25 cents. The system also operates the Capitol Park Trolley, which circles downtown and stops at major points between the State Capitol and city government complex.

LSU students, faculty, and staff members who display their LSU identification cards and LSU visitors who display acceptable identification are afforded access to the entire CATS transit system. In turn the general public is afforded access to the First Transit LSU routes. Most CATS buses can carry passengers in a wheelchair. If you can't use regular CATS buses at all because of a disability, you may be eligible for CATS On Demand, special transportation for people with disabilities. Many buses are equipped with bike racks. Routes, schedules, time changes, game day routes, and current updates are posted at www.brcats.com.

i A 2.5-mile bike path extends from the end of the downtown riverfront promenade just north of the I-10 Mississippi River bridge to Skip Bertman Drive at LSU. The 15-foot-wide path includes separate lanes for bicycles and walkers/joggers as well as lighting, seating, and water fountains. The bike path links to the 1-mile downtown promenade that is beautifully lit at night. Parking is available at a trailhead located under the Mississippi River bridge.

Taxis and Limousines

Taxi transportation is available into downtown as well as to hotels and residences throughout the city. Fares are regulated by the city. In town taxis charge $2.50 for the first mile and $1.50 for each additional mile. Cab fare from the airport should be $15 to $17 for one person to downtown. A total fare for one person from the airport to one of the hotel districts will run approximately $20. Ask about credit cards and check with your cab driver about your fare before leaving the airport. Limousines are popular for special events, including everything from conventions and concerts to football games and high school proms. Some limousine services also offer plantation tours, casino tours, swamp tours, and historical tours. Companies offering service include:

ABC TAXI CAB SERVICE
(225) 355-3133

MACKIE'S AIRPORT CAB SERVICE
(225) 357-4883

RIVERSIDE LIMOUSINES
(225) 928-5466

SHANNON'S CAR SERVICE
(225) 300-7363

TIGER TAXI AND TOURS
(225) 921-9199, (225) 225-635-4641

YELLOW CAB (OPEN 24 HOURS)
(225) 926-6400

HISTORY

Baton Rouge's history begins in the mist of time and the dynamic flow of the Mississippi River. Ancient Indian mounds can be found throughout the region. Two mounds on the Louisiana State University main campus functioned as ceremonial centers. Radiocarbon dating shows mound builders came to the area more than 5,000 years ago. By the 1500s England, Spain, and France were becoming interested in colonizing the Mississippi River. Following the death of Hernando de Soto in 1542, his followers would have passed the site on their way to the Gulf of Mexico, but they didn't claim the land for their king. In 1682, René-Robert Cavelier, Sieur de la Salle, claimed Louisiana for Louis XIV, King of France.

In 1698 a French-Canadian, Pierre Le Moyne, Sieur d'Iberville, was commissioned by the French king to found a colony in Louisiana. Traveling in two long boats to explore the Mississippi River, Iberville and his men first saw the bluffs of Baton Rouge on March 17, 1699. In her *History of Baton Rouge 1699–1812*, Rose Meyers writes that the ship's daily log stated that the explorers landed near a small stream at three o'clock, and they found several cabins covered with palmetto leaves and a tall reddened pole on which there were fish heads. Members of the Houma tribe lived to the north of the red stick and Bayagoulas to the south. The explorers named the site Baton Rouge (Red Stick).

Although it is easy to find the date for the discovery of Baton Rouge, there is little information for the exact date of a settlement. It is alleged that the French constructed a fort in 1719, but it's doubtful the fort ever existed.

COLONIAL RULE

In the early 1700s a concession was made to a member or members of the distinguished Dartaguette family of France. An entry in Bernard Diron Dartaguette's journal dated December 31, 1722, called the settlement Dirombourg or Baton Rouge. According to Meyers, Diron Dartaguette reported the soil was very fine and good, and there were many prairies on the concession. The settlement appeared to be well on its way. However when Father Paul du Poisson camped overnight on June 4, 1727, he found the remains of a French settlement abandoned on account of wild animals—deer, rabbits, wild cats, and bears. What actually happened is a mystery, although it's possible that disease, death, and lack of supplies all played a role in the settlement's demise.

The area was transferred to England by the treaty of Paris in 1763. The British promptly established two forts: Fort Bute on the north bank of Bayou Manchac and Fort New Richmond in Baton Rouge. Baton Rouge was renamed New Richmond. Mark T. Carlton, in his book *River Capital: An Illustrated History of Baton Rouge*, states the "origins of Baton Rouge as a continuously settled community dates from the establishment of a military outpost at this time, making the area the southwestern corner of the British North America." A royal proclamation October 7, 1763, granted colonists the "rights and benefits of English law." The colony's first governor, Captain George Johnstone, was authorized to award land grants to officers and soldiers who served in the French and Indian War.

A colony of Pennsylvania German farmers, the "Dutch Highlanders," who settled at Manchac during the 1770s moved to higher ground in Spanish West Florida after floods damaged their land in 1784. The "Highlanders" established themselves south of Baton Rouge along Highland Road, Bayou Fountain, and Ward's Creek between Ben Hur Road and Siegen Lane. The families started growing cotton in the 1790s and added sugar cane cultivation in the 1830s. Among the significant "Highlander" families were the Kleinpeters, Garigs, Starings and Sharps. A number of major streets are named after these families.

REVOLUTION AND REVOLT

During the American Revolution, a number of planters from the Eastern Seaboard moved to West Florida because they were either loyal to Britain or chose to remain neutral. Baton Rouge residents enjoyed their rights as English citizens. Yet to the south, Governor Bernardo de Galvez of Spanish Louisiana was secretly helping rebelling American colonists. Captain James Willing of New Orleans attempted to get West Florida residents to join the fight for American independence, but they refused. He informed Congress that West Florida was a threat, and he was commissioned to take a well-armed force and demand that West Floridians take an oath of neutrality. In January 1788 he raided British plantations up and down the Mississippi. Houses were burned and livestock killed. After the raid the British sent more troops to Manchac and other posts along the Mississippi. They established a blockade on the river.

Spain formally declared war on Great Britain in June 1779. Galvez defeated the English at Fort Bute on Bayou Manchac. The first Battle of Baton Rouge took place September 21, 1779, and Galvez defeated British troops at Fort New Richmond. The outpost was renamed Fort San Carlos, and Baton Rouge began to develop as a city during the late 1700s. By 1805 two subdivisions, Spanish Town settled by Spanish and Canary

Islanders and Beauregard Town founded by Captain Elias Beauregard, were established. Spain's rule was never popular, and most older residents of British descent viewed the Spanish as enemies.

A DEVELOPING CITY: 1800–1900

In the Treaty of San Ildefonso in 1800, Napoleon Bonaparte induced Spain to give western Louisiana and New Orleans back to France. In 1803 Napoleon needed money to fight the British and sold the Louisiana Territory to the United States. The Louisiana Purchase left Spanish West Florida, including Baton Rouge, surrounded by the United States. In 1810 a group of American and British residents held secret meetings in the St. Francisville area north of Baton Rouge. They declared themselves independent and renamed the area the West Florida Republic. On September 23 the rebels overcame the Spanish garrison at Baton Rouge and unfurled the flag of the new republic, a single white star on a blue field. In a few months the territory was annexed by the United States as part of the Louisiana Purchase territory. Louisiana was admitted into the United States April 8, 1812. Baton Rouge was incorporated in 1817.

During the 19th century, Baton Rouge flourished as a strategic town on the Mississippi River. Agriculture and river commerce dominated the economy. In the antebellum era, plantations produced crops of cotton and sugar cane. Steamboats, barges, and flatboats plied the river, and passengers visited the town. Before long there were hotels, schools, churches, and city services. In 1825 the Marquis de Lafayette visited his Revolutionary War aide-de-camp and friend, Joseph Armand Allard Duplantier, owner of Magnolia Mound Plantation. In honor of the occasion, city fathers renamed Second Street "Lafayette Street," which it remains today.

Baton Rouge continued as a strategic location, and between 1819 and 1822 the U.S. government built the Pentagon Barracks, near the site of old Fort Carlos, as quarters for an infantry regiment. The officer supervising Pentagon con-

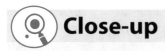 **Close-up**

Important Dates in Baton Rouge History

1699: French-Canadian explorers name area Baton Rouge (Red Stick).

1722: Dartaguette family of France establishes a settlement on a land grant called a concession.

1763: The area is transferred to England by the Treaty of Paris, and the settlement is renamed New Richmond. Baton Rouge becomes the southwestern corner of British North America.

1779: Spanish defeat the English at Fort Bute on Bayou Manchac and then capture Fort Richmond in Baton Rouge (first Battle of Baton Rouge).

1810: Spanish are overthrown by local settlers who declare themselves independent and rename the area the West Florida Republic. In a few months the territory is annexed by Louisiana and divided. East Baton Rouge Parish is created.

1812: Louisiana admitted into the United States.

1817: Baton Rouge incorporated as a city.

1825: Marquis de Lafayette visits Revolutionary War friend and local planter Joseph Armand Allard Duplantier, and city fathers rename Second Street "Lafayette Street," which it remains today.

1847: City begins construction on medieval-style capitol designed by James H. Dakin.

1848: General Zachary Taylor, local resident, elected president of the United States.

1849: Baton Rouge becomes the state capital.

1862: Civil War Battle of Baton Rouge takes place between Union and Confederate troops. The battle was a tactical success for the Confederates.

1869: Louisiana Seminary of Learning at Pineville moves to Baton Rouge and becomes Louisiana State University in 1870.

1877: LSU absorbs the State Agricultural and Mechanical College.

1882: The state capital, which was moved to New Orleans following the Civil War, is moved back to Baton Rouge.

1909: Standard Oil of New Jersey forms Standard Oil of Louisiana and starts building a refinery.

1914: Southern University relocated from New Orleans to Baton Rouge.

1928: Huey Long elected governor.

1932: Louisiana State Capitol completed.

1935: Huey P. Long is shot on September 8, 1935, and dies two days later.

1941: City businesses and residents participate in World War II. LSU educator and soldier General Troy H. Middleton, American Commander during World War II, makes the key tactical decision to hold Bastogne during the Battle of the Bulge, 1944–45.

1949: Baton Rouge citizens establish the city-parish plan of government.

1988: Citizens vote to amend government plan to provide for comprehensive master land use and development plan known as the Horizon Plan.

2004: Melvin L. "Kip" Holden elected the first African-American mayor-president of East Baton Rouge Parish.

2005: In August 2005, Holden leads city-parish in managing 200,000 evacuees from the New Orleans area following Hurricane Katrina.

2009: The LSU Tigers athletic teams are considered among the best in the nation. The men's baseball team has won six national championships in Omaha since 1991. With the football team winning the 2008 BCS National Championship Game, the Tigers became the first team to ever win two Bowl Championship Series titles.

struction was Colonel Zachary Taylor, a native of Virginia. He made Baton Rouge his residence and purchased cotton land in West Feliciana. Taylor advanced to the rank of major general and in 1845 led troops in the Mexican War. As the Whig nominee, Taylor was elected President of the United States in 1848. He left Baton Rouge for his inauguration in 1849 but never returned, dying the following year in Washington, D.C.

Baton Rouge was made Louisiana's capital city in 1846, and in 1847 New York architect James Dakin was hired to design and begin construction on a new capitol building. The legislature moved into the building in 1850. Dakin's medieval "castle" on a bluff overlooking the Mississippi River, complete with turrets and cupolas, is termed Neo-Gothic style. Samuel L. Clemens (Mark Twain), a steamboat pilot in the 1850s, didn't like the building. In *Life on the Mississippi*, he wrote: "It is pathetic enough that a whitewashed castle should ever have been built in this honorable place." Today, the old State Capitol is a treasured landmark.

i The performing arts came to Baton Rouge in the 1820s with traveling companies of comedians, minstrels, and actors. The first showboat to dock in Baton Rouge arrived in 1833. By 1841 the town had its own amateur theatrical organization, but the city had no public auditorium, theater, or meeting hall. Performances were staged in saloons, private halls, tents, or open air. The lack of a public auditorium continued until the 1970s.

Civil War Era

While Baton Rouge prospered, there also was turmoil. In his history, Mark Carlton writes, "The small but prosperous town was the capital of a slave state at a time when slavery's future in the United States had become seriously threatened." Following Abraham Lincoln's election in 1860, South Carolina left the Union, followed by Mississippi, Florida, Georgia, and Alabama. Louisiana legislature adopted an ordinance of secession January 26, 1861.

Baton Rouge raised a number of companies in the early stages of the Civil War. On January 12, 1861, seasoned veterans seized the Federal Pentagon barracks. In the spring of 1862 when New Orleans fell to a Union fleet under Admiral David Farragut, Confederate authorities abandoned Baton Rouge and moved the state government to Opelousas and then to Shreveport, which became the state's Confederate capital for the duration of the war. In the summer of 1862, Major General John C. Breckinridge led about 2,600 men in the third Battle of Baton Rouge. The plan was to squeeze the Federal army in Baton Rouge between Breckinridge's troops and the Confederate ship *Arkansas*, which was on its way downriver. Breckinridge started his attack August 5 just east of town. The battle was a tactical success for the Confederates who pushed the Federal army back through town to the protection of the Federal gunboats. However, the *Arkansas* never arrived, forcing Breckinridge to withdraw to the Comite River out of range. The town certainly was damaged, but it escaped complete devastation. Breckinridge moved his troops north of Baton Rouge to Port Hudson, which held out until July 1863, the longest siege in American military history.

i The Mississippi Riverfront was a busy docking area for steamboats and flatboats during the 1800s. Danger was always present on the river, and 19th-century steamboats often exploded. On Feb. 27, 1859, the *Princess* blew up just south of Baton Rouge, having departed from a local landing. A crowd of spectators witnessed the aftermath from the levee. Those still alive, though badly burned, were rowed ashore to Cottage Plantation on Conrad's Point where they were wrapped by slaves in sheets covered with flour, a standard treatment at the time for third-degree burns. Of 250 people on board, 70 were blown to pieces, drowned, or died.

Reconstruction

As veterans returned from war, Baton Rouge started rebuilding. However Federal troops remained in the city until the end of Reconstruction in 1877. In addition to cattle and crops destroyed, there was a sharp decline in property values and drying up of local investment capital. There was a mass migration of ex-slaves into the city. As the white population regained control of the state and city's government, segregation and Jim Crow laws were enforced.

Slowly the city began recovering. In 1869 Louisiana Seminary of Learning at Pineville moved to Baton Rouge and became Louisiana State University in 1870. Then LSU absorbed the State Agricultural and Mechanical College in 1877. Heading the university during the 1870s was David French Boyd, a member of the original 1860 faculty and a former Confederate officer. By 1880 the city's economy was rebounding. In 1882 the state capital, which had been moved to New Orleans by the Federal government, returned to Baton Rouge. Reconstruction politicians were replaced by middle-class white Democrats who detested the Republican party and preached white supremacy. This "Bourbon" era was short-lived in Baton Rouge and was replaced by a local style of conservatism in the 1890s. Civic-mindedness took hold. Railroad connections were established between Baton Rouge and New Orleans in 1883. By 1893 a municipal streetcar line encircled the town. Cotton and sugar prices began to rise, and 1896 marked the arrival of the Coca-Cola Bottling Company, a branch of the Atlanta company. The passage of several large bond issues led to the construction of public buildings, new schools, paving of streets, drainage and sewer improvements, and a municipal public health department. As the 19th century came to a close, Baton Rougeans had more time for play. Some took up golf and tennis, and on Saturdays many went to LSU to watch students kick a ball down a field.

P. B. S. Pinchback

During the Reconstruction era in Baton Rouge, P. B. S. Pinchback, the son of a slave woman and a wealthy planter from Mississippi, became the first black governor of Louisiana. This also made him the first black governor of an American state. He served for 36 days from December 9, 1872, to the inauguration of W. P. Kellogg on January 13, 1873. As a leader of the Louisiana Republican Party, Pinchback held or claimed offices including state senator, president pro tempore of the senate and acting lieutenant governor, de facto director of the New Orleans schools and police force, governor, U.S. representative, and U.S. senator.

ℹ️ LSU chemistry professor Charles E. Coates organized the first "Fighting Tigers" football team with himself as coach. The team played only one game that year with Tulane and lost 34-0. Ruffin G. Pleasant, team captain, became a lawyer after graduating. In 1916 he was elected governor of Louisiana. While recent governors have been LSU football fans, Pleasant is the only governor to have played the sport for LSU.

1900–1930: WEALTH AND POLITICS

By the beginning of the 20th century, Baton Rouge was flourishing. The Elks' Theater opened on May 26, 1900, and motion pictures soon followed. The last major threat of yellow fever occurred in 1905. A parish board of health was created and a quarantine enacted. Southern University was relocated from New Orleans to Scotlandville, just north of town, and opened

March 9, 1914. The city was becoming a center for the production of petroleum and natural gas.

Standard Oil Arrives

In 1909 Standard Oil Company, the predecessor of present-day ExxonMobil, established the Standard Oil Company of Louisiana. The company was capitalized in the amount of $5 million divided into 50,000 shares worth $100 each. The five company directors owned 1,000 shares, while the remaining 49,000 shares remained the property of Standard Oil Company of New Jersey. The new facility, built just north of town, became a lure to other firms. Today the company employs more than 4,000 people. Despite World War I, Baton Rouge continued to grow economically and socially throughout the 1920s.

Huey P. Long Era

The oil-based local economy buffered Baton Rouge from the worst during the Great Depression. However city leaders had plenty of stress with the dynamic personality of governor and United States senator Huey Pierce Long. Carlton writes, "Long's presence off and on between 1918 and 1935 was extremely unsettling to local tranquility and confidence."

Born on a farm near Winnfield, Winn Parish, Louisiana, on August 30, 1893, Huey Long was a larger-than-life figure. He worked as a book peddler, auctioneer, and salesman before studying law at Tulane in New Orleans. He was admitted to the bar in 1915. In 1918, at the age of 25, he was elected to the state railroad commission. For the next six years, he defended utilities consumers, railroad customers, and small pipeline companies, becoming a spokesman of Louisiana's common folk. In the process, he became the enemy of utility companies, railroads, and Standard Oil. Long ran as the Democratic nominee for governor in 1924 and lost. Four years later he ran again and served as governor from 1928 to 1932 and as a U.S. senator from 1932 to 1935 when he was assassinated.

Long revolutionized Louisiana in many ways, and he became nationally known for his radi-

cal populist policies. In Louisiana, his popularity and power grew as he paved roads, provided free textbooks for schoolchildren, and upgraded public education and state hospitals. Nationally he split with Franklin D. Roosevelt in June 1933 and created his own Share Our Wealth program, which would have taxed the super rich to provide a free college education for all qualified students, guaranteed family incomes, and offered other benefits. With the motto "Every Man a King," he proposed wealth distribution measures in the form of a net asset tax on corporations and individuals to curb the poverty and crime resulting from the Great Depression. Long, nicknamed "The Kingfish," was accused by his opponents of dictatorial tendencies for his near-total control of state government. He was aggressive, determined, blunt, and often insensitive. Long was shot September 8, 1935, in the Louisiana State Capitol in Baton Rouge. He died two days later at the age of 42. It is unclear whether he was assassinated by Dr. Carl Austin Weiss Jr. or accidentally killed by bodyguards who believed an assassination attempt was in progress. Tens of thousands crowded in front of the new State Capitol on September 10, 1935, for Long's funeral. He was buried on the grounds in front of the building, which he had built in 1932. People can visit the statue at his gravesite.

Long's legacy still affects Louisiana today. In his four-year term as governor, he doubled the size of the state's road system. He built 111 bridges and started construction on the Huey P. Long Bridge in Jefferson Parish, near New Orleans. The Huey P. Long Bridge in Baton Rouge, a combined railroad and highway bridge, was started in 1937. Long expanded the public school system, expanded funding for LSU, lowered tuition, and established scholarships for low-income students. He founded the LSU School of Medicine in New Orleans and doubled funding for the public Charity Hospital System. The political machine Long established was weakened but remained for decades after his death. His brother Earl K. Long was twice elected governor and served an unexpired term as well. Another brother George S. Long was elected to Congress in 1952. Long's older son, Russell B. Long, served as one of Louisiana's two U.S. senators from 1949 to 1987. Numerous other relatives have served in both state and federal offices.

Huey P. Long was the inspiration for Robert Penn Warren's 1946 Pulitzer Prize–winning novel, *All the King's Men*. In 1970 T. Harry Williams won the Pulitzer Prize for his biography *Huey Long*. Long's life has inspired numerous additional writers, filmmakers, and composers.

1940s–1980s: WORLD WAR II AND AFTERMATH

With the bombing of Pearl Harbor by the Japanese in 1941, Baton Rouge joined the nation in the war efforts. Military demand for increased production contributed to the growth of the city. Standard Oil spent $17 million for plant expansion, principally to produce aviation fuel. The company's new Chemical Products Division began to produce synthetic rubber because sources of natural rubber in the Dutch East Indies had been seized by the Japanese. Almost overnight Harding Field was constructed north of town to train fighter pilots. At the same time hundreds of south Louisiana men and women served in the armed forces. Navy Ensign Rodney S. Foss of Baton Rouge was killed in the Pearl Harbor attack, and a destroyer escort was later named the USS *Foss* in his honor. The Congressional Medal of Honor was awarded to Army Staff Sergeant Homer L. Wise for extraordinary heroism in an engagement with Germans in Italy. LSU continued its tradition of military training. By 1943, 15 of its graduates were serving as generals in the armed forces. The most outstanding World War II general from Baton Rouge, Lieutenant General Troy H. Middleton, had served on the LSU faculty and returned after the war to become its president. He became renowned after he, as American commander, made the key decision to hold Bastogne, Belgium, during the Battle of the Bulge.

Following World War II, new families flocked to East Baton Rouge Parish. The population pushed outward beyond the city limits and into new subdivisions. In 1949 the citizens established the city-parish form of government, one of the first in the nation to adopt such a plan. It provided for an elected mayor-president as the chief executive responsible for the administrative work of the government and for a parish council made up of elected representatives. It consolidated the major departments of government. There still exists a Sheriff's Office and a City Police Department with overlapping jurisdiction. In the 1950s a comprehensive zoning ordinance was adopted regulating subdivision development in both the city and the parish.

During the early years of America's civil rights movement, civic leaders in Baton Rouge's black community were among the first to seek justice. Baton Rouge was the site of the first bus boycott of the movement. On June 29, 1953, black citizens began an organized boycott of the municipal bus system that lasted eight days. It became the template for the famous Montgomery Bus Boycott in 1955–56 led by Dr. Martin Luther King Jr. The Baton Rouge boycott was led by the newly formed United Defense League (UDL), under the direction of Reverend T. J. Jemison of Mt. Zion Baptist Church, attorney Johnnie A. Jones Sr., and Raymond Scott. A volunteer free ride system, coordinated through churches, supported the efforts. In response the Baton Rouge City Council agreed to a compromise that opened all seats—except for the front two rows, which would be for whites, and the back two rows for black riders. Counter-protests eventually led to an overturning of the ordinance by the Louisiana attorney general, but many historians view the event as a success since it led the way for larger organized efforts. By 1962 Baton Rouge buses were fully integrated.

Another major event occurred February 1, 1960, when seven Southern University students were arrested for sitting in at a Kress Lunch counter. The following day nine more students were arrested for sitting in at the Greyhound bus terminal, and the day after that, Southern student Major Johns led more than 3,000 students on a march to the state capitol to protest segregation and the arrests. Major Johns and the 16 students arrested for sitting in were expelled from Southern and barred from all public colleges and universities in the state. Southern University students organized a class boycott to win reinstatement of the expelled students. Eventually the United States Supreme Court overturned the convictions of the students; in 2004, they were awarded honorary degrees by Southern, and the state legislature passed a resolution in their honor.

Through the 1970s Baton Rouge continued to grow with new subdivisions and shopping areas. Many businesses moved to the suburbs. April 16, 1988, citizens voted to amend the Plan of Government to provide for a comprehensive master land use and development plan, more commonly known as the Horizon Plan. The plan focuses on seven major planning elements: land use; transportation; wastewater, solid waste, and drainage; conservation and environmental resources; recreation and open space; housing and public services; and public building and health and human services. Along with government's interest in planned growth came a drive to revitalize the original central business district.

CURRENT

Today new state office buildings reflect the Art Deco architecture of the State Capitol. Enhancing the city's quality of life are activities at the RiverCenter, which includes the Theatre for the Performing Arts, an arena, and exhibition halls. Old buildings on Third Street have been renovated to house popular bars and restaurants. The Louisiana Arts and Science Museum and Planetarium, the USS *Kidd* and Veterans Memorial, and the Shaw Center for the Arts draw crowds with special events and exhibitions. Performing arts groups, including the Baton Rouge Symphony, Baton Rouge Ballet Theater, Baton Rouge

Little Theater, Playmakers, and others are thriving. Equally vibrant is the range of art galleries found throughout the city.

In 2004 Melvin L. "Kip" Holden was elected the first African-American mayor-president of East Baton Rouge Parish. He was re-elected to a second term October 4, 2009, carrying every precinct in the parish for the first time in history. Born in New Orleans on August 12, 1952, Holden earned a bachelor's degree in journalism from LSU, a master's degree in journalism from Southern University, and a juris doctorate from Southern University School of Law. He was invited to study at the Oxford University Round Table in England. Prior to 2004 he had a distinguished 20-year career in public service, including serving as a Louisiana state senator.

Mayor Holden has received numerous awards and honors. He has been recognized nationally for his leadership during the aftermath of Hurricane Katrina in August 2005 when he managed a city-parish that became a place of refuge for more than 200,000 evacuees from south Louisiana in less than a week. By the time Hurricane Gustav hit the city September 1, 2008, the city's first responders and residents had become far better prepared at handling emergencies. During his second term in office, Holden has made public safety a top priority. Under his direction the city-parish Green Light Plan is a $690 million program to improve traffic flow on key surface roads.

As the 21st century progresses, the historical riverfront city will no doubt face many challenges. Baton Rouge residents are resilient and proud of their past, and they are always ready to welcome newcomers. It doesn't take long to understand the city's motto, "Authentic Louisiana at every turn."

ACCOMMODATIONS

Baton Rouge offers travelers a wide selection of places to stay. There are hotels to suit every taste and budget. Two major hotels are downtown, within walking distance of state and city governmental offices and a number of major attractions. Numerous others are situated at major intersections along I-10 and I-12, where they are convenient to Louisiana State University, business complexes, shopping centers, and medical facilities. Depending on the location this can include easy access to the Mall of Louisiana, Towne Center, Cortana Mall, or Baton Rouge General and Our Lady of the Lake hospitals. Several new hotels are situated near the Baton Rouge Metro Airport.

Baton Rouge attracts visitors year round, but the busiest times are most often linked to football weekends at LSU and Southern University. Rooms also fill up quickly for other collegiate events, including baseball and basketball games, as well as high school regional tournaments. In fact, the town is sports-fan friendly. Arrive as a team or with a team, and you'll find welcoming hotel staffs. Seasonal events, such as Mardi Gras (usually in February or March) are also busy times.

Equally available are hotels with facilities designed for businessmen and -women working in the greater Baton Rouge region. Travelers with governmental meetings or assignments with any of the area's petrochemical industries can easily find a quiet room with an up-to-date work space and that offers a solid night's rest.

Hotels with large facilities for weddings, large charitable events, and conventions tend to have higher rates. Budget hotels can be found along the interstates and Airline Highway (U.S. 61).

Price Code

Nailing down hotel rates in today's economy is always tricky. Rates fluctuate with the market, and all accommodations offer a range of rates. Prices will top out during big game weekends and special events in New Orleans, such as Mardi Gras and Super Bowl. You should note that state, local, sales, and use taxes plus room tax total up to 13 percent, so be sure to factor this into your travel budget.

$.................... $59 to $89
$$ .... $90 to $109
$$$ .... over $110

HOTELS AND BED-AND-BREAKFASTS

BATON ROUGE MARRIOTT $$$
5500 Hilton Ave.
(225) 924-5000
www.marriott.com
One of the city's major hotels, the Baton Rouge Marriott has more than 300 guest rooms and 20,000 square feet of banquet and meeting space. Numerous business and social functions are held at the Marriott. Spacious guest rooms have plush feather comforters and down surround pillows. Wireless Internet is available in all rooms, as well as color remote cable TV, individual climate control, in-room coffee makers, irons, and ironing boards. The hotel features four concierge level floors. There's a pool and out-

door parking. Guests frequently comment on the friendliness of the staff and their willingness to go out of their way to help. Five handicapped rooms are available on the third floor. No pets accepted.

CAMBRIA SUITES $$$
4964 Constitution Blvd.
(225) 925-1005
www.cambriasuites.com
Designed for the way modern America travels and lives, Cambria Suites provides spacious guest rooms. Suites are decorated in pale gold and cream with red and black accents. The handy workspace has an oversize desk and ergonomic chair—everything you need to plug in for efficient business. The spacious open lobby is sectioned off with club seating and a large-screen media wall. The breakfast buffet features everything from cereal to omelets to Belgian waffles. The barista bar features specialty coffees by Wolfgang Puck. Enjoy the indoor pool and spa, and pick up healthy and organic food 24 hours a day. Suites for disabled guests include rooms with wider doors, handle bars, and other adaptations. One room features a roll-in shower. No pets are allowed.

> **i** Baton Rouge's first hotels were prospering by 1835. They included the Baton Rouge, Union, Exchange, and Madame Legendre's. The Harney House, built on Lafayette Street in the late 1840s, survived into the 20th century as the Louisian Hotel.

THE COOK HOTEL $$$
3848 West Lakeshore Dr.
(225) 383-2665
www.thecookhotel.com
One of the best-kept secrets in town is the four-star hotel and conference center located on the Louisiana State University campus. The hotel is designed to accommodate visiting lecturers, athletes, and alumni. It's a fan's delight with décor in the university's colors—purple and gold—repeated in subtle ways (never gaudy) throughout. Every guest room features plush Sealy Posturpedic beds and luxurious triple sheeting

and duvet comforters. Upgrade to a spacious suite or mega-suite complete with fireplace and Jacuzzi tub. You'll find high-speed Internet, a 24-hour business center, and a fitness center. Step into a fascinating LSU sports museum and a gift shop with everything from tasteful purple-and-gold dress shirts to items for the kids. An excellent full breakfast buffet is complimentary. Best of all, you never know when you'll rub shoulders with a star athlete or academic genius enjoying a cup of coffee in the dining area. Rooms are usually booked game days. Accommodations are usually available during holidays or when classes are not in session. Seven rooms are designed for disabled guests. No pets.

CROWNE PLAZA $$$
4728 Constitution Ave.
(225) 925-2244
www.crowneplazabatonrouge.com
This full-service hotel invites guests to relax in updated rooms with Serta pillowtop mattresses, plush duvets, and luxury sheets. Sleep amenities include an eye mask, drapery clip to darken the room, earplugs, and lavender spray. Newly updated baths feature travertine walls and granite countertops. Executive level rooms on the fifth floor feature 42-inch plasma TVs and access to the lounge for evening cocktails and morning breakfast. The comfortable Patio Grille restaurant serves a varied menu. Choose from the breakfast buffet or order from the menu. There's an outdoor pool, gift shop, and a tremendous amount of meeting space. Local organizations frequently book the spacious rooms for meetings and large events. Rooms for disabled guests include door bells, night lights, roll-in showers, and shower chairs. Pets accepted with a $30 pet fee.

DRURY INN & SUITES BATON ROUGE $$$
7939 Essen Park Ave.
(225) 766-2022
www.druryhotels.com
A new hotel situated just off I-10 at Essen Lane, the Drury Inn is across from the LSU Rural Life Museum, one of Louisiana's premiere attractions. Also nearby is Our Lady of the Lake Hospital, a

24-hour drug store, a grocery store, and restaurants. The handsomely furnished lobby features a lounge, wide-screen TV, and real fireplace. Displayed in the public areas are historic black-and-white photographs of old Baton Rouge. Spacious guest rooms feature luxurious beds and dark wood furniture. Burgundy-and-gold bedspreads, drapery, and carpets lend a sense of luxury to the rooms. Large baths are accented with granite counters. The hotel features an indoor-outdoor swimming pool with a swim-through, a Jacuzzi spa, and an excellent workout facility. The hotel starts serving complimentary popcorn and snacks at 3 p.m. and offers an evening beverage reception with beer, wine, and cocktails. The complimentary hot breakfast includes eggs, sausage, waffles, danish, and cereals. There's free high-speed Internet and a free one-hour long distance call every night. Rooms for disabled guests include roll-in shower and are equipped for the deaf. Pets are welcomed.

EMBASSY SUITES $$$
4914 Constitution
(225) 924-6566
www.embassysuites.com
Located just minutes from any major attraction in Baton Rouge, Embassy Suites features complete two-room suites. Each suite includes a roomy bedroom, comfortable sleeper sofa in the living room, and two televisions with full cable, pay-per-view, and computer games. High-speed Internet is complimentary. The suites include mini-refrigerator, coffee maker, and microwave, so guests can relax and dine in without leaving the room. However the Baton Rouge hotel has a delightful atrium with lush tropical plants and an excellent restaurant. Enjoy a fully cooked-to-order breakfast and a manager's reception with your favorite beverage. There's a relaxing indoor swimming pool, sauna, steam room, and three-hole putting green. The hotel also offers a complimentary shuttle service. Suites for the disabled are available. Pets are not accepted.

ℹ The Baton Rouge metropolitan area has more than 90 hotels and 9,718 rooms. In times of disaster, such as Hurricane Katrina, the Baton Rouge Hospitality Management Association encourages member hotels to offer accommodations to first responders.

HILTON CAPITOL CENTER $$$
201 Lafayette St.
(225) 906-5700
www.hiltoncapitolcenter.com
Baton Rouge's only historical hotel, located downtown on the Mississippi River, offers 290 guest rooms that have been designed with contemporary comforts while maintaining the appeal of the building's original facades. Built in 1927 as the Heidelberg Hotel, the building became a favorite haunt of Governor Huey P. Long. In 1931 the hotel briefly served as the state capitol during a dispute between Long and Lieutenant Governor Paul Cyr. The lobby and other public areas reflect the Art Deco motifs of the 1930s. The Kingfish Restaurant offers a delicious breakfast buffet. Lunch features soup and salad along with the a la carte menu. Dinner is a la carte. Executive suite rooms overlooking the Mississippi River have access to the executive lounge with a continental breakfast and evening reception. Ask for a tour of the hotel's elaborate ballroom with spectacular views of the Mississippi. The hotel is adjacent to the Shaw Center for the Arts and two blocks from the convention center. Also nearby are the Old State Capitol, Louisiana Arts and Science Museum and Planetarium, and USS *Kidd* and Veterans Memorial. There is a $75 nonrefundable pet fee. Wheelchair-accessible bathrooms feature roll-in showers.

HILTON GARDEN INN BATON ROUGE AIRPORT $$$
3330 Harding Blvd.
(225) 357-6177
www.batonrougeairport.stayhgi.com
This new hotel offers the services and amenities that a frequent business or leisure traveler needs

to be comfortable. Features include 42-inch flat screen plasma TVs, remote printing, and wireless high-speed Internet access. There's a 24-hour business center, fitness center, and pavilion pantry. The full-service restaurant serves breakfast, lunch, and dinner. The hotel is within a short drive of Southern University and the towns of Baker and Zachary. No pets allowed. Rooms are available for disabled travelers.

i The landmark King Hotel, 200 Lafayette Street, constructed in the 1920s, became the second most significant hotel in the downtown area for about 50 years. A legendary service tunnel connects the King Hotel with the Hilton Capitol Center (originally the Heidelberg Hotel). Currently undergoing complete renovation, the King Hotel is scheduled to open as an Indigo boutique hotel in late 2010.

HOLIDAY INN SOUTH $$
9940 Airline Hwy
(225) 924-7021
www.hibatonrougesouth.com
The Holiday Inn South is a full-service hotel offering 334 newly renovated guest rooms. Centrally located, it's within an easy drive to the Metro Airport, Cortana Mall, Women's Hospital, Southern University, and Baton Rouge Community College. Guest rooms feature a soft, warm décor along with color TVs with HBO, data port, wireless high-speed Internet, coffee maker, and ironing board. The Tower features a secure floor. We especially like the open-air atrium, with lush semi-tropical plants, that leads to meeting rooms and other public areas. Cafe Galvez, a complete full-service restaurant, offers burgers, sandwiches, pasta, and seafood as well as a complete breakfast buffet. There are three swimming pools—indoor/outdoor, children's pool, and outdoor pool. Other facilities include the Alamo Lounge, a business center, and fitness center with treadmills, elliptical stair climber, bicycles, and weight machine. No pets allowed. Handicapped rooms available.

HYATT PLACE BATON ROUGE $$$
6080 Bluebonnet Blvd.
(225) 769-4400
www.hyattplacebatonrouge.com
Situated just off I-10 and across from the Mall of Louisiana, Hyatt Place has 126 beautifully appointed rooms. Each room has the Hyatt Grand Bed, 42-inch flat screen TV, sectional sofa, and wet bar. Guests can purchase food 24 hours. Beer, wine, and Starbucks specialty coffees are available. An e-center is available for guests. Next door is Ralph and Kacoo's, one of Baton Rouge's signature restaurants featuring fresh seafood and steaks. All rooms for disabled feature one king-size bed and wheelchair-accessible baths. Pets are not accepted.

RADISSON HOTEL $$-$$$
2445 South Acadian Thruway
(225) 236-4000
www.radisson.com
The Radisson Hotel has undergone a major renovation. The spacious guest rooms, with interior corridor access, feature pillowtop beds, multi-head step-in showers, and rooms decorated in gold and brown tones. There's a delightful outdoor pool with waterfall and hot tub, fitness center, and business center. Wireless high-speed Internet is complimentary. The 225 Bistro Restaurant serves breakfast, lunch, and dinner, and guests enjoy gathering in the spacious lounge area. The hotel takes pride in its exceptionally friendly service. The Radisson is located within 2 miles of LSU and 5 miles of downtown. Rooms for disabled guests include tubs with handle bars and roll-in showers. There's also accessibility equipment for deaf. Pets are accepted, but there is a $20 fee per stay.

SHERATON BATON ROUGE
CONVENTION CENTER HOTEL $$$
102 France St.
(225) 242-2600
www.sheraton.com
Located in the heart of downtown at the foot of the I-10 bridge, the 10-story, 300-room Sheraton Hotel offers visitors dramatic views of the Missis-

sippi River and the Baton Rouge skyline. The hotel anchors the north entrance to the Catfish Town Atrium and is directly across from the convention center. Guest rooms feature pale gold and cream décor and Sheraton Sweet Sleeper beds. Other amenities include TV with cable channels, coffee maker, and desk with ergonomic chair. High-speed Internet is in all rooms, but there is a charge. From here you can take the elevator to the Belle of Baton Rouge Casino on the river or plan a twilight stroll on the levee's lighted walkway. Nearby attractions include the USS *Kidd* Naval Memorial, Louisiana Art and Science Museum and Planetarium, and Old State Capitol. Rooms are available for disabled guests. There's also a shuttle to the airport. Pets are accepted, and ask about a Sweet Sleeper dog bed.

THE STOCKADE BED AND
BREAKFAST $$$
8860 Highland Rd.
(225) 769-7358
www.thestockade.com
Conveniently located 3.5 miles from LSU on historic Highland Road, The Stockade is listed on the National Register as a Civil War site. Five guest accommodations are elegantly decorated. The large Great Room has a baby grand piano, origi-

nal art work, fireplace, and fountain. Two patios overlook lush, wooded grounds. Guests enjoy a full Southern breakfast in the dining room of lovely antiques and additional fine artwork.

CAMPGROUNDS

BREC'S FARR PARK HORSE
ACTIVITY CENTER
6402 River Rd.
(222) 769-7805
www.brec.org
Farr Park is the site of a fine equestrian facility and RV campground. There are 180 sites, many of which are pull-through. Activities are available for all horse lovers. There's horse boarding and riding lessons. Site fee is $20 per night.

KOA CAMPGROUND
7628 Vincent Rd., Denham Springs
(225) 664-7281
www.batonrougekoa.com
The campground offers quiet, shady sites. Features include a 50-foot heated pool, hot tub, concrete pull-through, and blacktop streets. Walking distance to Bass Pro Shops. Site fees range from $35 to $45 per night.

RESTAURANTS

South Louisiana has some of the best restaurants in the world. Food selection, preparation, and serving are almost an art form in private homes and restaurants. It's not unusual to hear men at a dinner conversation discussing where to find just the "right" seafood dish in town. Taking a lighthearted approach to local eating customs, a food aficionado recently remarked, "In Louisiana, when we eat breakfast, we talk about what we're going to have for lunch. At lunch, we talk about what we're going to have for dinner."

The cuisine in Plantation Country evolved from the region's rich cultural blend: French, English, Spanish, African American, German, and Italian. Add to this the more recent arrival of people from China, Thailand, India, and Vietnam. The ebb and flow of south Louisiana's economy also has played a role in the food. In eras of great wealth, elaborate dishes were prepared in wealthy mansions. When times were bad, sparse meals were created with simple ingredients enhanced with spices.

There's an abundance of fresh seafood from the Gulf of Mexico and the wetlands, and a long growing season allows an abundance of vegetables and herbs. The result is a diet heavy in seafood. Gumbo (an African word that means okra) is a staple in south Louisiana. Thickened with a rich roux (browned flour in oil), gumbo comes in many versions (shrimp, chicken, or vegetarian), and you will find it in almost every cafe, with the exception of most fast-food chains and ethnic restaurants. Since seafood is plentiful, local favorites include oysters on the half shell, shrimp and crawfish cooked every possible way, and fish fried, broiled, and baked. Always a meal in itself is the po'boy, a sandwich of sliced French bread packed with fried seafood, roast beef, meatballs, or other filling. The best po'boys feature French bread with a crusty top and soft interior. You will be asked if you want it "dressed," meaning served with lettuce, tomato, and mayonnaise. Po'boys and hamburgers are often served with a large helping of french fries.

Two dishes created in local kitchens are traditional favorites. Sensation salad, introduced by the former Bob and Jake's Restaurant, features a dressing of salad oil and lemon juice with plenty of garlic and grated Romano or Parmesan cheese over crisp shredded lettuce and a bit of parsley. Spinach Madeleine, created by a prominent local homemaker, is a blend of buttery cream sauce, melted jalapeño cheese, and spinach baked in a casserole. The recipe was printed in *River Road Recipes*, produced by the Baton Rouge Junior League, and is now legend. The most popular dessert in local restaurants is bread pudding, and there are seemingly hundreds of versions. The best bread puddings are topped with a sweet whiskey or rum sauce and served with hot steaming French roast coffee.

Mealtime here means more than just eating for nourishment. It's time to relax, enjoy the bounties from hard work, and visit with family and friends. A Sunday brunch can take hours. Dinner is often a complete evening of conversation and entertainment over an exquisite meal served with love.

There are more than 900 restaurants in the Baton Rouge area offering every type of menu. From fried green tomatoes topped with remoulade sauce to grilled shrimp pierced with sugar cane skewers, an abundance of innovative menus and dishes are found throughout the city. At the same time some of the simplest dishes served in the most humble restaurants—chicken and sausage gumbo, a roast beef po'boy—can be spectacular.

Whatever food you select, you will find most Baton Rouge restaurants are casual or dressy casual for evening. During the summer months, expect to see people in shorts and T-shirts in the college and tourist areas. Downtown, where state and city government offices are near tourist sites, you will see legislators and well-dressed businesspeople enjoying lunch side by side with tourists in casual garb. Some restaurants are "dress-up" by local standards, and male diners will feel more comfortable with a jacket. We've indicated these in the listings. Almost all restaurants are air-conditioned and women may want to wear a light wrap, especially in the evening.

The restaurant listings are arranged by cuisine. As a rule chain restaurants are not included, except for a few that offer a unique experience. Instead the list features restaurants owned or operated by local residents. In many you will find cuisine by award-winning chefs and chefs-in-training. Often a friendly waitstaff will include future restaurant owners and managers.

Most restaurants are open for lunch and dinner. Some close for a short time between meals. Most close up around 10 p.m.; a few stay open until midnight on Friday and Saturday. Most larger restaurants encourage reservations. Often, if you just show up and get your name on the waiting list, you will be given an approximate wait time. On game days, it's always wise to call and ask the length of wait time. Most restaurants accept credit cards.

Because of the Mediterranean culture of south Louisiana, drinking alcoholic beverages is acceptable and common when dining out. Wine, beer, and alcoholic cocktails are available at most restaurants. Often the bar is in a separate area from the main dining room or in a side room. Your waiter often will ask if you want a wine menu or a beverage from the bar. However, if you choose only water or a soft drink, you will be served quickly.

A particularly popular beverage in Louisiana, as well as throughout the South, is iced tea. During the long, hot summer, this beverage is particularly popular, but people drink it all year long. Expect the tea to be freshly brewed. You will be asked if you want sweet or unsweetened tea. If you choose sweet tea, you will receive a pre-sweetened beverage that can be very sugary. Many prefer to sweeten their beverage themselves with sugar or sweeteners available on the table.

Louisiana is famous for its rich, dark coffee. In south Louisiana, the hot beverage is enjoyed with meals and throughout the day. Hostesses often graciously ask if you would like coffee or another beverage as soon as you enter their home. Travelers from other states often expect to receive coffee with chicory. However this drink, which can be bitter, is rarely served in restaurants. Instead people usually prefer a well-brewed French roast coffee. Restaurants often serve a special restaurant blend that is full-bodied and delicious. Many local residents prefer to end their evening with this drink.

Smoking is not allowed in establishments that serve meals.

Price Code

The price key symbol found in each listing is the average price for dinner entrees—excluding cocktails, wine, appetizers, desserts, tax, and tip. Some restaurants have a wide variety of entrees, so some listings have a price range.

$................. Less than $20
$$ .... $21 to $40
$$$ .... $41 to $60
$$$$ .... More than $60

Some Baton Rouge restaurants that take reservations will seat patrons arriving late for their assigned time immediately. It pays to call ahead and ask about the reservation policy.

AMERICAN

BISTRO BYRONZ $$–$$$
5412 Government St.
(225) 218-1433
www.bistrobyronz.com

Bistro Byronz is a good place to relax and get excellent food at a reasonable price. The menu features delicious sandwiches on the restaurant's Byronz bread. The corn and shrimp soup and piquant shrimp remoulade are popular with patrons, as well as steak frite, chicken paillard, and more. Open for lunch and dinner Monday through Saturday, and Sunday, 11 a.m. to 3 p.m.

CAFE AMERICAIN $$–$$$
7521 Jefferson Hwy
(225) 924-9841
www.cafeamericainrest.com
Locally owned, this restaurant gets its name from Rick's Cafe, the setting for much of the action in the 1942 Humphrey Bogart movie *Casablanca*. Don't be fooled—the cuisine is far from exotic. It's American with a nod to Louisiana tastes. Try the pecan-crusted chicken salad with pecan-crusted grilled chicken over a bed of romaine lettuce, mandarin oranges, and almonds. The shrimp New Orleans features two shrimp stuffed with crab and wrapped in a thin catfish fillet, deep fried and topped with a brandy tarragon sauce. The restaurant also has a "create your own pasta dish" feature that allows patrons to choose various combinations of five meats, three pastas, and 10 vegetables. It's a vegetarian's dream dish. Open 11 a.m. to 9:30 p.m. Monday through Thursday, and 11 a.m to 10:30 p.m. Friday and Saturday.

THE CHIMES RESTAURANT $$
3357 Highland Rd.
(225) 383-1754

10870 Coursey Blvd.
(225) 296-4981
www.thechimes.com
Crowds have packed The Chimes restaurant, situated at the north gate of LSU, since it opened in the 1980s. You may not always hear the chimes from the nearby bell tower, but you will find students, alumni, and professors at almost every table. Expect lines on game days. Crawfish dishes with cream sauces are fantastic, and sandwiches, packed with meats or seafood, are meals in themselves. The restaurant has a large bar and features

some 120 beers from more than 60 countries. Oysters on the half shell are special 4 to 7 p.m. daily and all day Tuesday. Open for lunch and dinner daily. Kitchen closes at midnight Monday to Saturday. A second location on Coursey offers the same food at the same prices.

DOE'S EAT PLACE $$–$$$
3723 Government St.
(225) 387-5331
www.doesbatonrouge.com
A casual country-style setting, with checkered cloths and duck decoys on display, gives Doe's a down-home atmosphere for dining enjoyment. The restaurant has been serving world-famous steaks and hot tamales since 1941. *Bon Appetit* magazine ranked the steak here as third best in the country. For a sweet surprise try the eclair cake with layers of cake, a creamy custard filling, and chocolate icing. Hours are Monday to Saturday 4:30 to 9 p.m. and Friday 11 a.m. to 2 p.m.; extended hours game days.

i Monday is traditionally "red beans and rice" day in south Louisiana. Creamy red beans are often served with spicy sausage and white rice. The dish is served on Mondays in many restaurants, not just those specializing in Cajun and Creole food.

FRENCH MARKET BISTRO $$$–$$$$
16645 Highland Rd.
(225) 753-3500
www.frenchmarketbistro.com
The art of fine food is served in this beautiful setting featuring local artwork and handmade furniture. The contemporary, eclectic cuisine includes a variety of steaks, seafood, pasta, and nightly chef selections inspired by flavors from around the world. Take-out and catering available. Lunch served Monday through Saturday, 11 a.m. to 2 p.m.; dinner served Tuesday through Saturday beginning at 5:30 p.m.

KINGFISH RESTAURANT $$–$$$
Hilton Capitol Center
201 Lafayette St.
(225) 753-3500
www.hiltoncapitolcenter.com
The Kingfish is the main restaurant in the Hilton Capitol Center Hotel. It is named after Huey P. Long, Louisiana's flamboyant governor and senator who was assassinated in 1935. He once held court in the hotel, even turning it into a makeshift capitol briefly during a dispute with the lieutenant governor. The restaurant's name is taken from Long's nickname, "The Kingfish." Specialties are the aged Angus beef steaks and fresh Louisiana seafood. Simply delicious is the crab asiago bisque made with lump crabmeat, cream, and butter. The appointments are sparkling and the staff exceptionally friendly. It's fun to dine here when the Louisiana legislature is in session. You never know who's going to be sitting at the next table. Hours are 6:30 a.m. to 11 p.m.

LOUIE'S CAFE $
209 West State St.
(225) 346-8221
www.louiescafe.org
A Baton Rouge institution, Louie's has been in business since 1941. Generations of college students have eaten in this small greasy-spoon cafe just outside the LSU north gate. One of the few 24-hour spots in town, you can get fantastic breakfasts at Louie's. Order a simple omelet or one filled with grilled onions and vegetables. The hash brown potatoes are seasoned with Cajun spices, and the biscuits are huge and fluffy. Gumbo and hamburgers are also a specialty.

SAMMY'S GRILL $$
8635 Highland Rd.
(225) 766-7650
4760 Old Scenic Hwy, Zachary
(225) 654-5355
Sammy's is a casual south Baton Rouge dining spot, great for a stop after work or at lunch. Especially well prepared and seasoned are the crawfish étouffée and crabmeat au gratin, both traditional Louisiana dishes. A variety of steaks, salads, hamburgers, and large Louisiana po'boys on crusty French bread are hard to pass up. Open lunch and dinner Monday to Saturday. Sunday brunch dishes, including eggs Benedict, are especially great. Sunday hours are 10:30 a.m. to 10 p.m. The Zachary location is open 11 a.m. to 10 p.m. Daily.

> **i** The muffuletta, which originated at Central Grocery in New Orleans, is a popular sandwich that is a complete meal in itself. The large, round loaf of Italian bread is packed with Genoa salami, provolone cheese, mortadella ham, and olive salad. It easily makes a meal for two. Versions of the sandwich can be found in numerous restaurants around Baton Rouge.

SILVER SPOON $$
7731 Jefferson Hwy
(225) 926-1172
www.thesilverspoonbr.com
The Silver Spoon in Bocage Village has been a preferred lunch spot for Baton Rougeans for more than a decade. Travelers will recognize the bistro's California casual atmosphere (yes, you can get sprouts on your sandwich). For something different, try the Jamaican jerk crawfish salad with jerk-dusted fried crawfish tails set over greens with sweet bacon and Dijon dressing. Or order the maple chicken sandwich featuring maple-grilled chicken, sprouts, avocado, bacon, smoked cheddar, and sun-dried tomato aioli on rosemary foccacia served with fries. Most sandwiches are served with Zapp's chips, the wonderfully crunchy potato chips produced in Louisiana. Open Monday to Saturday, 11 a.m. to 2 p.m.

SPORTING NEWS GRILL $$–$$$
4848 Constitution Ave.
(225) 636-5347
The Sporting News Grill offers an appealing menu. Look for items under listings such as Greens and Bowls (salad and soups) or Slam Dunk (burgers and entrees). The sporty atmosphere is perfect in Baton Rouge, a city filled with avid sports fans. Watch your favorite sport while enjoying a hearty meal at breakfast, lunch, or

dinner. For an appetizer try the succulent tequila lime shrimp with a tangy, fresh tequila lime salsa. If you're really hungry, go for the flame-broiled 20-ounce rib-eye steak cooked to your request and served with butter sauce and garlic mashed potatoes. Open daily 6 a.m. to 11 p.m.

VOODOO BBQ & GRILL　　　　**$–$$**
3510 Drusilla Lane
(225) 926-3003

3347 Nicholson Dr.
North of LSU campus
(225) 248-6793

6409 Bluebonnet Blvd.
Mall of Louisiana
(225) 767-7267
www.voodoobbqandgrill.com
Let's face it. In the South everyone has their own "best barbecue" spot. Baton Rougeans are no different. So the taste that's just right is up to the individual. That being said, VooDoo BBQ dishes up tasty slow-smoked meats in a casual atmosphere. Line up at the counter to pick out your choice of smoked brisket, pulled pork, jerk chicken, Cajun smoked sausage, or rack of ribs. The eatery's signature side dishes are Southern delights, including corn pudding, gris gris greens, and macaroni and cheese. The menu includes salads, burgers, and soft drinks. After you pay, your food is delivered to your table. In a hurry? Ask for carry out. Open Monday to Thursday, 11 a.m. to 10 p.m.; Friday to Saturday, 11 a.m. to 11 p.m.; and Sunday, 11 a.m. to 9 p.m.

ZEA ROTISSERIE & GRILL　　　**$$–$$$**
2380 Towne Center Blvd.
(225) 927-9917
www.zearestaurants.com
Located in Towne Center, one of Baton Rouge's newest shopping complexes, Zea specializes in American cuisine with regional flavors created around a wood-burning grill and rotisserie. In Louisiana, "regional" flavors means fresh seafood grilled to perfection and other dishes enhanced with herbs and spices. Most diners rave about the Mediterranean hummus appetizer made with sun-dried tomatoes, kalamata olives, feta cheese, roasted garlic, and olive oil. The seared tuna steak with a soy marinade and cooked to order comes with orange basil butter. Zea's huge rack of St. Louis–style spare ribs slow roasted and grilled with a wet hickory sauce are fall-off-the-bone tender. The contemporary décor of the restaurant is soft and pleasant. Families and friends gather here around large tables for the excellent food and conversation.

ASIAN

DEREK CHANG'S KOTO　　　　**$$**
2562 Citiplace Court
(225) 924-1980
www.kotoofjapan.com
Key to this restaurant are the fresh ingredients of its outstanding sushi. Enjoy dining around 12 hibachi grills and an 18-foot waterfall. Explore the artful presentation of Japanese ingredients. The salmon teriyaki is delightful as is the hibachi steak and shrimp. Lunch and dinner are served Monday through Saturday.

HUNAN CHINESE RESTAURANT　　**$$**
4215 South Sherwood Forest Blvd.
(225) 292-4462
www.hunanbr.com
Jeffery Cheng established his restaurant in 1979 with the realization that the people of Hunan province in China and the people of Louisiana have a lot in common: fertile wetlands, bountiful seafood, and a taste for spicy foods. The restaurant has built a reputation as one of the top Chinese restaurants in the area. The large menu offers both mild and spicy dishes. Try the walnut chicken with broccoli and sweetened walnuts or the delightful mu shu pork with pancakes and plum sauce. Families gather at Hunan's after Sunday church services for a lavish luncheon buffet. Lunch and dinner are served daily.

**ICHIBAN JAPANESE
GRILL & SUSHI**　　　　**$$–$$$**
5741 Essen Lane
(225) 767-2288
www.ichibanbr.com

Noted for its fresh seafood and hibachi grill, Ichiban Sushi offers a large menu with numerous selections. For starters choose the crisp salty edamame, boiled whole soybeans, or vegetable spring rolls made with sliced beef, asparagus, and carrots. The sushi is known for being fresh and well constructed. Try the Kani Naruto roll that is served with a tangy, lemony sweet sauce. The California and Philadelphia rolls are always popular. If you are really hungry, two can easily share the Ichiban Boat, an assortment of sushi and sashimi with shrimp, vegetable tempura, and an Ichiban roll. It includes a tempura banana with vanilla ice cream for dessert. The restaurant serves lunch specials Monday through Friday, 11 a.m. to 2:30 p.m. Additional hours are dinner Monday to Thursday, 5 p.m. to 10 pm; Friday to Saturday, 5 p.m. to 10:30 p.m., and Sunday 11:30 a.m. to 9 p.m.

INDIA'S $$
5230 Essen Lane
(225) 769-0600

While it's not the only Indian restaurant in Baton Rouge, India's offers an excellent choice of exotic dishes highly flavored with curried sauces and served with condiments, such as coconut chutney. The lamb curry, chicken tikka masala, and vegetable samosa are favorites. The large lunch buffet gives customers a chance to choose from mild to highly spiced dishes. Mango ice cream is the perfect ending to a meal. Open for lunch and dinner.

A TASTE OF ASIA NGUYEN BISTRO $$–$$$
3651 South Sherwood Forest Blvd.
(225) 291-2222
www.nguyenbistro.com

A Taste of Asia is a remarkable restaurant that serves Vietnamese, Thai, traditional Chinese, and fusion cuisine. Each dish is bursting with texture and flavors and served with a sense of artistry. Meals can start with Vietnamese spring rolls or 5-spice dragon wings. Try the shredded green papaya salad or the Cantonese birdnest with chicken. Catch the slight tang in the sauce in the orange beef or the piquant curry bite in Thai crispy chili fish. The waitstaff is very accommodat-

ing. For example you can order curries peppery hot or as mild as you choose. The setting is lovely, and the food is even better.

THAI KITCHEN RESTAURANT $$
4335 Perkins Rd.
(225) 346-1230
www.thaikitchen.com

The spicy foods of Thailand appeal to Louisiana residents who have developed a taste for exquisitely prepared dishes with subtle blends of flavors. Thai Kitchen more than meets those criteria with both hot and spicy foods as well as mild dishes. The restaurant's tom kah (chicken coconut soup) is a delicate blend of coconut milk, lemongrass, lime juice, and a touch of chili pepper. The somewhat unusual peanut sauce salad combines lettuce, tomato, red onions, and cucumber with a hot and sour vinaigrette peanut dressing. A distinctive dish is goong op mor din, which features baked butterfly shrimp with silver noodles, garlic, gingerroot, cilantro, white pepper, and scallions served in a clay pot. The restaurant is popular for its lunchtime buffet. Carved wood furniture and artwork from Thailand add beauty and charm to this neighborhood restaurant. Hours are 11 a.m. to 2 p.m. and 5 to 9:30 p.m. Monday through Thursday; 11 a.m. to 2 p.m. and 5 to 10:30 p.m. Friday; and 5 to 10:30 p.m. Saturday. Closed Sunday.

TSUNAMI SUSHI $$
100 Lafayette St., 6th floor
(225) 346-5100
www.servingsushi.com

Experience one of the most beautiful and romantic views of the Mississippi River at Tsunami. The downtown restaurant on the sixth floor of the Shaw Center for the Arts is the fashionable place to be seen, especially at sunset. Tsunami offers an extensive list of sushi and sashimi. Dinner menu includes succulent Pacific Rim ribs cooked in sake and pineapple juice served with a mango barbecue sauce, and crispy duck served with sugary snap beans with a raspberry hoisin drizzle. Lunch and dinner are served Tuesday through Saturday. Closed Sunday and Monday.

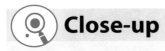

Close-up

What's the Difference Between Cajun and Creole Cuisine?

Visitors often ask about the difference between Cajun and Creole cuisine. Their confusion is understandable, especially when some restaurants carry both styles on the same menu.

John D. Folse, internationally known award-winning chef who has been called Louisiana's Culinary Ambassador to the World, has the best answer. In his book, *The Encyclopedia of Cajun and Creole Cuisine*, an 11-pound masterpiece, Chef Folse explains. Louisiana cooking is best defined as cuisine based on French cookery, which evolved around indigenous ingredients. He writes:

"Generally Cajun cooking is home-style cuisine served over or with cooked white rice. Most often it is found simmering in a cast-iron pot with its main ingredients harvested from the abundance of the land, swamps, bayous, and streams.

In comparison, Creole cuisine is a more sophisticated cousin. Creole is the cuisine of cooks and chefs and is based on European techniques. Wine- or liquor-based sauces often enhance the subtle, delicate flavors. Though Creole cuisine has French roots as well, it has been greatly influenced by other cultures, including Native American, Spain, Germany, England, Africa, and Italy. In general, Creole cooking is more sophisticated fare."

To dine on either style in Louisiana is a special treat. People who live here recognize that they are spoiled when it comes to dining. They expect their meals to be flavored properly, cooked properly, and served properly. A restaurant that doesn't meet with local approval rarely lasts more than a month or two.

CAJUN AND CREOLE

**BOUTIN'S CAJUN MUSIC
AND DINING** $$
8322 Bluebonnet Blvd.
(225) 819-9862
www.boutins.com

For an authentic Cajun dining and dancing experience, don't miss Boutin's. Stop by for lunch or dinner or just to enjoy live Cajun music. Watch patrons waltz or two-step around the large dance floor while others dine in surrounding areas. For a taste of Louisiana tradition, order a platter of steaming boiled crawfish or a fried crawfish platter. Perfect for a family outing and visitors who want to capture some Cajun flair. Meeting rooms and banquet facilities are available. Lunch and dinner served daily.

BRUNET'S CAJUN RESTAURANT $$
135 South Flannery Rd. and U.S. 190
(225) 272-6226
www.brunetscajunrestaurant.com

Ready for a "real" Cajun experience? Check out the fried seafood platters piled high with catfish, shrimp, oysters, soft shell crab, and frog legs. Choose from various platter combinations. Appetizers include oysters on the half shell, marinated crab fingers, and fried white boudin balls. Chicken fingers will appeal to the youngsters in the family. If you get there for lunch, try the catfish courtbouillon or shrimp fettuccini. Cajun bands perform Wednesday through Saturday nights. Bring your dancing shoes. Hours are Monday 5 to 9:30 p.m.; Tuesday through Thursday 11 a.m. to 9:30 p.m.; and Friday and Saturday, 11 a.m. to 10 p.m.

JUBAN'S RESTAURANT $$$–$$$$
3739 Perkins Rd.
(225) 346-8422
www.jubans.com

Creole-inspired cuisine becomes an exceptional fine dining experience complemented by one of the region's finest wine cellars, which was awarded *Wine Spectator*'s Best of Award of Excel-

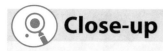

Close-up

Local Hangouts

Every town has its down-home restaurants that are cherished by locals. Downtown Baton Rouge has three such "hangouts." They all serve excellent, well-prepared popular meals, but the company and the conversation are even better. Prices are reasonable, but each spot is worth its weight in gold for atmosphere.

Christina's Restaurant (320 St. Charles St., 225-336-9512) is a neighborhood cafe that's a comfort to natives. Get there early for lunch to beat the downtown crowd of lawyers and judges. It's close enough to the courthouse that you can even get a meal while waiting for jury call. End a typical southern plate lunch with a chocolatey Mississippi mud pie. Join regulars on Saturday morning for great biscuits, coffee, and local gossip.

Pastime Restaurant and Lounge (252 South Blvd., 225-343-5490, www.pastimerestaurant .com), sits beneath the I-10 Mississippi River Bridge. Generations of LSU alumni (starting in the 1940s) return here frequently to stand in line ordering their favorite po'boy or pizza covered in meats and veggies. The old standby lounge is famous for its funky dark bar, reasonably priced drinks, and LSU memorabilia on the wall. Stay till the 2 a.m. closing to be part of the "in" crowd.

Poor Boy Lloyd's (201 Florida St., 225-387-2271) packs in weekday lunch crowds enjoying traditional gumbo, fried shrimp, or crawfish po'boys on crusty French bread. Off-duty deputies, police, legal eagles, office workers, and lobbyists line up to read the day's menu off the blackboard and then grab a table. No alcohol is served. No one leaves without getting a large peppermint or two before walking out the door. Check out the live music on Friday and Saturday nights.

lence. Exceptional entrees range from the signature Hallelujah Crab to an excellent selection of veal, beef, lamb, and duck. The rich gumbo is superb and 25-cent martinis are featured for lunch. Reservations suggested. Open for dinner Monday through Saturday. Lunch is served Tuesday through Friday. Dress is business casual to dressy. Reservations suggested.

**MANSURS ON THE
BOULEVARD** $$$–$$$$
5720-A Corporate Blvd.
(225) 923-3366
www.mansursontheboulevard.com

Fine Creole cuisine and inviting surroundings are enormously popular with locals and visitors alike for some of the finest dining in Baton Rouge. Award-winning dishes include the exquisite cream of brie and crabmeat soup, as well as the prime rib and cedar-roasted redfish entrees. Live

jazz piano music completes your dining experience. Softly lit side rooms are perfect for private parties that can be fun or formal. Off-premises catering is available. Mansurs is open for lunch, midday, and dinner. Reservations suggested. Dress is business casual to dressy.

EUROPEAN

DIGIULIO BROTHERS ITALIAN CAFÉ $$
2903 Perkins Rd.
(225) 383-4203
www.digiulios.com

Located in the culture district near the Perkins Road overpass, DiGiulio's is a small neighborhood cafe with great atmosphere and excellent wine bar. A specialty of the house is the delicious meatless lasagna with five cheeses—ricotta, parmigiana, romano, provolone, and mozzarella—topped with a rich marinara sauce. Pizzas are made fresh to order. The veal picatta with veal sauteed in wine, lemon juice, and capers is a delightful light dish. A favorite Sunday brunch dish is the pasta frittata. Open for lunch Monday through Friday and for dinner Monday through Saturday. Sunday brunch is 10:30 a.m. to 2 p.m.

i Sicilian immigrants to south Louisiana in the late 1800s brought with them their centuries-old traditions of St. Joseph's Day altars. On March 19, the feast day of the Catholic saint, altars in homes and churches are filled with regional foods. A parish priest usually blesses the altar the night before the feast day. Following a brief religious ceremony, everyone who visits the altar receives a gift of cookies, fava beans, St. Joseph's bread, and sometimes prayer cards. According to legend the tradition evolved from a drought in the Middle Ages. When people prayed to St. Joseph, the patron saint of Italy, for guidance, the countryside finally received rain. The tradition of thanksgiving honors the saint. The altars can be found in Baton Rouge and in small towns throughout south Louisiana. In many communities locals as well as visiting strangers are offered a simple meal of spaghetti and a meatless red sauce.

ENOTECA MARCELLO'S WINE BAR & CAFÉ
$$-$$$
4205 Perkins Rd.
(225) 379-7662
www.enotecamarcellos.com
Definitely designed for sophisticated tastes, Marcello's in the Southdowns Shopping Center is as much a restaurant as a wine bar. Diners enjoy authentic Italian food in an Old World setting. Marcello's was planned by owner Gene Tedaro, whose family has been in the restaurant and liquor business for at least three generations. You might want to start a meal with calamari fritti with freshly made marinara sauce, or go for the Italian version of mac-n-cheese, a penne pasta with creamy fontina, havarti, and pecorino Romano cheeses with crispy pancetta and white truffle oil. Choose veal or chicken for pan-sautéed

meats cooked in a variety of styles. For example the Palermo features sautéed scaloppini topped with fresh tomatoes, mushrooms, capers, and garlic in a lemon butter sauce. The Anatra con Risotto is seared duck breast topped with rosemary demi-glace and served with the chef's daily risotto creation. Dishes at Marcello's are designed to be accompanied by specific wines, which can be bought by the bottle or glass. Hours are 11 a.m. to 2 p.m. for lunch on Friday only, and for dinner 5:30 to 10 p.m., Tuesday through Saturday. Closed Sunday.

GALATOIRE'S BISTRO $$$-$$$$
17451 Perkins Rd.
(225) 753-4864
www.galatoires.com
Galatoire's Bistro opened in Baton Rouge in November 2005 when this famed New Orleans restaurant celebrated its 100th anniversary. Local gourmands consider themselves fortunate that the restaurant has become a part of the city's fine dining choices. A remarkable dish is the Louisiana Seafood Eggplant Cake featuring crabmeat, boiled shrimp, and eggplant in a béchamel-bound cake with a spicy remoulade aioli topped with jumbo crab meat. Open for lunch and dinner Tuesday through Friday. Dinner only on Saturday, and Sunday brunch, 11 a.m. to 3 p.m. Dress is business casual to dressy.

GINO'S $$-$$$
4542 Bennington
(225) 927-7156
www.ginosrestaurant.com
This family-owned Italian restaurant has the distinction of being voted Best Italian Restaurant in the city. Outstanding southern Italian dishes include a rich baked lasagna, Italian sausage with pasta and red sauce, and arancine stuffed with ground meat, peas, rice, sauce, and Parmigiana. The extensive menu also features grilled seafood, poultry, and steaks. Lounge is open Monday through Saturday with live entertainment Thursday through Saturday. Open for lunch and dinner Monday through Friday and for dinner only on Saturday. Closed Sunday. Dress is business casual.

MAISON LACOUR FRENCH
RESTAURANT $$$$
11025 North Harrell's Ferry Rd.
(225) 275-3755
www.maisonlacour.com
Chef Michael Jetty offers a wide range of French cuisine including seafood, game, veal, lamb, and beef. Guests are served in a pleasant French cottage setting. Elegant entree menu includes such dishes as grilled filet topped with crawfish tails in a spicy red butter sauce and young squab marinated in port, stuffed with veal, pork, shallots, and pistachio and baked with port wine sauce. Dressy casual attire welcomed. Reservations recommended. Hours for lunch are Monday through Friday, 11:30 a.m. to 2 p.m.; and for dinner, Monday through Thursday, 5:30 to 8 p.m. and Friday and Saturday until 8:30 p.m. Dress is business casual to dressy.

MEDITERRANEAN

ALBASHA GREEK & LEBANESE
RESTAURANT $$
5454 Bluebonnet Rd.
(225) 292-7988
4520 South Sherwood Forest Blvd.
(225) 293-1100
2561 Cityplace Court, Suite 500
(225) 216-1444
www.albashabr.com
Enjoy the flavors of the Middle East in a pleasant setting. Albasha offers a variety of shawarma and gyro plates and salads. If you're hungry, order the lamb shank plate that includes rice pilaf topped with toasted pine nuts. Lunch and dinner served daily.

CAFE MEDITERRANEAN $$
4347 Perkins Rd.
(225) 336-4501
This unpretentious neighborhood cafe features food from throughout the Mediterranean region, including Lebanese, Greek, and Italian. Exceptional dishes are the lasagna and eggplant Parmigiana, both topped with a luscious thick, rich marinara sauce. Chicken shawarma and gyros sandwiches and plates are packed with meats

flavored with Lebanese spices and garlic. Greek and Italian salads are served with cold, fresh ingredients. Lunch and dinner are served Monday through Saturday. Closed Sunday.

SEROP'S CAFE $$
7474 Corporate Blvd.
(225) 201-8100
6301 Perkins Rd.
(225) 767-5500
www.seropscafe.com
This popular cafe attracts local residents with freshly cooked Lebanese cuisine, handy for brief business lunches or a casual evening meal. Among favorites are Fish and Shrimp in a creamy dill sauce served with rice pilaf and vegetables. Grilled lamb, beef, chicken and kafta kebobs are served with fluffy rice pilaf and hummus. We recommend the creamy lentils as a side dish. The Corporate Boulevard location is open daily for lunch and dinner, but the Perkins Road location is closed weekends.

SEROP'S EXPRESS $–$$
712 Jefferson Hwy
(225) 248-9500
504 Main St.
(225) 338-1211
www.seropscafe.com
This Lebanese version of a fast-food restaurant attracts locals with its cafeteria setup. Customers can select from meats, vegetables, salads, and desserts and create their own plates. The food is well seasoned and cooked with fresh ingredients. Tables are available for sit-down dining, or ask for carry-out service. Lunch and dinner are served Monday through Friday, 10:30 a.m. to 7 p.m. at the Jefferson Highway location; the Main Street location closes at 2 p.m. Closed Saturday and Sunday.

MEXICAN

LOS GALLOS MEXICAN GRILL
AND CANTINA $$
6606 Siegen Lane
(225) 293-6480
www.losgallosmexicangrill.com

Los Gallos, a comfortable, family-style restaurant, offers a large menu of regional dishes from Mexico as well as Tex-Mex favorites. Crispy empanadas (small fried pies) filled with a lightly seasoned ground beef and served with fresh pico de gallo make a great appetizer for two. For a light touch, the chicken lime soup is a delicate chicken broth packed with diced potato, yellow squash, zucchini, and chicken. This is one of the few restaurants in Baton Rouge where you can get a chicken enchilada topped with a thick mole sauce, a blend of chile powders, ground nuts, and chocolate. Iced tea is served in large pitchers. Margaritas and other cocktails are available from the bar. Open for lunch and dinner daily.

MESTIZO LOUISIANA
MEXICAN RESTAURANT $$
2323 Acadian
(225) 387-2699
www.mestizorestaurant.com
Mestizo does an excellent job of blending the flavors of Mexico's Pacific and Atlantic coasts with the fresh seafood tastes of Louisiana. Start with the shrimp and crab queso dip served with icy margaritas. Entrees vary, but we recommend the shrimp and crab enchiladas, topped with creamy melted cheese and served with pico de gallo. For a different touch, try the Louisiana salad of fried crawfish tails in a sweet potato batter over a bed of lettuce with tomatoes, chives, and guacamole in a fried tortilla shell. Open for lunch and dinner daily.

SERRANOS SALSA COMPANY $$
3347 Highland Rd.
(225) 344-2354
www.serannossalsacompany.com
Join the collegiate crowd at Serrano's located near LSU's north gate. The restaurant takes an original approach to Latin American cuisine. The menu features Tex-Mex favorites as well as grilled dishes from Mexico and Central America blended with the flavors of Louisiana. Serranos has the largest selection of tequilas, rums, and Latin wines on the Gulf Coast. Hours are Wednesday through Saturday 11 a.m. to 11 p.m. and Sunday through Tuesday, 11 a.m. to 10 p.m.

SUPERIOR GRILL $$–$$$
5435 Government St.
(225) 927-2022
www.superiorgrill.com
Fashioned after large Mexican restaurants along the U.S.-Mexico border, Superior Grill puts you in the mood for margaritas and corn tortillas the minute you walk in the door. The landmark restaurant, decorated with posters, colored lights, and antler chandeliers, serves an incredible array of dishes, so take your time reading the menu. It's famous for sizzling steak fajitas served with flour tortillas, rice, beans, black bean soup or tortilla soup, pico de gallo, guacamole, and sour cream. For something different try the Yucatan camarones salad or meat and chicken dishes prepared over a mesquite grill. Patrons are devoted to the margaritas made with freshly squeezed lime juice. There's live music Thursday through Saturday, 6:30 to 10 p.m. Happy hour is daily, 4:30 to 6:30 p.m. Open daily for lunch and dinner. Breakfast served 7:30 a.m. to 2 p.m. Saturday and Sunday.

SEAFOOD

HALF SHELL RESTAURANT AND
OYSTER BAR $–$$
9828 Bluebonnet Blvd.
(225) 767-3667
37390 Perkins Rd., Prairieville
(225) 673-1951
www.onthehalfshell.biz
Even if you don't eat oysters, it's fascinating to watch oysters being shucked almost as fast as people can eat the briny mollusks. The Half Shell serves oysters up faster than you can order another dozen. You can get them raw or chargrilled, Bienville, Casso, Rockefeller, or Piccante di Formaggio. Then there's a dish called Oysters in Heaven. It includes grilled oysters in an eggplant, shrimp, and crab casserole. Patrons also enjoy seafood cooked every way imaginable. The restaurant also grills steaks and serves a variety of veggies, including corn maque choux and sweet potato fries. Regional bands crank up at 6 p.m. Tuesday through Saturday nights. Hours are 11 a.m. to 9

p.m., Monday through Thursday, and 11 a.m. to 10 p.m. Friday and Saturday. Closed Sunday.

HEADS AND TAILS SEAFOOD $$
2070 Silverside Dr.
(225) 767-2525
www.headsandtailsseafood.com

Heads and Tails has served Baton Rouge customers for more than 20 years. This cozy small cafe (off Perkins Road near Essen Lane) offers down-home bayou cooking. The seafood gumbo here was voted Number One by the *Wall Street Journal*. Try the grilled fish of the day topped with crabmeat or crawfish tails. The po'boys served on crispy fresh French bread are packed with your choice of oysters, shrimp, crawfish tails, catfish, sausage, chicken, roast beef, or ham and cheese. Then there's the Poor Sloppy Pierre Po'Boy featuring fried crawfish tails topped with homemade étouffée. The restaurant also serves seafood platters and burgers. Place your order at the counter. Help yourself to a soft drink and wait for the delicious food. Open Monday through Saturday, 9:30 a.m. to 7 p.m.

i While it's off the beaten path for most visitors, Tony's Seafood Market & Deli, 5215 Plank Road, is Louisiana's largest seafood market. You can select fresh fish or shrimp from the day's offering, find all the right seasonings, and find the right equipment you need to create your own seafood feast. Or, line up with locals in the deli area to order a take-out plate lunch or sandwich. Fried catfish, shrimp, and hush puppies are top choices along with southern home-cooked sides, such as yams and turnip greens. Tony's will pack its Cajun specialties to travel or to ship nationwide. Open daily.

MIKE ANDERSON'S $$-$$$
1031 West Lee Dr.
(225) 766-7823
www.mikeandersons.com

Mike Anderson's, established in the 1970s by a former LSU All-American football player, started in a small cottage just outside the university's south gate. The restaurant has grown into a landmark eatery, famed for its fresh Louisiana seafood. Signature dishes include fried or broiled fish topped with crab and crawfish in rich sauces. For a special treat, order a huge platter of crisp onion rings or artichoke, spinach, and shrimp dip with thin fried catfish "chips." Stop at the bar for a cold beer and outstanding charbroiled oysters. Lunch and dinner served daily.

PARRAIN'S SEAFOOD
RESTAURANT $$-$$$
3225 Perkins Rd.
(225) 381-9922
www.parrains.com

Dine here for nouveau Cajun cuisine served in a pure Louisiana setting. Every day, the restaurant has two lunch specials, and one is always seafood. Try the oysters—only 25 cents each—all day Tuesday. A new outside deck is a great spot to relax and enjoy the atmosphere. Parrain's packs in crowds on weekends. Go early or late to avoid the rush. Happy hour is 4 to 7 p.m. Monday through Friday in the Hammerhead Bar. Lunch and dinner are served daily. Brunch is offered on Sunday.

RALPH & KACOO'S $$-$$$
6110 Bluebonnet Blvd.
(225) 766-2113
www.ralphandkacoos.com

Ralph and Kacoo's, across from the Mall of Louisiana, features a variety of fresh seafood dishes with Cajun flavor, including daily grilled specials. Dine here when you anticipate a seafood platter piled high with fantastic fish, shrimp, oysters, stuffed crab, and more. For sheer dining pleasure, try the crabmeat au gratin. R&K's old-fashioned deep-fried cornmeal hush puppies may be the best in the South. Lunch and dinner served daily.

SWEETS AND COFFEE

COFFEE CALL $
3132 College Dr.
(225) 925-9493

Stay in Baton Rouge long enough and you'll find yourself in Coffee Call. Modeled after the legend-

CC's Coffee House

CC's coffee houses can be found throughout town. Based in Baton Rouge, Community Coffee is the largest family-based coffee company in America. The company's aromatic hot-brewed coffees suit Louisiana residents' passion for the beverage. Drop in with friends or enjoy a book or newspaper in a corner for a few moments of solitude. The line includes espresso drinks and frozen beverages. Relax and enjoy a delicious muffin or pastry and the coffee of the day. Also try the signature Mochasippi, a creamy frozen espresso drink with the flavor of your choice. One of the main locations is at 327 North Blvd., (225) 389-0511, www.communitycoffee.com. Other CC's locations may be found below:

1375 Coursey Blvd. (225) 752-7170	6971 Siegen Lane (225) 292-6622
10711 Coursey Blvd. (225) 292-3938	2 Roosevelt Dr. (Southern University Campus) Paul M. Hebert Law Center (225) 578-0263
7960 Jefferson Hwy. (225) 926-2511	Middleton Library (LSU Campus) (225) 578-3719
3930 Burbank Dr. (225) 767-6203	
4161 Perkins Rd. (225) 381-8187	Our Lady of the Lake–St. Mary's Tower (225) 765-1393
9757 Perkins Rd. (225) 767-6406	Our Lady of the Lake–Medical Plaza (225) 765-1129

ary coffee houses in the New Orleans French Quarter, this is the spot to be for hot beignets, heavily dusted with powdered sugar. Steaming coffee (black or au lait) and hot chocolate complete your experience. Locals head to Coffee Call at all hours from early in the morning until late at night. Don't mind the slight dusting of sugar you're likely to find on your sleeve. It's a sign of a truly pleasurable interlude. Open 24 hours.

COPELAND'S CHEESECAKE BISTRO $$
6171 Bluebonnet Blvd.
(225) 761-1110
www.copelandscheesecakebistro.com
While Copeland's Cheesecake Bistro is a full-scale restaurant with a comprehensive menu, we consider it one of the best places in Baton Rouge for dessert lovers. Every dessert is huge and delicious. There's a large selection of truly decadent

cheesecakes with any number of lush toppings, or choose a monster slice of chocolate or carrot cake to satisfy that sweet tooth. Open daily for lunch and dinner. Friday and Saturday hours extend until midnight. Reservations suggested.

PJ'S $
100 Lafayette St.
(225) 381-1875
Ralph Semmes Rd. (LSU Union)
(225) 578-5124
7329 Highland Rd.
(225) 769-2191

7248 Perkins Rd.
(225) 753-3573
www.pjscoffee.com
P.J's Coffee House specializes in a variety of New Orleans–style coffees from dark roast to cafe au lait, a rich espresso mingled with steamed milk. For something special treat yourself to a white chocolate cappuccino enhanced with Ghirardelli white chocolate and topped with whipped cream. PJ's offers a complete array of frozen and blended coffees.

NIGHTLIFE AND ENTERTAINMENT

South Louisiana has a long history of partying after dark, from local residents lighting streets with flares for the earliest Mardi Gras parades to today's spectacular illuminations. The Creole joie de vivre is infectious. Join locals who know how to embrace the best parts of life. People frequently gather in neighborhood pubs or bars after work for relaxing and socializing. These hangouts are especially popular on game days when you can watch favorite teams on big-screen televisions. Dancing, a practice brought to Louisiana by early settlers, also is a strong tradition. So, you can expect a dance floor in many establishments. Don't be surprised to see a dad waltzing with his young daughter, or two women joining hands to two-step around the floor.

Through the years nightlife has matured in Baton Rouge, especially for the over-21 crowd. Pubs offering a variety of wines, beers, and cocktails are growing in popularity. Several upscale restaurants feature classy bars that are destinations in themselves, and don't overlook well-stocked lounges in the hotels. Many are excellent. Young professionals and singles are drawn to places where they can mingle and meet in comfort and style. Sports bars and cozy neighborhood spots continue to have strong appeal to families enjoying a night out.

The downtown entertainment district, centered on Third Street, is booming, especially on Friday and Saturday nights. Twentysomethings and thirtysomethings gather inside popular spots and spill out onto the well-lit street to see and be seen. Couples, singles, and groups of friends schmooze, drink, and nibble on bar food and items such as hamburgers and pizza. A number of venues here have been adding live bands as regular entertainment on weekends. Usually there's a $5 to $10 entertainment cover charge. The scene is reminiscent of Austin's Sixth Street when music clubs were just beginning to take hold. In keeping with city regulations, bars and nightspots close at 2 a.m.

Other popular areas where you'll find nightly entertainment include the Perkins Road Overpass area, CitiPlace shopping complex, Towne Centre, and Mall of Louisiana.

Official closing hour in Baton Rouge is 2 a.m.

BARS, PUBS, WINE BARS

333 BISTREAUX
333 Third St.
(225) 381-9385
The 333 Bistro is a lounge and restaurant. Formerly the Avoyelles' Third Street Bistreaux, the restored downtown building has great atmosphere with wood floors and old brick walls. Take the stairs to the second floor lounge with a long bar and wood floor made for dancing. A balcony at the back offers views of the Mississippi River.

A DJ plays pop favorites on Friday and Saturday nights. There's a cover charge for special events. The first floor bistro has a definite New Orleans atmosphere and serves Louisiana seafood and steaks at lunch and dinner. Try the seafood manicotti. Hours are 7 a.m. to 2 a.m.

BOUDREAUX & THIBODEAUX
214 Third St.
(225) 636-2442
www.myspace.com/boudreauxdowntown

Boudreaux & Thibodeaux offers two stories of Louisiana fun. If you know something about the goofy Cajun "Boudreaux and Thibodeaux" jokes, then you know how this place acquired its name. Selected best nightclub 2008 by *225 Baton Rouge* magazine, this is one hot spot. The Balcony Bar with French Quarter atmosphere offers the best people-watching seat. Step outside for a great view of downtown. The downstairs nightclub, sporting fishing camp décor, features live entertainment three nights a week. There's great music variety from alternative to Cajun and Zydeco groups, as well as new rock and country acts. Cover fee is $5. Night club closes at 1 a.m.

There have always been bars and taverns in Baton Rouge. In 1859 one of the most colorful was the Rainbow House Saloon on Third St. Decorated in purple and gold, it offered patrons wines, liquors, and "segars."

BULLDOG
4385 Perkins Rd.
(225) 303-9400
www.bulldog-batonrouge.draftfreak.com
A perfect place to bring your four-footed friend, Bulldog invites customers to park their pets in a special area while enjoying a pint or two. The beer tavern features 50 beers on tap from all over the world as well as an extensive bottle selection. You'll find lots of warm, dark wood, wooden benches, stools, and a long wood bar. Or choose to sit in the comfy leather couches. The outdoor patio has a great beer-tap fountain, a fire pit, and umbrellas to ward off the sun or raindrops. Let your Labrador or bulldog curl up at your feet and enjoy the outing. The pub grub (sandwiches and salads) is super. So is the Abita root beer. Open until 2 a.m. on Friday and Saturday.

CHELSEA'S CAFE
2857 Perkins Rd.
(225) 387-3679
www.chelseascafe.com
Chelsea's Cafe is located under the historic Perkins Road overpass. It is a great place to catch live musi-

cal acts such as New Orleans' own Dirty Dozen Brass Band and the legendary bassist from the Funky Meters, George Porter Jr. Music and food are dished out in an intimate, casual atmosphere.

THE COVE
CitiPlace Court
(225) 201-9900
www.portroyallounge.com
This pirate-themed bar is simply too cool to pass. Walk through a small entrance and enter the long, wide hall with a 65-foot bar. Several large coolers hold a massive beer collection. The Cove offers 400 beers and 200 types of scotch. Check out the back wall with a giant octopus taking down a sailing ship. Open Monday through Saturday. Closes at 2 a.m.

FLEMING'S
7321 Corporate Blvd.
(225) 925-2710
www.flemingssteakhouse.com/wine
The wine bar at Fleming's attracts a mature crowd that enjoys the sophisticated clubhouse atmosphere and opportunity to choose from 100 different wines. Each wine is available by taste, glass, flight, or bottle. Stop by here on your way to a concert or film showing. Stay longer and indulge in a fine steak from this chain restaurant. Open dinner hours Monday through Thursday, 5 to 10 pm.; Friday and Saturday, 5 to 11 p.m.; and Sunday, 5 to 9 p.m.

GEORGE'S
2943 Perkins Rd.
(225) 343-2363

George's South Side
8905 Highland Rd.
(225) 768-8899

George's O'Neal Road
15321 George O'Neal Rd.
(225) 755-5700

George's Feliciana
5632 South Commerce St., St. Francisville
(225) 635-4711
www.georgesbr.com

The original George's, situated by the I-10 Perkins Road Overpass, has both character and top-drawer food and drinks. It's a great place for anyone seeking a late-night snack. There's a friendly bar that serves mixed drinks, wine, and beer. The current owner, City-Parish Councilman Rodney "Smokie" Bourgeois, said the spot was named for a previous owner. When you enter the oddly shaped building, you may be told that the structure lost a section when I-10 was constructed through this part of town. There's a tradition here that satisfied customers will staple dollar bills to the ceiling—be sure to look up at the signed bills. George's was honored for having "the best burger in town" by *225 Baton Rouge* magazine, but it has a complete menu including fish, steaks, salads, desserts, and great seafood gumbo. Dishes are cooked properly with only fresh ingredients. While Perkins Road is the original, you also can visit three other George's in the area.

THE GRAPE
10111 Perkins Rd.
(225) 763-2288
www.yourgrape.com

This chic wine bar and bistro in Perkins Row Shopping Center attracts wine lovers, as well as neophytes to wine drinking. The bistro removes all the worry about selecting wines by listing a "suggested" wine to go with each item on the menu. The first section of the menu is devoted to wines, grouped from one to ten and varying in price. Wine can be ordered by glass, half glass, or bottle. The menu's second section is devoted to food. The Grape's cuisine is created to be paired with wines. If in doubt, ask for a splash, a tiny tasting of a wine that you can try.

HAPPY'S IRISH PUB
136 Third St.
(225) 389-1282
www.happysirishpub.com

All this pub needs to make you really feel like you're in Ireland is a TV in the corner showing thoroughbred races. Happy's has a true pub setting with dark woods, Tiffany-style stained-glass fixtures, and simulated stained-glass panels in the ceiling. Some 16 beers on draft, including Guinness and Bass, are served from taps at the long bar. Get there early on St. Patrick's Day if you want to get inside. Hours are 6 p.m. to 2 a.m.

IVAR'S SPORTS BAR AND GRILL
2954 Perkins Rd.
(225) 388-0021
www.ivars.com

This small, funky bar and grill is a favorite of Baton Rouge's twentysomethings. The bar's motto? "Where Beautiful People Come to Get Ugly." There's a definite Irish sense of humor in play here where people love to hang out before and after the annual St. Patrick's Day Parade. Tucked under the I-10 Overpass on Perkins Road, Ivar's is always busy. Beers on tap include Abita Amber, Bass, Guinness, Newcastle, Blue Moon, and Dos Equis. Menu items have sporty names: Sugar Ray Rings, Maravich Mushrooms, the Daily Double Spud. Happy hour is Monday through Friday, 2 to 7 p.m. with special prices on beers and cocktails. Hours are 2 p.m. to 2 a.m. Monday; 11 am. to 2 a.m. Tuesday to Saturday; and 11 a.m. to midnight Sunday.

KINGFISH LOUNGE
201 Lafayette St.
(225) 344-5866
www.hiltoncapitolcenter.com

Located downtown inside the Historic Capitol House Hilton Hotel, the Kingfish is a stylish, small, intimate lounge just off the hotel's lobby. It's patronized by hotel guests and the upscale crowd. Bar snacks and comfortable chairs entice you to settle down and relax. Expect excellent bar service with half-price martinis on Tuesdays. The Kingfish Restaurant next door serves American cuisine with Louisiana specialties daily.

NORTH GATE TAVERN
136 West Chimes
(225) 346-6784
www.northgatetavern.com

Just across the street from the LSU campus, North Gate Tavern started as Joe's Library. A number of other bars followed. Now spruced up under current owners, the nightspot books aspiring rock acts from throughout the nation and local bands that may one day appear on the nearby Varsity Theatre's larger stage. North Gate offers drink specials and is open nightly Monday to Saturday.

ℹ️ People who want to cruise the night-spots in downtown Baton Rouge will find the Third St. area extremely well lighted. Friendly city police officers patrol the area on a regular basis.

SCHLITZ AND GIGGLES
301 Third St.
(225) 248-6846
www.schlittzandgiggles.com

Getting hunger pains during a night out downtown? Head to this lighthearted beer and pizza hangout located across the street from the landmark Coca-Cola sign. Order a great pizza or panini and watch at the counter while they make it for you, or grab a seat at the bar or at tables located both downstairs and upstairs. Beer is available in cans or on draft. Name your cocktail and watch the bartender work his or her magic. There's a bright, shiny newness here with chrome and aluminum appointments. You can't miss the place, because the outside overhang is illuminated with hundreds of red, green, and yellow lights. Schlitz and Giggles sponsors the Red Stick Roller Derby. Happy hour is 3 to 6 p.m. with $10 buckets of beer. Open until 2 a.m.

SPANISH MOON
1109 Highland Rd.
(225)383-6666
www.thespanishmoon.com

Located between LSU and downtown, Spanish Moon attracts patrons with modern rock, hip-hop, and dance nights. The first floor is a dance hall with a seating area. The second floor is more like a pool hall. It's known for its friendly bartenders. National touring bands, such as Isis and the Manchester Orchestra, as well as regional and local groups, appear at Spanish Moon.

THE STATION SPORTS BAR AND GRILL
4608 Bennington
(225) 926-0631
www.stationsportsbar.com

If you're an avid LSU Tigers sports fan, The Station is not to be missed. The place is made up of old railroad cars turned into a nightspot. Every space on the walls and ceilings is filled with neon beer signs, framed covers of vintage magazines, and the lead pages of sports sections. Hundreds of photographs of sports and movie celebrities—many of which are signed—are everywhere. The sports memorabilia include football and basketball jerseys. One room is set up with a bar—lighted with zany jellyfish lamps—a dance floor, and a band stand. A second intimate bar is located in a smaller room. Local cover bands perform popular '80s and '90s music Thursday through Saturday. Wednesday is Above Ground comedy night at 8 p.m.

SULLIVAN'S RINGSIDE
5252 Corporate Blvd.
(225) 237-3055
www.sullivansteakhouse.com

Savvy bar hoppers frequent Sullivan's Ringside, the jazzy nightspot just inside Sullivan's Steakhouse, named after the famed bare-knuckle boxer J. L. Sullivan. Order your favorite drink and listen to live contemporary jazz and pop music. The stage, which resembles a boxing ring, is set in the corner of the room with a bar around it. Order a light meal from the bar menu. The Ringside Bar is open Thursday, Friday, and Saturday from 9 p.m. to 2 a.m. A second bar, called the Main Bar, is open daily from 11 a.m. to 2 a.m. Music groups perform live jazz and pop music in both bars.

THE VARSITY THEATRE
3353 Highland Rd.
(225) 383-7018
www.varsitytheare.com

With its 300-person capacity, the Varsity Theatre is one of Baton Rouge's larger clubs. Featured performers have included singer-songwriter Robert Earl Keen, rising modern-rock band Red Jumpsuit Apparatus, and a number of tribute bands. It also features retro, Latin, and other dance nights. The Varsity opens at 8 or 9 p.m. depending on the show. Cover charge.

THE WINE LOFT
304 Laurel St.
(225) 346-8454
www.thewineloft.net
Walk into the Wine Loft on weekends to see and be seen. Situated in the historic Fuqua Buildings, the urban-chic wine bar is popular with young professionals. It features soft lighting and deep red accents against a black background. An extensive wine list gives you a chance to explore new tastes. It also serves a light cuisine.

BILLIARDS

CLICKS
5124 Corporate Blvd.
(225) 925-0806
This is an immense pool hall and bar. There's more than enough room for 14 pool tables, two of which are 9-foot competition tables. Electric guitars decorate the overhang above the large circular bar. There's a dance floor and stage for nights when Clicks features live bands. This is an 18-and-over club. Most patrons range from their mid-20s to mid-30s. No food is served at Clicks.

FOX AND HOUND PUB AND CIGAR BAR
5246 Corporate Blvd.
(225) 926-1444
Billiards is the main entertainment at Fox and Hound, which fashions itself as an English pub and grille. However the games and the food are more suited to American tastes. Guests sit at tables near the pool tables or may opt to sit in the cigar bar area. About 15 flat screen TVs (spaced about 5 feet apart) encircle walls above the dining tables and booths in this area. If pool is not your cup of tea, then Fox and Hound also offers dart boards and shuffleboard. There's also a handsome green room for private parties. The place features a complete menu, including freshly baked Bavarian pretzels, Napa Valley spinach salad, and Newcastle fish and chips. Order your favorite draft beer or a fancy fruit-flavored cocktail. Lunch is served Monday through Friday. Fox and Hound is in the same complex as Sullivan's, Hooters, and Clicks. Open 11 a.m. to 2 a.m. daily. Closed Sunday.

CASINOS AND GAMBLING

BELLE OF BATON ROUGE CASINO
103 France St.
(800) 676-4847
www.belleofbatonrouge.com
This three-deck paddlewheel casino is permanently docked on the Mississippi River downtown at the foot of the I-10 Mississippi River bridge. Across from the convention center, it's open 24 hours daily. Concerts and other live entertainment, including boxing, are booked throughout the year. Food is available on board and in the casino's landside facilities, including a seafood restaurant and casino buffet. The casino is next to the 10-story Sheraton Baton Rouge Hotel. The gaming area is 28,000 square feet of live poker, slots, table games, and video poker. Valet parking and entry are free.

HOLLYWOOD CASINO
1717 River Rd. North
(225) 709-7777
www.hollywoodbr.com
Upriver from downtown, Hollywood Casino's Studio 7 presents music on Fridays and Saturdays. Featured performers have included swamp-pop acts Charles Mann and T. K. Hulin, zydeco favorite Geno Delafose, and Fats Domino tribute act Al "Lil' Fats" Jackson. Dine in style at the Steakhouse or choose meals at the Take 2 Deli or the Epic Buffet. Gaming activities include more than 1,100 slots. Open daily 24 hours. Easy and convenient parking.

COMEDY CLUB

FUNNY BONE/TRIPLE A BAR
4715 Bennington
(225) 927-3222
www.funnybonebatonarouge.com
www.tripleabatonrouge.com
Plan your night out just right and you can get double your fun at the Funny Bone and Triple A. The side-by-side lounges are housed in one building and separated by a double sound-proof wall. This lets entertainers perform in the Funny Bone, while a separate party can be taking place

in the Triple A. Host Tom Hirschey, who's been with the club 22 years, introduces comedians at the Funny Bone. Shows take place at 8 and 9 p.m. on Friday and Saturday and at 9 p.m. on Thursday. The club features both newcomers to the comedy circuit as well as top-name comedians. Among those who have performed on the stage are Dave Coulier, who played Uncle Joey on *Full House*, and Jon Reep. John Morgan, known as the Ragin' Cajun, has played the club for 16 years. Other top comedians who have appeared at the club over the years include Jeff Foxworthy, Ron "Tater Salad" White, Rahn Ramey, and Phyllis Diller. Funny Bone can seat 310 guests. A 60-foot bar lines one side of the room, and a DJ stage is tucked into one corner.

The place is arranged so that guests can arrive at the Triple A Bar early or stay late after either first or second show at the Funny Bone. They can enjoy music and dancing on a large dance floor or just relax in comfy lounge chairs. Patrons also can gather around the large rectangular bar and watch sports or popular shows on four extra-large television screens. For something different they can saunter into the pool room for additional fun. The Funny Bone is open to ages 18 and over. Guests may be asked to show IDs at the door. Those ages 18 to 21 are given wristbands in one color marked with XXXXs and will not be served alcohol; those 21 and over get wristbands in another color.

JAZZ AND BLUES

PHIL BRADY'S
4848 Government St.
(225) 927-3785
www.philbradys.org
Located in mid-city Baton Rouge, Phil Brady's is well known for its Thursday night blues jam. It also books local, regional, and sometimes national blues and rock acts during the weekends. Patrons can order from a wide variety of beer and mixed drinks from the bar. Lunch and dinner are served. Ask about lunch specials. Hours are 11 a.m. to 2 a.m. Monday through Friday and 3 p.m. to 2 a.m. Saturday.

i Baton Rouge blues is a genre of music that is more of a swamp and country sound than the Delta blues. The prime example is the music of Slim Harpo. The Rolling Stones used one of his songs on their first album. Others who have performed Harpo's music are Van Morrison, the Kinks, Moody Blues, and Hank Williams. Visitors will find Baton Rouge blues performed in a number of nightspots in the city.

RED DRAGON
2401 Florida St.
(225) 939-7783
rdlrbr@gmail.com
This listening club is a labor of love for owner Chris Maxwell. The music genre varies from week to week, but the Red Dragon specializes in singer-songwriters, including Jimmy LaFave, Slaid Cleaves, and country and gospel legend Charlie Louvin. Concerts take place in a large street-level room and are scheduled once or twice a month. Admission fees go directly to participating entertainers. No food or drink is served.

TEDDY'S JUKE JOINT
17001 Old Scenic Hwy, Zachary
(225) 892-0064, (225) 658-8029
www.teddysjukejoint.com
One of the city's busiest clubs, Teddy's is an authentic juke joint created by owner and DJ Teddy Johnson. The colorful atmosphere includes Christmas lights everywhere. North of town not far from the airport, Teddy's has developed an international reputation as an authentic American blues venue. Weekends are often booked with well-known blues performers. A jam is held every Saturday. Try the food from Nancy's Kitchen. A bass player, Teddy Johnson's newest album is "Super Cooper" with Teddy's Sharecroppers." Among the performers who have appeared at Teddy's Juke Joint are Kenny Neal Band, Larry Garner, Henry Gray, Greg Wright, and Big Red and the Soul Benders.

LIVE MUSIC AND DANCING

MELLOW MUSHROOM
4250 Burbank Dr.
(225) 490-6355
www.mellowmushroom.com
The Mellow Mushroom dishes up pizza and plenty of fun. The bar features daily drink specials with 100 different beers and 25 on draft. The Mushroom is also a great, casual place to watch your favorite game on one of 12 HD televisions. Tuesday night features open mic night. Wednesday night features Teen Trivia and Karaoke. Thursday and Friday night the action is turned over to some of Baton Rouge's best local musicians. Open Sunday through Thursday, 11 a.m. to 10 p.m; Friday and Saturday, 11 a.m. to 10:30 p.m.

ROUX HOUSE
143 Third St.
(225) 344-2583
www.rouxhousebr.com
The Roux House is in the same location that used to be Swamp Mama's, and before that it was M's Mello Cafe. The club is popular with LSU students, and there are live bands every night. Patrons gather in front of the band to dance as couples or singles. Cajun food is served upstairs. The outdoor patio is packed on no-rain nights and is a great spot when breezes are blowing off the Mississippi River. Hours are 6 p.m. to 2 a.m.

THE TEXAS CLUB
456 North Donmoor
(225) 928-4655
www.thetexasclub.com
The Texas Club, designed to hold a large crowd, is one of Baton Rouge's largest concert halls. This landmark club in a former Continental Trailways building presents country stars, such as Jason Aldean and Randy Owen, as well as popular Louisiana musicians, including Wayne Toups and Zydecajun. Drop in on a Saturday night for country dancing and "U Call It" happy hour.

DOWNTOWN THEATERS AND CITY ARENAS

MANSHIP THEATRE
100 Lafayette St.
(225) 344-0334
www.manshiptheatre.com
Situated in the Shaw Center for the Arts, the Manship Theatre's schedule has ranged from New Orleans music master Dr. John to singer-songwriter Randy Newman. The Manship books some of the world's top musicians. The small auditorium is perfect for the serious fan. There is no public dancing here. See the Culture and Arts chapter for more.

RIVERCENTER ARENA
RiverCenter Complex downtown
275 South River Rd.
(225) 389-3030
www.brrivercenter.com
Located in the city-parish government complex, the arena is the main venue for large entertainment productions. People flock here to see big name entertainers in rock shows, gospel shows, mass choir productions, truck pulls, sporting events, and trade shows. The annual Ice Skating on the River event takes place here during the Christmas season. Parking garages operated by the city are conveniently located nearby. For information on events and tickets, check the Web site.

RIVER CENTER THEATRE FOR THE PERFORMING ARTS
275 South River Rd.
(225) 389-3030
www.brrivercenter.com
The Theatre for the Performing Arts is the home of the Baton Rouge Symphony Orchestra. The annual production of *The Nutcracker*, presented by Baton Rouge Ballet Theater, also is presented here. Traveling Broadway drama and musicals, as well as opera, one-man shows, magic acts, dance competitions, and recitals have appeared here. See the chapter on Culture and Arts. For a schedule of events, check the Web site.

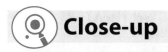

Close-up

Dancing to Louisiana's Music

Visitors to Baton Rouge any time of year will soon discover that dancing is very much a part of the social scene. When you walk into a Cajun restaurant, you'll often find tables surrounding a dance floor and a small stage where a local band will be playing traditional Cajun tunes or perhaps zydeco music. Dancing here is not only relegated to Cajun music; the custom applies to any rhythmic music that gets you up on your feet and moving. If looking for something more lively at one of the city's nightspots, you'll find a similar scene. Couples will be out on the floor dancing and swaying to the drumbeats of jazz, rock, pop, salsa, and fusion music. However, the most popular dance patterns are the waltz, the two-step, and the jig.

You may find yourself attending a festival in downtown Baton Rouge or one of its suburbs. There's seldom a festival without two or three stages where local and guest musicians will be performing as early as 10 a.m. After an hour or two, another band takes over and the music continues throughout the day and into the night. Some festivals set up in halls where there's a smooth floor for dancing. Most outdoor events simply leave space near the stages so people will have room for impromptu dancing.

In Louisiana current forms of dancing and music have evolved from the early arrivals of Europeans and Africans to the new world. The Cajun waltz progresses slowly around the floor and is characterized by a subtle swaying of the hips and steps very close to walking. In Louisiana's Acadian country, families would gather in their homes, push back the furniture, bring in a fiddler, and have a dance called a *fais do do*. These gatherings celebrated special occasions such as a birthday or a season such as harvest, when the hard work of fall was completed.

The two-step developed later in America's history. The original two-step caught on with the public when John Phillip Sousa came out with "The Washington Post March" in 1891. This was done with a skip in each step and in 2/4 or 4/4 time. Basically it's a quick step or quick-quick-slow.

The jig is danced to lively folk tunes, making it easily adapted to Louisiana's music. The name is possibly derived from French *giguer* or Italian *giga*, meaning "to jump." The Cajun jig, popular in the 1980s and 1990s, remains a mainstay of local dancers. The hopping steps can be alternated with other patterns and enjoyed indoors or at outdoor festivals. Variations of handholds combined with turns give dancers numerous options.

At any given dance, people are likely to apply the steps to various forms of Louisiana music. Some bands deftly switch styles to give dancers a change of pace.

Creole, Cajun, and zydeco music and dance are a blend of European, African, and Native American traditions found only in southwest Louisiana. In his monograph *Cajun Music: Its Origins and Development*, Dr. Barry Jean Ancelet, author and professor of Francophone Studies at University of Louisiana-Lafayette, explains that Acadians who came to Louisiana in 1755 brought with them music that had its origins in France but had already been changed by New World encounters with British settlers and Native Americans.

In the 1800s the music of the Acadians in Louisiana was transformed by new influences, including African rhythms and Native American singing. Some fiddle tunes and a few ballads came from Anglo-American sources. Even the Spanish contributed a few melodies, according to Ancelet. German immigrants brought the accordion to Louisiana in the late 1800s. Because the accordion was tuned in keys that did not match the "open string" tuning of the fiddlers, the instrument was not immediately incorporated into Acadian music. With the introduction around 1925 of accordions tuned in C and D, Cajun music found a sound that carried well during noisy dances. Today, a typical Cajun band will include the fiddle, accordion, and triangle.

Many slaves who gained their freedom during French and Spanish rule before the Louisiana Purchase were of mixed racial ancestry and identified themselves as Creole. Their music drew on French traditions, as did Cajun music, but it included rhythms of the Caribbean and the melodies of the blues. Creole music played in the old style, including the fiddle, was known as "la-la music." By the 1920s musicians were exposed to music from other areas of the United States. Clifton Chenier, born in 1925, learned la-la music as well as other genres. Chenier, who became the King of Zydeco, and his brother Cleveland, who played the washboard, performed in Texas and Louisiana clubs in the late 1940s. Cleveland began using corrugated tin, played at first with spoons and then bottle openers. Clifton had a metal worker in Port Arthur, Texas, shape a board with shoulder straps, inventing the frottoir, the distinctive instrument of zydeco. Eventually Chenier's band included saxophone, horns, and keyboard on some numbers. Visit a zydeco dance hall and you'll see the floor filled with people dancing 21st-century style: a combination of jig, jitterbug, and swing patterns.

When rock 'n' roll became popular during the 1950s, a number of Louisiana musicians with Cajun roots started producing a style known as swamp pop, a blend of Cajun, hillbilly melodies, and New Orleans style R&B music. Performers, including Van Broussard, Rod Bernard, and Warren Storm, became household names.

Today, you can listen and dance to all the styles of Louisiana music. Discover for yourself the innovative spirit of such performers such as Wayne Toups, who coined the name *zydecajun* to describe his fusion of rock, Cajun, and zydeco. Geno Delafose and Keith Frank are among zydeco players who record some songs in French as well as English. In recent years, many musicians, such as Dewey Balfa, Canray Fontenot, and Alphonse "Bois Sec" Ardoin, have worked to preserve traditional Cajun and Creole music. In 2008 the Grammy Awards created an award for the Best Zydeco or Cajun Music Album. The 2008 award went to Terrance Simien and the Zydeco Experience for *Live! Worldwide*. In 2009 the award was presented to BeauSoleil avec Michael Doucet for *Live at the 2008 New Orleans Jazz & Heritage Festival*.

In Baton Rouge visit Boutin's and Brunet's for dinner and to waltz or dance the two-step to authentic Cajun, Creole, or zydeco music. Mulate's at Breaux Bridge is a must for food and dancing (see the Day Trips chapter). Extend a trip to Eunice, west of Opelousas, on U.S. 190 to attend a performance of *Rendezvous Des Cajuns*, a live Cajun radio and TV show, in the Liberty Theater. The show runs 6 to 7:30 p.m. every Saturday night. Tickets are $5 for general seating, and there's a dance floor right in front of the stage. Waltz next door to the Prairie Acadian Cultural Center, a unit of Jean Lafitte National Historical Park and Preserve, open Tuesday through Friday, 8 a.m. to 5 p.m. and Saturday, 8 am. to 6 p.m. Free Cajun music and dancing takes place every Saturday at 3 p.m. Volunteers will teach you how to dance Cajun style. Free cooking demonstrations take place every Saturday at 4 p.m. Rangers and volunteers share the secrets of gumbo, étoufée, and other favorites. While in town you can stop by the Savoy Music Center for a Saturday jam session, 9 a.m. to noon. Contact www.eunice-la.com.

Become thoroughly immersed in south Louisiana music by attending one of the many festivals found throughout the area. The Zydeco Festival in Plaisance, near Opelousas, is a major event in August with dancing, music, seminars, food, and a grand parade. Visit www.zydeco .org. Festivals Acadiens in Lafayette is a free event downtown in October celebrating both the Acadian and Creole cultures. Visit www.festivalsacadiens.com. In recent years, Gonzales, just south of Baton Rouge, has hosted the Swamp Pop Music Festival in July. If you're planning to dance outdoors, wear comfortable, cool clothing. Most folks wear tennis shoes, but they can be awkward when trying to dance a gliding waltz. However, not having the proper shoes never stops Louisianians from hitting the dance floor.

Because space is limited in this guide, many famed musicians, nightspots, and dance halls are not mentioned. I suggest you start by browsing the Internet and search for historical background, recordings of authentic Louisiana music, and special events. I highly recommend "A Brief History of Cajun, Creole & Zydeco Music" posted on the Web site www.lsue.edu/acadgate/ music/history.htm. For more on folk dance, visit www.history.com/encyclopedia. Also look for performances by Lousiana musicians posted on YouTube.

i Baton Rouge residents tend to dress more casually than people in other cities. However, men wear suits and ties and women dressy outfits for symphony concerts in the main theaters. Formal wear is chosen for invitational events, such as Mardi Gras balls. Dressy casual is acceptable for most recitals, art shows, and jazz ensembles in small venues. Call ahead and ask, if in doubt.

MOVIE THEATERS

Most Baton Rouge movie theaters are situated in major shopping centers. They are designed with multiple theaters and can handle large crowds, although first-run films will sell out early. Since the city has hot and humid weather from mid-spring to mid-fall, the theaters are highly air-conditioned. Bring a light jacket if you tend to get chilled. There is no movie theater downtown. However the Manship Theatre in the Shaw Center does feature some special art films from time to time. See the Culture and Arts chapter.

CINEMARK PERKINS ROW
Perkins Road and Bluebonnet Boulevard
(225) 761-7844
www.cinemark.com
Cinemark is situated in the center of the upscale Perkins Row Center. It offers stadium seating with reclining chairs. Tickets are $6.75 for children age 11 and under and seniors; $6.75 for adult bargain matinees (until 6 p.m. each day); and $5 for the first matinee seven days a week. Adult admission is $8.50 Sunday through Thursday and $8.75 Friday and Saturday after 6 p.m.; students $7. Tickets and showtimes are available on the Web site.

GRAND CINEMA
15365 George O'Neal Rd.
(225) 755-8888
www.thegrandcinema.com
Grand Cinema provides excellent movie entertainment with all stadium seating and digital sound. All tickets are $5 for showings before 1:30 p.m. All tickets for showings 1:30 to 6 p.m. are $6.

Adult tickets after 6 p.m. are $8; children age 12 and under and seniors 55 and over are $6; students and military, $7.

RAVE BATON ROUGE 16
16040 Hatteras
(225) 753-2710
www.ravemotionpictures.com
With stadium seating and ample parking, this multi-theater facility can be crowded on weekends. All tickets are $7 for showings before 6 p.m. daily. Regular adult admission, $9; children 3-11, $7; senior citizens, $8; students with I.D. (Sunday evening-Thursday), $8; and military $8. The 3D shows before 6 p.m. are $9.50; other 3D shows are adults, $11.50, and children, $9.50.

RAVE MALL OF LOUISIANA 15
6401 Bluebonnet Blvd.
(225) 769-5176
www.ravemotionpictures.com
There are two Rave Motion Pictures in Baton Rouge. They offer stadium seating and complete digital projection. The theaters are relatively new and well-maintained. First-run movies will sell out quickly, especially on Friday and Saturday nights. For group sales and events, call (866) 878-7068.

This Rave is located at the Mall of Louisiana. Friday and Saturday nights are extremely busy, but there is ample parking. All tickets are $7 for showings before 6 p.m. daily. Regular adult admission is $9; children 3 to 11, $7; senior citizens, $8; students with ID, $8; military, $8. All 3D shows before 6 p.m. are $9.50. The 3D shows after 6 p.m. are $9.50 for children and $11.50 for adults.

UNITED ARTIST CITIPLACE 11
2610 CitiPlace
(225) 216-0056
www.regmovies.com
There is one United Artist Theater in Baton Rouge. All tickets are $6.75 for all showings before 6 p.m. daily. Regular adult admission is $8.75; students, $7.75; children and senior citizens, $6.75. On Friday and Saturday nights, all patrons under age 17 must be accompanied by an adult age 21 or older. Valid IDs may be requested.

SHOPPING

From its early days as a river port, Baton Rouge residents developed a penchant for living well. River boats traveling down the Mississippi River from the north brought innovative products and fancy goods from cities, such as St. Louis. Boats traveling up the river from New Orleans brought goods from as far away as Cuba and France. Today there's an amazing variety of shopping experiences available. Much of Baton Rouge's shopping now takes place in expansive malls and new mixed-use lifestyle centers. However, from downtown to the farthest edge of town, there are boutiques and quaint shops that attract seekers of unusual one-of-a kind items. Enjoy the glitz of the malls. A selection of specialty shops is listed here, but explore Baton Rouge's neighborhood shops and find places that appeal to your own sense of adventure. Extend your search to nearby towns to browse through clusters of antique shops and boutiques.

MALLS AND SHOPPING AREAS

MALL AT CORTANA
Florida Boulevard at Airline Highway
(225) 927-6747
www.themallatcortana.com
A landmark of Baton Rouge for more than 30 years, the Mall at Cortana is a tradition with more than 1 million square feet of shopping, including Macy's, Dillard's, JCPenney, Sears, and numerous restaurants. Cortana hosts regular events for families and children. Parking areas are huge, with easy access.

MALL OF LOUISIANA
6401 Bluebonnet Blvd. at I-10
(225) 927-6747
www.malloflouisiana.com
The Mall of Louisiana, one of south Louisiana's premier shopping complexes, features dramatic décor, a carousel for the kids, a large food court, and some 155 stores on two levels. Outside on the Boulevard is a pedestrian-friendly, tree-lined walkway with more than 25 upscale retailers. Check out Louisiana's first Apple Store, Ann Taylor Loft, Sephora, L'Occitane en Provence, Jos. A. Bank, Williams Sonoma, Pottery Barn, Coach, and others. Satellite facilities include a brew house, an Italian restaurant, a bookstore, and Rave Motion Pictures.

PERKINS ROW
Bluebonnet at Perkins
(225) 761-6905
www.perkinsrow.com
Perkins Row is an upscale mixed-use living complex with contemporary condos, a gourmet market, wine bars, lively restaurants, and a 16-screen movie theater. Shops include Anthropologie, Sur La Table, J. Crew, Z Gallerie, Barnes & Noble, and White House/Black Market. For a different dining experience, try Texas de Brazil, where grilled meats keep coming to your table until you shout "stop."

SIEGEN CORRIDOR
Siegen Lane
Siegen Lane is a major street connecting any number of neighborhoods across the southern region of Baton Rouge. It runs from Burbank Drive southeasterly until it connects with South Sherwood Forest Drive at Airline. Major shopping areas include Siegen Park Mall (Sam's Club, Wal-Mart, and Lowe's) as well as Target Plaza, with several satellite shops. Along the route are banks, car dealers, home supply companies, and numerous commercial establishments. The area also has Italian, Mexican, and American restaurants, fast-food chains, and hotels.

TANGER OUTLET CENTER
I-10, Exit 177 at La. 30
(225) 647-9383
www.tangeroutlet.com
This outlet complex, with 55 stores, is an easy drive from Baton Rouge. Stores include Banana Republic, Gap, Nike, Harry & David, Old Navy, Ann Taylor, and Aeropostale. Restaurants within the complex include Cracker Barrel and Chili's. Just across the street is Cabela's, a world-class sports outfitter.

TOWNE CENTER AT CEDAR LODGE
Corporate Boulevard at Jefferson Highway
(225) 925-2344
www.townecenteratcedarlodge.com
Towne Center at Cedar Lodge is one of Baton Rouge's newest venues. The handsome open-air complex features sidewalks to stroll, great restaurants, and beautiful landscaping. Stores include Gap, Banana Republic, Chico's, Talbots, Coldwater Creek, American Eagle Outfitters, and New Orleans jewelers Adler's and Mignon Faget. There's also a Whole Foods Market, Don Juan Cigar Company, Relax the Back, and Ricky Heroman's Florist and Gifts. Just across the intersection is Bocage Village, the city's oldest upscale shopping center offering everything from fine jewelry to day spas. Located here is Jules Madere Jewelry, La Madeleine, Dearman's Soda Shop with an authentic 1950s theme, and Calvin's Bocage Supermarket specializing in Louisiana produced items, including Steen's Cane Syrup, TABASCO hot sauces, Zapp's potato chips, and Tony Chachere's original Creole seasoning.

i Jefferson Highway, which runs through the center of Baton Rouge, is named for Thomas Jefferson, who brokered the Louisiana Purchase in 1803. It is the longest remaining stretch of the original Jefferson Highway, called "Old Jeff" by auto enthusiasts, that starts in Winnipeg, Canada, and runs through the Louisiana Purchase territory to New Orleans. Along the Baton Rouge route, you'll find several upscale shopping centers and beautiful neighborhoods.

SPECIALTY SHOPS

BRIAN'S FURNITURE AND APPLIANCES
515 Court St., Port Allen
(800) 259-0896
www.briansfurniture.com
Brian's is a fascinating experience for anyone planning to landscape a lawn, garden, or patio. The company has the largest selection of rust-free cast aluminum furniture in the South. Check out the iron and fiberglass sugar kettles that can be turned into ponds or water fountains. The kettles are reproduced from those found on Louisiana sugar cane plantations.

CIRCA 1857
1857 Government St.
(225) 387-8667
www.circa1857.com
You never know what you will find at Circa 1857. Browse for antiques, retro clothing, or original art. Anyone who loves old handcrafted woodwork, fencing, grates, or gates incorporated into their home will enjoy browsing through architectural salvage from around the world. See the Culture and Arts chapter.

i The Baton Rouge Arts Market, North Fifth St. at Main, takes place the first Saturday of each month. This open-air market and cultural event features more than 50 Louisiana artists. It's an excellent place to find oils and watercolors of Louisiana scenes, as well as subjects such as herons, pelicans, and waterfowl. Browse for one-of-a-kind necklaces and earrings, woodwork, and pottery fashioned from Louisiana clay. A project of the Arts Council of Baton Rouge, the market runs from 8 a.m. to noon.

COYOTE MOON
1938-A Perkins Rd.
(225) 344-4448
www.coyotemoonbr.com
Coyote Moon tempts the pocketbook with gifts and books that make your heart sing. Special

items include jewelry, crystals and minerals, and aromatherapy products. Local psychic readers are available Thursday through Sunday 10 a.m. to 6 p.m. The shop offers classes in meditation, self-improvement, and healing on a periodic basis.

DENHAM SPRINGS ANTIQUE VILLAGE
Range Avenue
(225) 791-1116
www.denhamspringsantiquedistrict.com
The antique district in Denham Springs is a hot spot for antiques roadies. More than 25 shops feature everything from hard-to-find collectibles to jewelry and fine antiques. Drop by Theatre Antique Mall, 228 N. Range Ave., to browse for old books, knives, and cookware. Benton Brothers Antiques, 115 N. Range Ave., features porcelains, silver, and handsome Victorian and East Lake furniture. Local cafes offer Louisiana cuisine, including sandwiches and desserts. For lunch stop by Patty Denham Restaurant, 31899 La. 16, for a huge hamburger and an order of fried pickles or fried mushrooms.

FIRESIDE ANTIQUES
14007 Perkins Rd.
(225) 752-9565
www.firesideantiques.com
Fireside Antiques has fine quality French, Italian, English, and Swedish antiques. Eight showrooms display significantly important armoires, tables, sofas, and chairs as well as delicate decorative pieces. In addition Fireside is a great source for mirrors, tall case clocks, chandeliers, and home decor accessories. In keeping with the southern tradition, the store has a large collection of elegant European garden statuary, including limestone fountains, planters, birdbaths, and sundials.

GOODWOOD HARDWARE & OUTDOORS
7539 Jefferson Hwy
(225) 926-0040
www.goodwoodonline.com
Goodwood Hardware is a destination in itself. You'll find a whole lot more than electric and plumbing supplies. Goodwood, across from Towne Center at Cedar Lodge, is a major source for barbecue grills and supplies, as well as hundreds of kitchen supplies and pots and pans. Before you leave, head for the rear of the store where you'll find a super collection of cookbooks for smoking and barbecuing outdoors. The store also features handsome outdoor furniture and a purple-and-gold LSU area with shirts, ponchos, dishes, glassware, baby clothes, and dog collars—all in celebration of Louisiana's flagship university.

GRANDMOTHER'S BUTTONS
9814 Royal St., St. Francisville
(800) 580-6941
www.grandmothersbuttons.com
Grandmother's Buttons started when Susan Davis and her 95-year-old grandmother were sifting through tins and boxes filled with a lifetime's worth of collected buttons—dazzling jet glass, carved pearl, and decorative brass buttons. Davis turned the buttons into one-of-a-kind jewelry and started a business that is now recognized nationwide. The firm is based in a turn-of-the-century old bank building. After you're done browsing the button jewelry and accessories, step into the old bank vault to view the amazing Button Museum.

HIGHLAND ROAD SHOPPING VILLAGE
16255 Highland Rd.
(225) 752-1762, (225) 756-2000
www.highlandroadantiques.com
This small complex of simple cottages contains a number of highly innovative shops. Included are Rudolph's Christmas Store, Highland Road Antiques and Gifts, Highland Gifts, Renaissance Fine Photography, Houchin's Art and Frame, and A Cottage Path Florist. You'll find one-of-a-kind Christmas items, antique books, weapons, china, garden art, and jewelry and linens from France. Visit Highland Road's Web site for information on each of its shops.

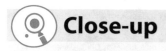

Homegrown Treasures

The Baton Rouge region is home to some highly respected food products. You'll find them on the shelves and in the refrigerators in most Louisiana homes. Many stem from the region's agricultural industry and from entrepreneurs who turned their favorite foods into businesses. Others evolved from South Louisiana's seafaring trade that brought raw products from other countries into the ports of New Orleans and Baton Rouge. From candy to coffee, hot sauce to ice cream, the area produces homegrown treasures.

Included here are items made in Baton Rouge or in towns within a day's trip of the city. You can always take a sample home to enjoy or to introduce the flavors of Louisiana to friends.

CHEF JOHN FOLSE & COMPANY

Chef John Folse, restaurateur, author, and entrepreneur, created his food marketing division in 1990. Based in Gonzales south of Baton Rouge, Folse's Bittersweet Plantation Dairy, one of the only specialty artisan dairies in Louisiana, produces cream cheeses, butters, and ice cream using Louisiana milk. The company's lightly salted hand-churned butter is an old-world-styled butter that's higher in fat and lower in moisture. Other products include Fleur-de-Lis, a soft, ripened triple cream cheese; Feliciana nevat, a cow and goat mixed-milk cheese patterned after the Catalonia nevat; and a Bulgarian-style feta, a creamy feta firm enough to hold its shape when sliced. The company's line of Creole Cream Cheese ice creams gets rave reviews from local cooks. Folse, who owns White Oak Landing, a catering division in Baton Rouge, is an avid supporter of Louisiana's Cultural Economy initiatives. He is producer and host of an international PBS television series as well as *Stirrin' It Up with Chef John Folse & Company*, a radio cooking talk show. Check out his products at www.jfolse.com.

ELMER'S CANDY CO.

Ponchatoula is home to the oldest family-owned chocolate company in the United States. The company is the leading manufacturer of seasonal chocolates in the country, including the familiar heart-shaped box at Valentine's Day. Other famous products are Gold Brick, Pecan, and Heavenly Hash eggs. The company was founded in 1855 by Christopher Henry Miller, a German immigrant who had moved to New Orleans. His daughter married Augustus Elmer, and the company became the Miller-Elmer Co. In 1914 with the addition of Augustus Elmer's sons, the business became the Elmer Candy Co. In 1963, Roy Nelson purchased the company. In 1970 the Nelson family moved the company to Ponchatoula. Generations of children have found Elmer's eggs in their Easter baskets. Other family members receive the familiar chocolates at Christmas and other occasions. Today the company employs about 300 people, making it the largest employer in Ponchatoula. Visit www.elmercandy.com.

JACK MILLER'S BAR-B-QUE SAUCE

Founded in 1955, Jack Miller's Bar-B-Que sauce was produced in Miller's restaurant, the American Inn in Ville Platte, north of Lafayette. In 1955 the tangy product was placed on the open market in south Louisiana and later in other states. Millions of bottles later, Jack's son, Kermit, oversees operations. He has added two new products to the line, Cajun Dipping & Cocktail Sauce and Cajun All-Purpose Seasoning. Visit www.jackmillers.com.

KLEINPETER FARMS DAIRY

Kleinpeter is a household world in Baton Rouge. The family's history dates from 1774 when members, originally from Switzerland, traveled by flatboat down the Ohio and Mississippi Rivers to the Baton Rouge area. In early 1913 Sebastian Louis Kleinpeter started a small dairy with Guernsey cows. In 1982 the original farm ceased operations, but Kleinpeter Dairy continued to process raw milk purchased from local Louisiana dairy farmers. In 1997 the company reopened the Kleinpeter Farm on 1,600 acres in Montpelier. The current line of products includes milk, orange juice, butter, oleo, eggs, cottage cheese, and yogurt. Kleinpeter's recently introduced a new line of delicious ice cream made with Louisiana-produced ingredients, including Gold Brick, Peach, Banana Foster, and Cafe' Au Lait. Visit www.kleinpeterdairy.com.

LOUISIANA FISH FRY

The Pizzolato family of Baton Rouge founded Louisiana Fish Fry Products more than 18 years ago as an offshoot of Tony's Seafood Market, 5215 Plank Rd. Founder Tony Pizzolato started with a small produce market in Donaldsonville and then expanded his business to include seafood. The company now produces some 30 products, including its number-one-selling fish fry. Other products include hush puppy mix, various seafood boils and seasonings, cocktail sauce, tartar sauce, and remoulade dressing. Today Tony's Seafood is the largest seafood market in the South. Visit this old-fashioned, one-stop market for fresh or frozen seafood, seasonings, and other grocery products. A deli on one side of the store does a brisk take-out business with lunches featuring everything from fried catfish and oysters to southern cooked greens and sweet potatoes. Check out www.louisianafishfry.com.

MANDA FINE MEATS

The Baton Rouge–based Manda Fine Meats has been around since 1947. Smoked sausages, Cajun andouille, and boudin are some of the meat products the company produces. Manda products are distributed to more than 30 states. The company operates with three high-tech processing facilities and one modern distribution facility. Visit www.mandafinemeats.com.

RIVER ROAD COFFEES

In the late 1800s Stanislaus and Marie Melancon began River Road Coffees in a small country store along River Road. It started with their idea that family and neighbors could come together and share stories over a cup of coffee. Today a new generation of the Melancon family continues the tradition of making fine coffee blends. The company is owned and operated by 30-year coffee industry veteran John "The Coffee Man" Melancon. The Web site is www.river roadcoffees.com/riverroadcoffees.

TABASCO

When traveling around the globe from Louisiana to New York—or to Paris, Budapest, and Tokyo—we have been handed a bottle of TABASCO when we asked for hot sauce. Owned by Louisiana's McIlhenny family, TABASCO has been around for more than 140 years. It was started by Edmund McIlhenny of Avery Island. Given seeds of *Capsicum frutescens* peppers from Mexico or Central America, he sowed the seeds and delighted in the peppers' spicy flavor. Following the Civil War and during Reconstruction, available food was bland, so he crushed the reddest peppers and mixed them with Avery Island salt and French white wine vinegar. The "mash" set for at least 30 days, and then he transferred the mixture into small cologne-type bottles. McIlhenny grew his first commercial pepper crop in 1868 and secured a patent in the 1870s. Today TABASCO is labeled in 22 languages and dialects and sold in more than 160 countries. You will always find it in Baton Rouge, and you can visit the company's plant and store on a day trip to Avery Island, near New Iberia. In fact about half of the company's 200 employees actually live on Avery Island, with many of their parents and grandparents having worked and lived there as well. Paul McIlhenny, current president, is the sixth McIlhenny in a chain of direct descendants who have preserved the legacy and traditions of the company. See the Day Trips chapter. Check out www.tabasco.com.

ℹ️ Because of ongoing renovation of the Louisiana State Capitol's observation deck, the Shop at the Top has moved to the Louisiana State Museum–Baton Rouge, 660 Fourth St. This is a good place to pick up postcards and Louisiana souvenirs, including books, caps, and jewelry. Museum hours are Tuesday through Saturday 9 a.m. to 5 p.m., and Sunday noon to 5 p.m.

LITTLE WARS
7517 Jefferson Hwy
(225) 924-6304
www.littlewars.com
Looking for somewhere to role-play with friends? The Louisiana Little Wars shop is a treasure trove for those who enjoy the modern hobby of miniature war gaming and toy collecting. The shop has a 2,000-square-foot showroom with 10 gaming tables and hosts between two and four tournaments a month. It offers a wide selection of games, miniatures, and books.

ROYAL STANDARD
2877 Perkins Rd.
(225) 344-2311
16016 Perkins Rd.
(225) 751-0009
www.theroyalstandard.com

Walk through pathways and little rooms filled with imaginative gift items for every occasion. You'll see estate jewelry as well as contemporary accessories. Look for items for any room in the house, from kitchen to bedroom. Perhaps you're seeking garden and architectural elements that will complete the exact home décor you're trying to achieve. The 2877 Perkins Rd. store is more intimate, but both locations offer a great shopping experience.

ℹ️ The LSU Rural Life Museum, I-10 at Essen, Louisiana, (225) 765-2437, has an excellent gift shop featuring handcrafted woodworks, paintings, pottery, and metal sculptures by Louisiana artisans. In addition, shoppers will find cookbooks and books on Louisiana history as well as handmade soaps and candles.

SANCTUARY
7480 Highland Rd.
(225) 757-0927
Located in the former Greater Morning Star Baptist Church, the Sanctuary is a nifty upscale gift shop. You'll find gifts for weddings, birthdays, and christenings. There's also innovative jewelry, pottery, china, glassware, and more. Don't miss the specialized LSU items for both men and women.

ATTRACTIONS

Want to feel the drama of the wide Mississippi River where French explorers found the first high land above the flowing water? Step into an old arsenal built by U.S. Army troops to defend America's frontier? Watch politicians and lobbyists dance a few side-steps? Sip a mint julep and stroll the 19th-century gardens around a plantation mansion? Or you may prefer to attend a knock-'em-dead football game, with wide-screen digitized scoreboards and thousands of screaming fans.

If ever there was a place to do it all—in a week, a year, or just one day—it's Baton Rouge. Louisiana's capital city is a destination that appeals to just about everyone. No matter what your age, gender, or ethnicity, you'll find attractions that fit your interests. Some recall glory days of the past. Others provoke thoughts of romance, power, or fame. Turn one corner and absorb an expansive landscape. At another spot, just enjoy plain fun.

Price Code

The price code represents the average cost for one adult, without tax. Admission costs for children and seniors are less. Almost all attractions in Louisiana are closed on major holidays. Some may close for special events. Hours can change, so it's usually best to call ahead.

$......................Under $5
$$ ....$6 to $10
$$$ .... $11 to $20

DOWNTOWN

Start your visit with downtown Baton Rouge, a city with remarkable landmarks. Start with the State Capitol area and stroll streets filled with historic museums and fascinating old homes. Then head toward Third Street where a revitalization program is bringing new life to the downtown. From there it's an easy walk to the historic Old State Capitol, RiverCenter, Shaw Center for the Arts, USS *Kidd* and Veterans Memorial, and more. An exceptionally well-designed walking tour brochure, created by the Foundation for Historic Louisiana, is available at welcome centers.

BEAUREGARD TOWN HISTORIC DISTRICT   FREE
Neighborhood bordered by Government St. on the north, South Blvd. on the south, the Mississippi River on the west, and East Boulevard on the east

In 1806 Elias Beauregard, a retired captain of the Louisiana Regiment, offered Baton Rouge citizens plans for a complete community situated on the banks of the Mississippi River, bordered by North Boulevard, South Boulevard, and East Street. His vision followed the grand European manner of town design with tree-lined boulevards, fountains, squares, and formal gardens. He envisioned a Palace Royal on the Grand Rue which would be approached by four diagonal streets. Although the plans were never fully realized, the area became a fashionable neighborhood for many leading families following the Civil War. Drive through the area to see romantic and classic structures used as residences and offices.

BOGAN FIRE STATION   FREE
427 Laurel St.
(225) 344-8558
Multicolored glazed terra cotta tiles adorn the facade of this 1914 Gothic Revival brick firehouse.

The building was named the Bogan Fire Station in 1959 after Robert A. Bogan, the city's first paid fire chief, who served from 1918 to 1959. The firefighters' museum contains two antique fire trucks, fire-fighting equipment, and historic photographs of early firefighters. The building also is home to the Arts Council and Community Fund for the Arts. Hours are 9 a.m. to 5 p.m. Monday through Friday.

CAPITOL COMPLEX AND
BUILDINGS   FREE
Clustered around Louisiana Capitol Park
Capitol Welcome Center
(225) 342-7317

Beginning at the end of the 20th century and into the 21st, Louisiana began consolidating the offices of various state departments in the downtown area. Most are located around the large Louisiana State Park extending from the front of the Capitol building beginning at State Capitol Drive. The buildings were inspired by the 1930s Art Deco style of the State Capitol. Historical names such as Bienville, Iberville, and Lafayette adorn their facades. Public parking garages blend in and carry out the same Art Deco design. The weekly Red Stick Farmer's Market, the monthly Arts Market, and a food court are located within this area.

CAPITOL PARK/HUEY LONG
GRAVE   FREE
State Capitol Dr.
Capitol Park Center
(225) 219-1200

Beautifully landscaped formal gardens stretch out in front of the State Capitol. Designed by Jungle Gardens of Avery Island, the park is filled with ancient oaks, magnolias, and more than 300 varieties of plants. Paved walks wind through the garden. Governor and senator Huey P. Long, one of the state's most controversial political figures, is buried in the garden in front of the capitol where he was fatally wounded by an assassin in 1935. Long's statue here faces the capitol, which he built.

CATFISH TOWN AND
MUNICIPAL COMPLEX   FREE
River Road and Government Street

Once a pocket of Beauregard Town, Catfish Town takes its name from an early era when neighborhood residents caught many a catfish from their front porches when flood waters receded. Five attractive brick warehouses from the 1880s have been restored. The Sheraton Hotel anchors one end, and there's direct access to the Belle of Baton Rouge Casino. The Municipal Complex combines the RiverCenter (convention and exhibition halls and an arena), the Performing Arts Theater, and the downtown branch of the city-parish library. They are linked by three plazas, the Bicentennial Plaza, Mestrovic Court, and Galvez Plaza. Fountains here provide tranquil settings for residents and visitors alike. Across from the RiverCenter, on the Mississippi River, is a fountain and the *Red Stick* sculpture by artist Frank Hayden. From here, steps lead to the docking area (nicknamed the Paper Clip dock) for steamboats and other pleasure vessels visiting Baton Rouge.

LOUISIANA ARTS AND SCIENCE
MUSEUM AND IRENE W.
PENNINGTON PLANETARIUM $$
100 South River Rd.
(225) 344-9478
www.lasm.org

Housed in the historic Yazoo & Mississippi Valley Railway Station, LASM includes fine art galleries that showcase special exhibitions and works from the museum's collection. Also featured are the Ivan Mestrovic sculpture atrium and an Ancient Egypt Gallery, complete with mummy. The Irene W. Pennington Planetarium, a world-class attraction, houses a 60-foot domed theater presenting large-format films, sky shows, and visual music shows using the most advanced visual and sound technology available. Learn about the seasonal night sky and current celestial events, and explore the solar system. LASM and the Planetarium bring art and science together. Numerous programs are planned for children and adults alike. Hours are 10 a.m. to 3 p.m., Tuesday through Friday; 10 a.m. to 5 p.m. Saturday (planetarium open until 8 p.m.); and 1 to 4 p.m. Sunday.

LOUISIANA GOVERNOR'S
MANSION   FREE
1001 Capitol Access Rd.
(225) 342-5855
www.lamansionfoundation.org
Situated on Capitol Lake, the Louisiana Governor's Mansion is a stately home built in 1962 by then Governor Jimmie Davis. The white-brick mansion follows the style of plantation homes seen along River Road. The interior showcases Louisiana artists and craftsmen. Of special interest is the mural of Louisiana scenes painted by Auekils Ozols. Current residents are Governor Bobby Jindal and his family. Tours can be scheduled by appointment 9:30 a.m. to 3:30 p.m. (with the exception of the lunch hour, noon to 1 p.m.) Tuesday, Wednesday, and Thursday.

LOUISIANA STATE CAPITOL   FREE
State Capitol Drive
(225) 342-7317
www.nps.gov/nr/travel/louisiana/cap.htm
An Art Deco masterpiece, the Louisiana State Capitol was completed in 1932 by Governor Huey P. Long at a cost of $5 million, including $1 million worth of art. A small army of craftsmen and artists joined builders to create the building as a symbol of Louisiana. Designed by Weiss, Dreyfous, and Seiferth, the building is the tallest capitol in the United States. Famed sculptor Lorado Taft directed much of the statuary work. Sculpture, murals, and detailed bronze work can be found on both the exterior and interior. Forty-nine granite steps lead the way to the capitol's entrance. The 13 original colonies are represented by the first 13 steps. The rest of the states follow with the dates of entrance into the union. The Latin motto of the United States, "E Pluribus Unum," along with the names of the last two states admitted, Alaska, 1958, and Hawaii, 1959, are engraved on the top step. A magnificent historical frieze at the fifth-floor level depicts scenes from the early explorations through World War I. The frieze is repeated high on the wall of Memorial Hall inside the entrance. Centering the hall's floor is a bronze map of Louisiana with symbols showing the products of each area, circled by a list of 64 parishes. As

you tour the building, see how often you can spot the symbol of the state's bird, the brown pelican. An observation deck on the 27th floor affords a spectacular view of the capital city. Hours are 8 a.m. to 4:30 p.m. daily.

ℹ️ The magnificent bronze elevator doors in the Louisiana State Capitol's Memorial Hall bear the likenesses of Louisiana's governors from 1812 to 1932, when the capitol was dedicated. When visiting, note the multiple portraits in three panels. Thirty-seven governors grace the doors. Governor Huey P. Long occupies the honored position at the top right of the door on the right.

LOUISIANA STATE MUSEUM–
BATON ROUGE   FREE
Spanish Town Road and 4th Street
(225) 342-5428
http://lsm.crt.state.la.us/br/br.htm
Packed with dynamic exhibits, the museum tells the story of Louisiana's cultural heritage and milestones, including wars, the 1927 flood, agriculture, history, cuisine, music, civil rights, and legendary persons. You can't help but smile at the exciting displays on jazz, blues, and swamp pop. Colorful Mardi Gras displays feature dazzling costumes as well as rustic outfits for rural country horseback rides. Hours are 9 a.m. to 5 p.m. Tuesday through Saturday and noon to 5 p.m. Sunday.

MAIN STREET MARKET AND RED STICK
FARMERS MARKET   FREE
501 Main St.
(225) 267-5060
www.mainstreetmarketbr.org
Main Street Market creates a public marketplace for local farmers, artists, and entrepreneurs. It's located on one side of the Galvez Parking Garage in the center of downtown. Small cafes in a food court offer everything from designer sandwiches to Chinese take-out. The lunch crowd gathers here to pick up a bite or relax at white cast-iron tables and chairs. Musicians from the Baton Rouge Symphony give mini-concerts here, as do

other performers. Market hours are 7:30 a.m. to 4 p.m. Monday through Friday and 8 a.m. to 1 p.m. Sunday. Red Stick Farmers Market operates every Saturday, 8 a.m. to noon. The Arts Market takes place here the first Saturday of the month.

OLD ARSENAL MUSEUM   FREE
State Capitol Grounds
(225) 342-0401
www.sos.louisiana.gov/museums
Constructed in 1838, this structure was built by the U.S. Army as a powder magazine with 54-inch-thick walls and a 10-foot-high fence. The magazine was used by the United States military during the Mexican and Civil Wars. The museum contains exhibits about the structure's design and construction as well as the history of the State Capitol grounds. Open Tuesday through Saturday, 9 a.m. to 4 p.m.

OLD GOVERNOR'S MANSION $$
502 North Blvd.
(225) 387-2464
www.fhl.org
The Old Governor's Mansion is a historic house museum. Built by Huey P. Long in 1930 and nicknamed "Louisiana's White House," it served as the official residence for nine governors and their families. The Georgian mansion is on the National Register of Historic Places and serves as a venue for weddings, receptions, and special events. It is the headquarters of the Foundation for Historical Louisiana. Open Tuesday through Friday, 9 a.m. to 4 p.m. Last tour starts at 3 p.m.

SHAW CENTER FOR THE ARTS $$
101 Lafayette St.
(225) 346-5001
www.shawcenter.org
A blend of new and vintage buildings, the Shaw Center for the Arts is the cornerstone of the downtown entertainment district. It is home to The Manship Theatre, art galleries, the LSU Museum of Art, LSU School Museum of Art, and museum shop. The center's Lafayette Street entrance features a dancing fountain that delights children especially during the summer. Across the street is shady Lafayette

Park where small open-air concerts often take place. Also here is the Baton Rouge Water Company's landmark Standpipe water tower, which was shipped to Baton Rouge in 1888. Building hours are 9 a.m. to 11 p.m. Tuesday through Saturday and 11 a.m. to 5 p.m. Sunday. LSU Museum of Art hours are 10 a.m. to 5 p.m. Tuesday through Saturday and 1 to 5 p.m. Sunday.

SPANISH TOWN HISTORIC
DISTRICT   FREE
Bordered by State Capitol Dr. on the north, North St. on the south, North Fifth St. on the east, and North Ninth St. on the west.
Stroll through this district's narrow streets and imagine life here in the early 1800s. One of Baton Rouge's first formally planned communities, Spanish Town was commissioned in 1805 by Don Carlos de Grandpre, governor of Spanish West Florida. During the city's early years, Canary Islanders and some of the Spanish population settled in this area. The major thoroughfare has always been Spanish Town Road. Stroll through the streets on a quiet day and view the array of architectural styles in this neighborhood, from antebellum to American bungalow. Residents are fiercely loyal and protective of the district. The Spanish Town Mardi Gras parade has become the most famous of any Baton Rouge parade. Thousands attend it every year to see Louisiana's politics and politicians spoofed and roasted. Everywhere is the parade's symbol, the pink flamingo.

ST. JAMES EPISCOPAL CHURCH
205 North Fourth St.
(225) 387-5141
www.stjamesbr.org
The congregation of this church was organized in 1819 and received its charter in 1844. Mrs. Zachary Taylor was one of the original founders. Built in 1895, the church is Gothic Revival style and features magnificent Tiffany windows behind the altar. Fourth Street was originally named Church Street.

ST. JOSEPH CATHEDRAL
Main St. at North Fourth St.
(225) 387-5928
www.cathedralofstjoseph.org

This Gothic Revival church is the third to stand on land donated in 1809 by Don Antonio Gras, a Spanish resident. It was designed by Jesuit architect Reverend John Cambiasco and constructed between 1853 and 1856. The steeple dates from 1891. Two important sculptures are at the church. A major work, a massive crucifix, by Ivan Mestrovic, assisted by Frank Hayden, is above the altar. A second sculpture, *Prodigal Son,* by Ivan Mestrovic, resides in the side garden.

THIRD STREET   FREE
Third Street east of the Mississippi River runs from North Blvd. to State Capitol Dr.
The historical heart of the city, Third Street has the atmosphere of an early 1900s town, with a mix of commercial architectural styles. The buildings house retail, office, residential, and night spots. It's the place to "see and be seen" during power lunches. The street is booming as an entertainment district with wine bars, cafes, and night spots.

During the day catch a ride here on the convenient trolley that circles the downtown district.

USS *KIDD* AND VETERANS MEMORIAL $$
305 South River Rd.
(225) 342-1942
www.usskidd.com
USS *Kidd*, a World War II Fletcher-class destroyer, was restored to 1945 configuration as a floating museum and national landmark. It floats during spring floods on the Mississippi River, and during the fall and winter, it rests in a specially designed cradle. The ship is named after Rear Admiral Isaac C. Kidd, who was killed aboard his flagship, the USS *Arizona*, during the surprise attack on Pearl Harbor. The museum contains the largest ship model collection in the South, historic artifacts, Veterans Hall of Honor, a riverboat pilothouse, USS *Constitution* gun deck exhibit, and the Louisiana Memorial Plaza with the names of more than 7,000 Louisiana natives killed in combat. Gift shop open daily 9 a.m. to 5 p.m.

ABOUT TOWN

While most attractions are found clustered in or near downtown, others can be found throughout East Baton Rouge Parish. They can be reached by driving your own vehicle, a rented car, or a taxi.

ENCHANTED MANSION:
A DOLL MUSEUM $
190 Lee Dr.
(225) 769-0005
www.enchantedmansion.org
Filled with fantasy and delight, the Enchanted Mansion is the land of angels, fairies, antiques, and exceptional one-of-a-kind dolls created by gifted artists. Gabrella, an animated fairy, greets guests as they enter. Visit Ted. E. Bear's playroom and walk through a life-sized Victorian dollhouse. The sole purpose of the museum is to benefit the handicapped. There is no fee for handicapped visitors.

LSU HILLTOP ARBORETUM   FREE
118 Highland Rd.
(225) 767-6916
http://hilltop.lsu.edu
A plant lover's haven, LSU Hilltop Arboretum showcases an extensive collection of Louisiana native trees and shrubs. Visitors cross an old footbridge overlooking a 20-foot-deep ravine and wander into the tranquil "cathedral" where tree canopies form a protective room. Enjoy Louisiana sunlight filtering through the trees or listen to mockingbirds, warblers, cardinals, and other birds stopping here on their migratory passage. Mr. and Mrs. Emory Smith developed this sanctuary, and in his 90th year in 1981, Smith gave 14 acres to LSU to be used as a teaching tool in the LSU School of Landscape Architecture and to be shared with the community. The arboretum sponsors plant sales and garden tours. Visit the Garden Book and Nature Shop. Open to the public during daylight hours daily. Call the office Tuesday through Friday, 9 a.m. to 3 p.m.

LSU RURAL LIFE MUSEUM $$
4560 Essen Lane (I-10 at Essen)
(225) 765-2437
http://rurallife.lsu.edu
Situated on 450 acres, the LSU Rural Life Museum and Windrush Gardens is a major outdoor folk

complex. Voted among the Top 10 Outdoor Museums in the World by British Museum, Rural Life gives visitors a look at 18th- and 19th-century rural life in Louisiana. It is home to an extensive collection of tools, household utensils, furniture, vehicles, and farming implements. Walk the grounds and see more than 25 authentic log cabins, cottages, and farm structures dating from the 1800s and early 1900s. Windrush Gardens features 25 acres of semiformal gardens filled with azaleas, iris, and native plants and designed by renowned landscape artist Steele Burden. The museum sponsors educational programs and special events throughout the year. It also serves as a conference host for national and international museum associations. Open daily 8:30 a.m. to 5 p.m.

**ODELL S. WILLIAMS NOW &
THEN MUSEUM OF AFRICAN
AMERICAN HISTORY** $
538 South Blvd.
(225) 343-4411
The Odell S. Williams Now & Then Museum of African American History is situated on the southern perimeter of Beauregard Town. The museum showcases African-American contributors in science, medicine, and politics. Also featured are displays on minority inventions, rural artifacts, and African art. The museum features Juneteenth memorabilia, marking the end of slavery in the U.S, and is a faith-based initiative of New St. Luke Baptist Church.

PLANTATIONS

Baton Rouge is the hub of Louisiana's Plantation Country, so called because early European colonists created large plantations in the late 1700s and early 1800s along both banks of the lower Mississippi River. With slave labor and access to the river, planters could ship their crops and various products to New Orleans and on to ports along the Eastern seaboard, the Caribbean Islands, Central and South America, and Europe. During this era it was fashionable for successful planters to show off their wealth with elegant mansions and lavish furnishings. Planta-

tion families were expected to entertain with generous hospitality. Larger plantations were self-contained, often operating like mini-villages. Books and films such as *Gone With the Wind* have created a romanticized view of plantation life. Certainly the good times existed, but plantation life also was fraught with many hazards, including yellow fever, floods, and fire. Visit the antebellum mansions and learn about both the bad times and the good times. Magnolia Mound, administered by the Recreation and Park Commission for the Parish of East Baton Rouge (BREC), is the only plantation house in Baton Rouge open daily for tours. Others are 20 to 45 minutes from town. Many are listed on the National Register of Historic Places. Some are still working plantations using modern farming techniques and equipment. To really see these houses, gardens, and fields, plan on seeing only two per day, perhaps with lunch or picnic in between. Included here are sites that are regularly open to the public except on major holidays and special occasions. Some operate as bed-and-breakfast inns. Others host special events, including fall and spring festivals, art shows, weddings, and conferences. Call ahead to verify hours and admission fees.

When planning a visit to an antebellum mansion along the Mississippi River, remember that many of these are still private homes. Your tour guide, who may even be the home's owner, will often regale you with colorful stories of his or her ancestors. As a courtesy return their hospitality with kind words and a gracious attitude.

AUDUBON STATE HISTORIC SITE $
11788 La. 965, St. Francisville
(225) 635-3739, (888) 677-2838
www.crt.state.la.us/parks/iaudubon.aspx
Oakley Plantation Home at Audubon State Historic Site is a West Indies–style home with unique features that helped relieve residents from summer heat. John James Audubon lived here for several months in 1821 while teaching the owner's daughter. While at Oakley, Audubon painted part

of his "Birds of America" series. Grounds include an outside kitchen, kitchen garden, two slave cabins, an 1870 barn, and a nature trail through magnolia and poplar trees. The well-organized museum contains details on the area and memorabilia from early residents and a picnic area. Open daily 9 a.m. to 5 p.m. House tours 10 a.m. to 4 p.m.

BOCAGE PLANTATION $$
3950 La. 942, Darrow
(225) 588-8000
www.bocageplantation.com
Bocage Plantation began as a Creole cottage built in 1801 by Marius Pons Bringier as a wedding gift for his daughter Francoise. She was married to Christophe Colomb, a French refugee and a direct descendant of Christopher Columbus. The current mansion, which faces the Mississippi River, was designed by architect James Dakin in 1837. Meticulously restored by Marion Rundell, it features his superb collection of antiques, including pieces by John Henry Butler, John and Joseph Meeks, and Charles Lee. The plantation takes bed-and-breakfast reservations. Tours are offered Thursday through Sunday.

BREC'S MAGNOLIA MOUND $$
2161 Nicholson Drive
(225) 343-4955
www.magnoliamound.org
A French Creole house built in the 1790s, Magnolia Mound is one of the oldest houses in Baton Rouge. The house contains carefully restored and documented Louisiana-made furnishings and decorative arts. Expect well-versed guides in costumes from the Federal Period. There's also a crop garden, pigeonnier, overseer's house, and museum store. Hours are Monday through Saturday, 10 a.m. to 4 p.m., and Sunday, 1 to 4 p.m.

BUTLER GREENWOOD $$
8345 U.S. 61, St. Francisville
(225) 635-6312
www.butlergreenwood.com
This plantation house built in the 1790s is still owned by the original family. View the impressive furniture original to the house and a fascinating collection of family heirlooms and artifacts. Along the drive to the house, view camellias, azaleas, and magnolias in gardens planted long ago. Butler Greenwood offers daily tours and bed-and-breakfast in whimsical private cottages. Tours daily 9 a.m. to 5 p.m.

COTTAGE PLANTATION $$
10528 U.S. 61, St. Francisville
(225) 635-3674
www.cottageplantation.com
The oldest plantation complex in the area, the house sits on its original Spanish land grant. The English country mansion features an exceptionally long front gallery. There are many buildings, including the old school house, milk house, carriage house, and slave houses. The cottage also operates as a bed-and-breakfast. Tours are offered 10 a.m. to 4 p.m.

DESTREHAN PLANTATION $$$
13034 River Rd., Destrehan
(985) 664-9315
www.destrehanplantation.org
Destrehan is the oldest surviving plantation house in the lower Mississippi Valley. It was built in 1787 by a free man of color for the wealthy Destrehan family. The two-story house features open galleries on three sides of the house. Costumed docents give visitors the history of the house and the families who lived there. Visit the gift shop and outbuildings.

EVERGREEN PLANTATION $$$
4677 La. 18, Edgard
(985) 497-3837
www.evergreenplantation.org
Evergreen Plantation, circa 1790, is the most intact plantation complex in the South with 37 buildings, including 22 slave houses in their original double row configuration. The plantation's history is heavily documented. Emphasis is placed on the plantation's early dependence on slave labor and, following the Civil War, on the labor of free African Americans. A visit includes the Main House, filled with an impressive collection of antiques, and a walk down an alley of 100

oak trees more than 100 years old. Gates open at 11 for the 11:30 tour and at 1:30 for a 2 p.m. tour.

GREENWOOD PLANTATION $$
6838 Highland Rd., St. Francisville
(225) 655-4475
www.greenwoodplantation.com
The 1830 Greek Revival mansion burned and was rebuilt by the Barnes family following detailed research. It has been featured in seven movies, including *Louisiana, Drango, North and South–Book I, North and South–Book II,* and *Sister, Sister.* Tours are offered in spring and summer 9 a.m. to 5 p.m. and winter 10 a.m. to 4 p.m. It also has bed-and-breakfast accommodations overlooking a scenic pond.

HOUMAS HOUSE $$$
40136 La. 942, Darrow
(225) 473-9380
www.houmashouse.com
Visitors experience the grandeur of Louisiana's golden era of plantations. Restored by Kevin Kelly, a New Orleans businessman, the site features 16 acres of magnificent fountains and gardens blooming year-round. The home has been the setting for a number of films, including *Hush, Hush Sweet Charlotte.* Tour the mansion's 14 rooms filled with period antiques and fine Louisiana artwork. Guests can enjoy the turtle bar, named after a gilded turtle-shaped chandelier, and Latil's, a fine dining restaurant offering exceptional wines. A luxurious gift shop includes a video on the estate. Open Monday through Tuesday, 9 a.m. to 7 p.m.

LAURA: A CREOLE PLANTATION $$$
2247 La. 18, Vacherie
(888) 799-7690
www.lauraplantation.com
Enter the world of early plantation life during an exceptional history tour. The award-winning 70-minute guided tour is based on Laura Locoul's *Plantation Memoirs,* firsthand accounts of 200 years of the lives of Creole owners, women, slaves, and children on this 1805 sugarcane plantation. View slave cabins and gardens with heri-

tage plantings. There is an extensive gift shop. Tours are available in French and English. Open daily 9:30 a.m. to 5 p.m. Tours are 10 a.m. to 4 p.m. daily.

MOUNT HOPE PLANTATION $
8151 Highland Rd.
(225) 761-7000
www.mounthopeplantation.net
Mount Hope is one of two surviving antebellum plantation homes in Baton Rouge. Located on Highland Road, the property was part of a land grant endowed in 1786 to Joseph Sharp, a German planter. Built in 1817, the one-and-a-half-story house features a central hall flanked by a pair of rooms, a gabled roof, and inviting wrap-around porches. Crystal chandeliers, oil paintings, and taffeta chair covers add a touch of 19th-century romance. The spacious grounds boast three legacy oak trees, a gorgeous fountain, and a patio area. The home is available for wedding ceremonies, receptions, and tea parties. Call about tours.

THE MYRTLES $$
7747 U.S. Hwy 61, St. Francisville
(800) 809-0565
www.myrtlesplantation.com
Mystery and myth surround this plantation home. The home, often called America's Most Haunted Home, has been featured on *Oprah* and *National Geographic Explorer* and on A&E and the Travel, History, and Learning channels, among others. Home décor includes gold-leaf French furniture, Aubusson tapestries, and Baccarat crystal chandeliers. Bed-and-breakfast rooms are in the main house and grounds. The Carriage House Restaurant, featuring regional cuisine, is a local favorite. Tours given daily 9 a.m. to 5 p.m. Mystery tours are given Friday and Saturday nights.

NOTTOWAY PLANTATION $$$
31025 La. 1, White Castle
(866) 527-6884
www.nottoway.com
Majestic Nottoway is the South's largest plantation home. Surrounded by sugar cane fields, this historic mansion was completed in 1859

by wealthy Virginia planter John Hampden Randolph for his wife, Emily Jane, and their 11 children. The mansion reopened in spring of 2009 following a multimillion-dollar restoration. Architectural details include intricate frieze work and innovative features for the era, including gas-lit chandeliers and indoor plumbing. The spectacular white ballroom is a popular wedding setting. Recently remodeled, Nottoway is a resort with bed-and-breakfast guest rooms with modern amenities in the main house, wings, and grounds. The property has a swimming pool and gift shop, and Randolph Hall is available for conferences. Dine in the mansion and enjoy Ramsay's Mansion Restaurant, serving breakfast, lunch, and dinner. Tours are given on the hour 9 a.m. to 5 p.m.

OAK ALLEY PLANTATION $$$
3645 La. 18, Vacherie
(225) 265-2151, (800) 442-5539
www.oakalleyplantation.com
Oak Alley is named for its dramatic quarter-mile alley of oaks, believed to be nearly 300 years old, leading to the classic Greek Revival–style antebellum home. Jacques Telesphore Roman and his wife Celine acquired the property in 1836 and started building the mansion. It features 28 columns surrounding the entire house and 13-foot verandas. Tours touch upon the mansion's history, architecture, antiques, and family memorabilia. Visitors can enjoy the restaurant and gift shop. Bed-and-breakfast cottages are located on the grounds. Open 9 a.m. to 5 p.m. daily. Last tour is at 4 p.m.

ROSEDOWN PLANTATION STATE
HISTORIC SITE $$
12501 La. 10, St. Francisville
(225) 635-3332
www.crt.state.la.us/parks/irosedown.aspx
Rosedown Plantation features a 28-acre garden, which is considered one of the nation's five most important historic gardens. Meander through paths with heritage camellias and other plants. Tour the 1835 plantation house that contains

most of its original furnishings. Throughout the year costumed staff and volunteers offer programs, which include open-hearth cooking, 19th-century crafts, and children's games. Visit the doctor's office and gift shop. Open daily 9 a.m. to 5 p.m. House tours are on the hour with the last tour at 4 p.m.

SAN FRANCISCO PLANTATION $$$
2646 La. 44, Garyville
(888) 322-1756
www.sanfranciscoplantation.org
San Francisco Plantation was built by Edmond Bozonier Marmillon in 1856. The house is so distinctive that it inspired novelist Frances Parkinson Keyes to write "Steamboat Gothic," a story about a family she imagined lived there. Viewed from some angles, the house closely resembles the ornate superstructure of a Mississippi riverboat. Fully restored, it is filled with handsome antique furniture by master craftsman John Henry Belter. Visit the slave cabin and schoolhouse. Tours are offered daily April through October from 9:30 a.m. to 4:30 p.m. and November through March, 9 a.m. to 4 p.m.

ST. JOSEPH PLANTATION
3535 La. 18, Vacherie
(888) 322-1756
www.stjosephplantation.com
This 1830 Creole antebellum plantation is home to one of Louisiana's most interesting families; it has been lovingly restored by Waguespack and Simon descendants who have owned the plantation for 130 years. Tours are often conducted by family members who point out paintings, photographs, and artifacts relating to their history. Selected tours in fall include mourning customs of the 19th century. View the detached kitchen, commissary, blacksmith, and original slave cabins and learn more about sugar cane agriculture. Tours are Monday through Saturday, 9:30 a.m. to 5 p.m., and Sunday, noon to 5 p.m. (last tour starts at 4 p.m.) April through September.

CULTURE AND THE ARTS

Baton Rouge enjoys a flourishing arts scene. The arts in this city just keep growing. In recent years city officials have recognized the importance the arts play in the city's overall image and quality of life. There's seldom a time when you can't find an ongoing cultural event that will enhance your stay.

The arts scene is diverse and widespread, thanks in part to the efforts of the Baton Rouge Arts Council and the work of students and professors of Louisiana State University, Southern University, and Baton Rouge Community College. Among those associated with these institutions are professional actors, musicians, and artists, many of whom have appeared in films, on stages, and at galleries throughout the world. Their contributions to the community are enormous. Equally important are the efforts of arts activists and businesses that contribute time and money to support regional events.

This chapter lists a number of venues, public and commercial galleries, and resources for the culture vulture and the art lover in all of us. Listings are grouped according to type (art, theater, dance, and cinema) and resources. You'll find descriptions of traditional and nontraditional performance spaces. A selection of major galleries is included, but you will find visual art throughout town in places such as restaurants and coffee shops. We have also included community theaters that present outstanding productions.

ART

BATON ROUGE GALLERY IN CITY PARK
1442 City Park Ave.
(225) 383-1470
www.batonrougegallery.org
Baton Rouge Gallery is a multimedia art gallery located in City Park, situated just off I-10 near LSU. An important aspect of Baton Rouge's arts community, it is one of the United States' oldest artist co-ops. It was founded in 1965 when eight artists formed a gallery to showcase not only their own work but also that of other local artists. Monthly exhibits open on first Wednesdays, 7 to 9 p.m., and are free to the public. Other activities include Sundays at 4 programs, including poetry readings and chamber concerts. No admission.

BRUNNER GALLERY
100 Lafayette St.
(225) 389-7224
www.brunnergallery.com

The Brunner Gallery, owned by Susan and Rick Brunner, is recognized as one of the top contemporary art galleries in the South. Located in the Shaw Center for the Arts, the gallery showcases paintings, sculpture, photography, and mixed media works by artists from Europe and the United States. It also hosts exhibitions of functional art objects of glass, ceramics, metal, paper, and wood. Open 10 a.m. to 5 p.m., Wednesday through Saturday. No admission.

i Step into the State Capitol Annex Building, 1051 N. Third St., to view the magnificent murals created in 1938 by Conrad Albrizio as a Works Progress Administration (WPA) project. The murals were designed to illustrate the achievements of the state program under the administration of Gov. Richard W. Leche.

CAFFERY GALLERY
4016 Government St.
(225) 388-9397
www.cafferygallery.com
Located inside a pink house in the Mid-City Arts and Design District, Caffery Gallery is not the average art venue. It features collections of ceramics, stained glass, and hand-blown art objects. The gallery, popular for its offbeat approach and bright colors, also exhibits works by Louisiana artists, including jewelry, sculpture, paintings, and more. Be enchanted with the gallery's approach to visual fantasy. Open Tuesday through Saturday, 10 a.m. to 5 p.m. No admission.

CIRCA 1857
1857 Government St.
(225) 387-8667
www.circa1857.com
Circa 1857, situated in a former drug store, features an eclectic mix of old and new antiques, original art, and artifacts. You may find fanciful hats from the 1950s or colorful teapots. The gallery offers everything from old musical instruments to recycled sculpture. The owners specialize in architectural salvage from around the world—an old doorframe, a garden gate, and more. Stay for lunch or dessert at Yvette Marie, a delightful small cafe open from 10:30 a.m. to 3 p.m. Circa 1857 also presents an open house on the third Thursday of the month, showcasing a featured local artist. Sister shops are Rue Cou Cou, a gallery and frame shop, and Mosaic Garden, a gift shop. No admission.

ELIZABETHAN GALLERY
680 Jefferson Hwy.
(225) 924-6437
www.elizabethangallery.com
This family-owned gallery entered the art and framing business in 1978 under the perceptive direction of owner Liz Walker. It's a popular gallery where local artists and visitors are given personalized service. The gallery carries a large stock of limited-edition prints, lithographs, graphic posters, etchings, serigraphs, antique prints, and original works. It's the only local store that provides custom framing orders right up until Christmas Eve. Hours are 9:30 a.m. to 6 p.m. Monday through Friday and 10 a.m. to 4 p.m. Saturday. No admission.

LOUISIANA ARTS AND SCIENCE MUSEUM AND PLANETARIUM
100 South River Rd.
(225) 344-5272
www.lasm.org
Viewing shows at the Louisiana Arts and Science Museum and Planetarium is sheer pleasure. Housed in the historic Yazoo & Mississippi Valley Railway Station, the museum's spacious galleries showcase changing fine art exhibitions and selections from a permanent collection that includes more than 3,000 artworks and artifacts. Changing displays are usually on view in two small galleries, the Soupcon and Colonnade, one on each floor of the museum. Two other exhibits from the permanent collection remain on view year-round. The Ivan Mestrovic Sculpture Gallery in the Bert S. Turner Family Atrium is dedicated to showing works by Croatian sculptor Ivan Mestrovic. One of the most popular spots in the museum is the Ancient Egypt Gallery featuring a mummy, circa 300 BC, resting inside a reconstructed Ptolemaic-era tomb. The museum staff is also skilled in organizing special exhibitions. The Irene W. Pennington Planetarium features sky shows, large-format films, visual music shows, and galleries devoted to astronomy and space science. LASM plans numerous creative and fun programs for children. It serves the community through lectures, workshops, classes, teacher services, camps, and other events. In the museum store, visitors can shop for unique handcrafted items, books, toys, and objects related to LASM's exhibits. The museum and planetarium are open Tuesday through Sunday. Hours vary for galleries and planetarium shows. With the exception of the family show, children under age 3 are not permitted in the theater. Admission to the museum is $7 for adults, $6 for children and seniors, and $5 per person for groups. Add $2 per person for tickets to planetarium shows. See the Kidstuff chapter for more information.

The dramatic Oliver Pollock Monument is a bronze sculpture situated in Galvez Plaza next to the Old State Capitol. Created by Frank Hayden in 1979, the sculpture commemorates Oliver Pollock, a hero of the American Revolution, who joined forces with Louisiana's last Spanish governor, Bernardo de Galvez, who led the Spanish forces to victory over the English in 1783 for control of Baton Rouge. Its companion sculpture is the Oliver Pollock Fountain.

LSU MUSEUM OF ART
100 Lafayette St.
(225) 389-7200
www.lsumoa.com
The LSU Museum of Art is located downtown in the Shaw Center for the Arts. The museum's permanent collection includes English and American 17th- to 20th-century portraiture, including works by William Hogarth, Joshua Reynolds, and Rembrandt Peale. Recent acquisitions include portraits by Diego Rivera, Yousuf Karsh, and Paul Jenkins. The museum also features New Orleans silver, Newcomb pottery and crafts, art by current and former LSU faculty and students, and modern and contemporary Southern paintings, drawings, and sculpture. The museum is open Tuesday through Saturday, 10:30 a.m. to 4 p.m., and Sunday, 1 to 5 p.m.

SOUTHERN UNIVERSITY MUSEUM OF ART
G. Netterville Dr.
(225) 771-4513
www.subr.edu
A mix of African, African-American, Spanish, French, and Creole cultures is on exhibit at the Southern University Museum of Art and the university's newly renovated Visual Arts Gallery. The Museum of Art, housed in Martin L. Harvey Hall, features an extensive collection of African and African-American art. Four galleries contain art from several regions of Africa. They comprise three major collections: the President Leon R. Tarver II Collection, the Steve and Mary L. Harvey

Collection, and the Dr. William Bertrand Collection. They include more than 3,000 artifacts, including ceremonial masks, clothing, and other functional artifacts. The Visual Arts Gallery in Frank Hayden Hall takes a look at the present and future. The gallery features a 64-piece art exhibit created by 29 fine arts majors at Southern. The gallery shows an array of original paintings, drawings, and sculptures by students. The stunning exhibit hall is a showplace, with hardwood floors, professional track lighting, and glass doors. A sculpture garden is in the planning. The Southern Museum of Art is open Monday through Friday, 10 a.m. to 5 p.m., and the Visual Arts Gallery is open Monday through Friday, 10 a.m. to 4 p.m. Free admission.

TAYLOR CLARK GALLERY
2623 Government St.
(225) 383-4929
www.taylorclark.com
Taylor Clark is a premier fine art gallery featuring paintings, prints, and handmade custom framing. Owned and run by three generations of the Clark family, the gallery remains focused on personal customer service and fine art. It is based in Baton Rouge but serves clients around the world. The gallery showcases works by local and regional artists. It is recognized as a dealer in the printed works of John James Audubon. Open Monday through Friday, 10 a.m. to 5 p.m., and Saturday, 10 a.m. to 3 p.m.

WEST BATON ROUGE MUSEUM
845 North Jefferson Ave., Port Allen
(225) 336-2422
www.westbatonrougemuseum.com
Situated in Port Allen on the west side of the Mississippi River, the West Baton Rouge Museum is a delightful small museum with enough space to present exhibits by local and regional painters, sculptors, and photographers. Much of the focus is on the cultural heritage of sugar plantation life. View the 22-foot working sugar mill model, the 1850 Allendale Slave Cabin and 1830 Aillet House, and a French plantation "big house." Guided tours are given of historic sugar planta-

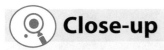

Close-up

Louisiana Lingo

In spite of its name, Baton Rouge never became a strong French community, but the French influence can be found here in food, music, and language. You will hear French expressions with roots in New Orleans and the Acadiana country sprinkled throughout our conversations. Mix those in with Native American, Spanish, and African names and expressions and you get a unique colloquial lingo. Stay a week or two and you'll be talking like a native.

Boudin (Boo-dan)—Cajun sausage made with pork and rice.

Cher (Share)—A term of endearment used to greet women of all ages.

Étoufée (A-too-fay)—A dish of shrimp or crawfish sauteed in butter, onions, celery, and green pepper.

Fais do do (Fay-doe-doe)—A traditional Cajun community dance.

Gris-gris (Gree-gree)—A good luck charm introduced by voodoo priestesses.

Gumbo (Gum-bow)—A succulent soup made with seafood or chicken and sausage.

Joie de vivre (Shwa-de-vie)—The joy of living.

Lagniappe (Lan-yap)—A little something extra; a courtesy gift.

Laissez les bon temps roulez (Laysay lay bon taun roo-lay)—Let the good times roll.

Neutral ground—Used to describe a median in the roadway.

Pirogue (Pee-row)—A shallow-draft wooden boat similar to a canoe.

Rue (Roo)—The French word for "street," found mostly in New Orleans and Acadiana.

Roux (Roo)—A sauce base used by Louisiana cooks that is made with flour and oil.

Zydeco (Zi-dee-ko)—Fast, lively music with French, Cajun, German, and African origins.

---

tion buildings. Free samples of locally produced Louisiana raw sugar are available for every visitor.

MUSIC

BATON ROUGE CONCERT BAND
www.batonrougeconcertband.org

Baton Rouge Concert Band is a nonprofit community organization under the direction of Sheily Bell and assistant director Wesley McCoy. Formed in June 1977 by Vernon Taranto, the band has been providing entertainment for 31 years. Musical selections range from military marches of John Philip Sousa to Broadway show tunes to symphonic band transcriptions, such as Tchaikovsky's *1812 Overture*. The band plays at various locations throughout the city, and annual concerts are presented on Memorial Day, the

Fourth of July, and Labor Day, and during the Christmas season. People especially enjoy attending concerts given on the steps of the Louisiana State Capitol.

BATON ROUGE SINFONIETTA
(225) 578-4010 (days)
(225) 766-3487
www.louisianasinfonietta.org

The Baton Rouge Sinfonietta is a nonprofit professional chamber orchestra composed of musicians led by internationally known composer and conductor Dinos Constantinides. The orchestra plays a wide variety of music from the Baroque through the Classical, Romantic, and 20th-century eras. Regional and international artists are featured as soloists. Sunday afternoon subscription series take place in the striking First Baptist Church downtown. Programs also are given at libraries and retirement communities.

BATON ROUGE SYMPHONY
7330 Highland Rd.
(225) 383-0500
www.brso.org
The premiere musical organization in the city, the Baton Rouge Symphony Orchestra was formed in 1947. Led by acclaimed conductor Timothy Muffitt, the orchestra presents a Master Works series in the RiverCenter Theatre for the Performing Arts. Performing with the orchestra is the Symphony Chorus conducted by Kenneth Fulton. Innovative concerts feature both classical and contemporary music. Guest artists have included Yo-Yo Ma, Itzhak Perlman, Van Cliburn, Joshua Bell, Renee Fleming, and Chris Botti. Other programs include Christmas Brass Concerts, Young People's Discovery Concerts, and the Lamar Family Chamber Series. The Louisiana Youth Orchestras, directed by David Torns, perform in Magnolia Theatre at the Baton Rouge Community College.

i The Baton Rouge Symphony is made up of musicians who are professors and students at the LSU College of Music and Dramatic Arts as well as teachers and professional musicians in the community. Many of these artists have performed with orchestras throughout the world. Along with the outstanding visual artists who reside here, they constantly add to the area's quality of life.

OPERA LOUISIANE
P.O. Box 4908, Baton Rouge
www.operalouisiane.com
Opera lovers will delight in the music of Opera Louisiane. This new organization was founded by local residents in 2006 with the help of Metropolitan Opera singer and LSU graduate Paul Groves and his former professor Robert Grayson. Serving as executive director, Grayson is a former lead tenor with the New York City Opera and noted teacher of international singers. Performances in the 2009–10 season included a "Bringing Out the Stars" gala featuring singers from Houston Opera, Dallas Opera, Lyric Opera of Chicago, and others. Also staged was *Hansel and Gretel,* based on the Brothers Grimm fairy tale.

THEATER

BATON ROUGE LITTLE THEATER
7155 Florida Blvd.
(225) 924-6496
www.brlt.org
Dramas, comedies, musicals, and one-act shows are presented by the Baton Rouge Little Theater. Founded in 1946, the BRLT is one of the oldest running regional theater companies in the U.S. In 1951 veteran actor/director Lee Edwards, who had studied under Lee Strasberg and Max Reinhardt, took over as director, and by 1959 the company began construction on its new theater building. Today, under the leadership of managing artistic director Keith Dixon, BRLT continues to offer outstanding productions such as *Agnes of God*, *Arsenic and Old Lace*, and *Elephant Man*. Summer musicals are always stellar. Performers include amateurs, drama students, and professional actors drawn from the community.

BATON ROUGE RIVERCENTER THEATRE FOR THE PERFORMING ARTS
RiverCenter Complex
275 South River Rd.
(225) 389-3030
www.brrivercenter.com
Entering the Theatre for the Performing Arts, the visitor is met with a contemporary setting of glass and wood. The hall features continental seating for up to 1,900 patrons. Every seat has an excellent view of the stage, guaranteed by the proscenium opening of 57 feet by 28 feet. Productions here include Broadway shows, ballets, magic acts, operas, comic acts, dance competitions, and recitals. The theatre has held performances including *Cats, Les Miserables, The Nutcracker, Miss Saigon*, and *Rent*. It's also the home stage for the Baton Rouge Symphony. There are no elevators

to the balcony, but seating for disabled patrons is available on the first floor, with a wheelchair ramp located at the side entrance.

Jimmie Davis, "Louisiana's Singing Governor," served a dual role as a country music singer and politician. In 1939 he composed and recorded "You Are My Sunshine," which was later recorded by Bing Crosby, Gene Autry, and others. Davis served as the state's governor in 1944–48 and again in 1960–64. He was elected to the Country Music Hall of Fame in Nashville in 1972.

LSU THEATRE AND SWINE PALACE
Music and Dramatic Arts Building
Dalrymple Drive, LSU Campus
(225) 578-3527
www.theatre.lsu.edu, www.swinepalace.org
LSU Theatre has a long tradition dating from 1928. The Claude Shafer Theater, within the university's multimillion-dollar renovation of the Music and Dramatic Arts Building, has been returned to its original concept with Art Deco details, comfortable seating, and modern lighting. Performances here are open to the public and include everything from heavy drama to lighthearted operettas. At the invitation of former LSU Department of Theatre chairperson Gresdna Doty, Swine Palace was founded in 1992 by Barry Kyle, former artistic director of the Royal Shakespeare Company's Swan Theatre in London. Today LSU Theatre remains one of the few programs in the country with an affiliate equity theater giving students the chance to work alongside leading professionals. The LSU productions give visitors access to some of the brightest young talent in the country. Many of LSU's theater graduates now work as actors, producers, directors, and professors throughout the United States. To attend a performance, contact the LSU box office at the number listed above.

MANSHIP THEATRE
100 Lafayette St.
(225) 344-0334
www.manshiptheater.org

Modeled after the classic European opera houses, the Manship Theatre in the Shaw Center for the Arts is a beautiful intimate theater. There are 325 front-row seats. Every audience member is placed eye-to-eye with the performers on stage. Presentations include all forms of performance: theater, musical theater, dance, music, and family programs. Among the celebrities who have appeared here are Jerry Seinfeld, Lyle Lovett, Branford Marsalis, and Kenny Barron. The venue also plays a role in the city's growing roster of art and film events, including a French film festival, a Jewish film festival, and the Red Stick Animation Festival.

PLAYMAKERS OF BATON ROUGE
100 Lafayette St.
(225) 389-7246
www.playmakers.net
Playmakers of Baton Rouge is a professional theater dedicated to bringing quality productions to young audiences. Founded in 1982, the company continues to provide educational and entertaining programs to children and adults through its Summer Neighborhood Tour, Spring Elementary School Tour, drama classes, and camps. Playmakers presents performances at various venues throughout Baton Rouge.

DANCE

BATON ROUGE BALLET THEATER
10745 Linkwood Court
(225) 766-8379
www.batonrougeballet.org
The Baton Rouge Ballet Theater, under the direction of Molly Buchmann and Sharon Mathews, was chartered in 1960 to promote ballet and maintain a first-rate dance company in Baton Rouge. Today its scope extends to communities outside the area. It also includes other forms of dance as well as ballet. Every year BRBT presents a dance series that includes two performances by the local company supplemented by outstanding guest artists and at least one performance by a major dance company. In addition the ballet company also invites world-renowned guest art-

ists to perform here. BRBT's unique production of *The Nutcracker, A Tale from the Bayou* sets the holiday classic in 19th-century Louisiana and draws sell-out audiences. Buchmann and Mathews also are co-owners of the Dancers' Workshop, www.dancersworkshop.com, which offers comprehensive dance classes.

CANGELOSI DANCE PROJECT
3749 Perkins Rd.
(225) 291-4587
www.cangelosidanceproject.com
Cangelosi Dance Project is a nonprofit dance company that promotes, educates, and serves all groups in developing contemporary dance through performances, workshops, and master classes. Professional and student performances are presented in the Manship Theatre, the Baton Rouge Little Theatre Stage 2, and other venues.

OF MOVING COLORS
1010 South Acadian Thruway
(225) 338-0804
www.ofmovingcolors.org
This youthful modern dance company dazzles audiences with performances that combine dance with theater, music, and live arts. The company offers outreach programs in dance and creative movement. Its full-scale multimedia performances have included *Looking Glass*, *Longitude*, and *Luminescence*. Performances take place in the Manship Theatre, Old State Capitol, and other venues throughout the area.

ART AND ARTISTS' ASSOCIATIONS

ARTS COUNCIL OF BATON ROUGE
427 Laurel St.
(225) 344-8558
www.artsbr.org

LOUISIANA ASSOCIATION OF MUSEUMS
P.O. Box 4434, Baton Rouge
(225) 383-6800
www.louisianamuseums.org

LOUISIANA PARTNERSHIP FOR THE ARTS
P.O. Box 82531, Baton Rouge
(225) 767-7640
www.lparts.com

PARKS AND RECREATION

Whether you're an avid sports enthusiast or simply want to spend a few moments outdoors enjoying green spaces and sunshine, Baton Rouge will more than fit the bill. There are also parklands nearby maintained by Louisiana State Parks, and even several national heritage parks within a day's drive. Many of the local parks and recreation facilities are free, but some have fees for certain programs. Jerry L. Stovall, president and CEO of the Baton Rouge Area Sports Foundation, said Baton Rouge's sports visitors (as spectators or participants) should consider three venues: Louisiana State University, Southern University, or BREC (the Baton Rouge Parks and Recreation Commission) facilities. Golf and tennis tournaments are held at country clubs or BREC parks. There's also Cypress Mounds, a privately owned sports park on Gardere Avenue. "The newspaper here does a wonderful job of reporting sports," says Stovall. "If something is going on from the high school level up, you can read about it in *The Advocate*."

BREC has one of the most comprehensive programs in the nation. Created by a state legislative act in 1946 as a separate and distinct body to develop, maintain, and operate public park and recreational properties and facilities for all people in East Baton Rouge Parish, BREC is a subdivision of the State of Louisiana and does not operate under city-parish government. You'll find walking, cycling, football, baseball, golf, tennis, fishing, fitness, and horseback riding. Then there's coach's pitch/tee ball, soccer, dodgeball, rugby, softball, swimming, volleyball, walking, track, and a skate park. There are garden walks, swamp strolls, yoga and tai chi classes, and more.

Birding is another popular outdoor activity. A number of parks within the city offer ample opportunity to view birds, as do protected refuges within an easy driving distance. Birding festivals in the area draw visitors who can register for canoe trips and walks with experts into forested areas to view birds. See the Annual Events chapter.

Whether you plan a visit to a city, state, or national park, keep south Louisiana's climate in mind. Temperatures can be very high in the summer, and humidity can be high year-round. Early morning visits are best from June through September. Also remember that you are the visitor in these natural settings. Regular inhabitants include birds, squirrels, and creatures that bite and sting, such as fire ants, bees, and mosquitoes. Pack repellent, sun block, and water if you plan on spending time outdoors. You're not likely to run into an alligator in city parks, but keep an eye out for snakes, both poisonous and nonpoisonous. Bites are rare, but if you are bitten, find help immediately. Six hospitals in Baton Rouge have 24-hour emergency rooms. See the Health Care chapter.

PARKS AND ZOOS

BREC PARKS
6201 Florida Blvd.
(225) 272-9200
www.brec.org
BREC stands for Baton Rouge Recreation. The award-winning agency is a member of the National Recreation and Park Association and has been nationally accredited and recognized as one of America's premier recreation and park departments. It maintains 184 neighborhood parks. It also operates the Highland Road Observatory for stargazing; Blackwater Conservation Area, Comite River area; Wampold Park and Beach on the LSU Lake; Cohn Arboretum, with plant collections and

walkways; Botanic Gardens for horticultural exhibits and education; the Baton Rouge Zoo; and Bluebonnet Swamp Nature Center (see Kidstuff). These all feature nature and educational programs year-round. Parks are closed between sunset and sunrise, except for special events and scheduled activities. Pets and animals must remain under control and on a leash at all times. Drugs, alcoholic beverages, firearms, and cursing are not allowed. BREC offers year-round sports action for all ages, youth through senior citizens. The agency will help place you on a team if you aren't already on one, or it will help you find additional players for your team if you need more people. The agency maintains a comprehensive Web site that is easy to read. For general rules of operation, a list of all parks and facilities, details on sports, contacts for sports teams, and more, visit the organization's Web site.

BREC'S BATON ROUGE ZOO
3601 Thomas Rd.
(225) 757-8905
www.brzoo.org
It's fun. Tigers glaring back at you. Monkeys hanging by their tails. The Baton Rouge Zoo is one of the top family attractions in the parish. Every visitor can view healthy animals and has a chance to participate in global wildlife conservation. Accredited by the Association of Zoos and Aquariums, the zoo is designed with sections on Africa, South America, Australia, North America, and Louisiana's Atchafalaya Basin. Native vegetation, enhanced with attractive landscaping, provides a park-like setting. There's a picnic area, Cypress Bayou Railroad, gift shop, educational programs, and more. See the Kidstuff chapter for more. Hours are 9 a.m. to 5 p.m. daily.

CITY BROOKS COMMUNITY PARK
1650 Eddie Robinson Sr. Dr.
(225) 272-9200
www.brec.org/index.cfm?md=pagebuilder&mp=home&cpid=436

City Brooks Community Park dates from the 1920s, and in 1927 a carousel pavilion was installed in the park. A Works Progress Administration project in the 1930s tripled the park in size, including the 50-acre City Park Lake. In 2008 the historical park got a multimillion-dollar facelift, turning the site into an urban jewel. The redesign improved the connection between City Park and neighboring Brooks Park. Improvements include Capitol One Tennis Center, a nine-hole golf course, basketball courts, recreation center, new walking trails and bike paths, informal gardens, a labyrinth, picnic areas, outdoor multiuse areas, contemporary outdoor lighting, and new way-finding signs. Take your pooch for a stroll in Raising Cane's Dog Park, or view works by local artists in Baton Rouge Gallery. I-10 runs across City Park Lake, and the park serves south Baton Rouge and the LSU area.

BOWLING

In recent years Baton Rouge has become recognized for its outstanding bowling facilities that provide year-round recreation and entertainment for people of all ages. The bowling lanes attract both regional and national competitions. The city's hotels and restaurants go out of their way to make bowlers and their families comfortable and welcomed during their stay. In 2012 the United States Bowling Congress will hold its national tournament in the city and will bring in some 13,000 teams over a period of six months.

CIRCLE BOWLING LANES
8878 Florida Blvd.
(225) 925-5471
www.circlebowl.com
Family-oriented Circle Bowling, across from Cortana Mall, has 25 bowling alleys and an arcade center. Part of the alley can be used as a dance floor, and a DJ is often playing the latest hits on weekends. Enjoy pizza and party-style bowling on special nights with lights and music. Prices vary by day and time selected for bowling. Check the Web site for details.

DON CARTER BATON ROUGE
9829 Airline Hwy
(225) 924-0124
www.dcbowl.com
Don Carter Baton Rouge is a 64-lane bowling center with activities geared toward the entire family. The staff is ready to assist you the minute you walk through the doors. In addition to adult leagues and tournaments, Don Carter arranges short-season leagues for bowlers with limited time. Hours, times, and fees are posted on the Web site. The facility offers corporate packages, including a complete catering menu. The Pro Shop at Don Carter features the latest in bowling balls and equipment. Check out the Mickey/Minnie pocket carriers for youngsters.

METRO BOWL
4388 Airline Hwy
(225) 356-1366
www.bowlmetro.com
A one-stop recreation center in Baton Rouge since 1959, Metro Bowl has 40 lanes. It caters to adult and youth leagues, tournaments, and the general public. Quibeca scoring has outstanding art graphics. Metro has a snack bar area. Clean and friendly, this is a great place for folks that enjoy bowling year-round. Ask about specials and events. Christian night is Wednesday, 9:30 p.m. to midnight. Visit the Web site for special events, prices, and hours.

FISHING AND HUNTING

Louisiana has long been called Sportsman's Paradise. For those who enjoy the outdoors, the state indeed has expansive wilderness areas and some of America's most spectacular wetlands. South Louisiana is laced with rivers, bayous, swamps, and lakes, providing numerous habitats for fish and game. Residents recognized early on the importance of preserving this unique environment. The first Louisiana wildlife conservation law was passed in 1857. Today the Louisiana Department of Wildlife and Fisheries oversees hunting and fishing activities on land and water. It shares that duty with the U.S. Forest Service and/or the

U.S. Army Corps of Engineers on federal lands. Basic hunting and fishing licenses are required for most people between the ages of 16 and 59. Those who turned 60 after 2000 are required to have a $5 Senior License covering both activities. Special licenses are required for archery and primitive weapons seasons.

You need a saltwater fishing license for trips to coastal waters and a big-game hunting license for taking deer, turkey, and bobcats. The state also offers lifetime licenses covering all those activities. If hunting waterfowl, you'll need a federal waterfowl stamp. All recreational licenses run from July 1 to June 30. Licenses differ between residents and nonresidents and vary according to season. Hunting and fishing licenses are issued after you present a driver's license to a state vendor. To find a vendor, call (888) 765-2602.

The agency enforces both state and federal laws dealing with hunting, fishing, and boating safety. It also enforces criminal laws in rural areas including DWI enforcement both on highways and waterways.

For detailed information on outdoor sports activities, visit the Louisiana Department of Wildlife and Fisheries at www.wlf.louisiana.gov. Additional information is available from the Louisiana Office of State Parks, www.crt.state.la.us; U.S. Forest Service, www.fs.fed.us; and U.S. Fish and Wildlife Service, www.fws.gov.

In East Baton Rouge Parish, you can fish in BREC's lakes. They include: City Park Lake, 2549 Dalrymple Dr.; Greenwood Park Lake, 13350 Hwy 19; Oak Villa Lake, 2615 Oak Villa Blvd.; Doyle's Bayou, 7801 Pride-Port Hudson Rd.; North Sherwood Forest Lake, 3140 North Sherwood Forest Dr.; and Blackwater Conservation Area, intersection of Blackwater and Hooper Roads. Fishing ponds at North Sherwood, Greenwood, and Oak Villa have been stocked with rainbow trout. Your best chances are at North Sherwood and Oak Villa ponds.

For fishing in BREC ponds, you do not need a special license, just a basic fishing license from the Louisiana Department of Wildlife and Fisheries. The limit is four fish a day. You can catch and release more than four.

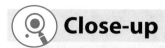 **Close-up**

Louisiana Brown Pelican

The Louisiana state bird—the eastern brown pelican—symbolizes the perseverance and spirit of the state. Early European settlers were impressed with the pelican's generous and nurturing attitude toward their young. Louisiana's official nickname is the Pelican State, and the bird appears on Louisiana's state flag, state seal, and official state painting. In Baton Rouge you will see the pelican symbols on state buildings and on souvenirs. It is also one of the Louisiana symbols displayed on the U.S. Mint's bicentennial quarter.

The brown pelican made headlines November 2009 when it was officially taken off the federal Endangered Species List. Although in decline since the late 1890s, the bird suffered when the use of pesticides such as DDT caused pelicans' eggs to be easily breakable with thin shells. Brown pelicans stopped nesting along the Louisiana coast in 1961, and the birds weren't spotted in the state at all in 1963. Louisiana undertook a reintroduction program from 1968 to 1980 and brought in 1,276 pelicans from Florida. Today there are numerous nesting colonies along coastal Louisiana.

Unique among the world's seven species of pelicans, the brown pelican nests from South Carolina to Brazil. It is found along ocean shores and not on inland lakes. It is the only dark pelican, and the only one that plunges from the air into the water to catch its food. The bird depends almost entirely on fish for food, scooping up quantities of water into its pouch as it seizes prey from salt waters. As the large bill is elevated the water dribbles from the mandibles, and the pouch contracts as the fish are swallowed. The average pelican, from the age of one month, consumes five pounds of fish a day.

Though the brown pelican is no longer on the Endangered Species List, environmentalists will be watching its progress. The coastal landscape the bird uses in Louisiana is disappearing. The bird will still have protection under the Migratory Bird Treaty Act.

BREC offers bank fishing only. No trout lines allowed. Louisiana Wildlife and Fisheries laws must be followed. Parks close at dark.

GOLF

No matter where you are in Baton Rouge, a good golf course is not far away. Golfers have access to a number of Louisiana's Audubon Golf Trail courses. These courses represent some of the best designed and most challenging courses in the country. Golfers are urged to phone ahead for information, accessibility, greens fees, and tee times.

BEAVER CREEK PARK AND GOLF COURSE
1100 Plains-Port Hudson Rd., Zachary
(225) 658-6338
www.brec.org

Beaver Creek Park, a BREC 18-hole course, has a windswept front nine and sheltered back nine. The course has an immense practice facility, a lighted driving range, putting green, and wedge chipping area. Stay for lunch at the Creekside Grill. Distance is 6,950 yards; course rating, 73.1; status, public. Green fees are $35 per person and $30, seniors age 55 and older, Friday through Sunday. Fees Monday through Thursday are $28 per person and $15, seniors.

COPPER MILL GOLF CLUB
2100 Copper Mill Blvd., Zachary
(225) 658-0656
www.coppermillgolf.com
Designers of this course are Max Maxwell and Nathan Crace. The 18-hole course is routed through its natural setting of fields of native grasses, ancient live oak trees, and cypress bayou.

Green fees are $50 weekdays and $60 weekends, including cart. Distance is 7,000 yards; course rating, 73.7 (black), 70.2 (copper), 66.9 (green), 67.6 (ladies/white); status, semiprivate.

GREYSTONE GOLF AND COUNTRY CLUB
9214 Greystone Dr.
Denham Springs
(225) 667-6744
www.greystonecountryclub.com

Greystone Golf and Country Club is just minutes from the new Juban Road Exit off I-12 and minutes from the Bass Pro Shop off of Range Ave. The 18-hole course incorporates natural wetlands and part of a hardwood forest. Distance is 7,054 yards; course rating, 74.3; slope, 143. Green fees are $65 weekdays and $75 weekends.

THE ISLAND COUNTRY CLUB
(Audubon Golf Trail)
23550 Myrtle Grove Rd., Plaquemine
(225) 685-0808
www.theislandgolf.com

This course is across the I-10 Mississippi River Bridge in Iberville Parish. Designed by Mike Young, the course has been featured on the Golf channel and in *Golf* magazine. Water comes into play on nine holes and 17 greens. The clubhouse overlooks holes 9 and 18. Distance is 7,010 yards; course rating, 74.4/135 championship, 71.8/130 standard; status, semiprivate.

LSU GOLF CLUB
Corner of Burbank Dr. and Nicholson Dr.
(225) 578-3394
www.golf.lsu.edu

Just across from the new Alex Box Baseball Stadium, this 18-hole course is located minutes from downtown. Driving range is open 7 a.m. to 8 p.m., and there's a nine-hole pitch and putt course. Distance is 6,772 yards; course rating 72.3 (blue); status, public course with full-service pro shop. Green fees on weekdays are $12, students; $15, faculty, staff, and seniors; $18, LSU alumni and public. Weekend fees are $14, students; $16, faculty; $18, seniors; and $23, alumni and public. Call about specials.

PELICAN POINT GOLF CLUB LINKS AND LAKES
6300 Championship Court, Suite 201, Gonzales
(225) 746-9900
www.golf.thepoint.com

Pelican Point is a semi-private club offering 36 holes of golf near the Mississippi River. The Links course was opened in 1997 followed by the Lakes in 2002. The club offers a pro shop and Mulligan's Grill, offering breakfast, lunch, and dinner. The grill features sandwiches, burgers, salads, and grilled entrees. Located by an upscale residential area in Ascension Parish, the course was selected in 2004 by *Golf Digest* as one of the best places to play. The Links course distance is 6,931 yards; rating 73.3; and slope; 129. Fees are $55, weekdays, and $65, weekends. The Lakes course distance is 6,513; rating, 71.3; slope, 126. Fees are $35, weekdays, and $45, weekends.

SANTA MARIA GOLF CLUB
18460 Santa Maria Parkway
(225) 752-9667
www.brec.org

Designed by Robert Trent Jones Sr., this is one of the newest BREC courses. Distance is 6,826 yards; course rating, 74.1 (gold), 71.8 (blue), 68.2 (white), and 70.7 (red); status, public. There's a driving range, practice facility, and workout facility. The cafe has hamburgers, sandwiches, and snacks.

Standard BREC Courses
FIRST TEE AT CLARK PARK GOLF COURSE
12702 La. 19
(225) 775-9008

HOWELL PARK GOLF COURSE
5511 Winbourne Ave.
Baton Rouge
(225) 357-9292

WEBB PARK MEMORIAL GOLF COURSE
1352 Country Club Dr.
(225) 383-4919

WOODROW DUMAS GOLF COURSE
(Greenwood Park)
2400 Lavey Lane, Baker
(225) 775-9166

TENNIS

Tennis enthusiasts play at BREC courses and at private clubs. The Greater Baton Rouge Community Tennis Association actively supports the sport and local tournaments, providing residents with many opportunities for competitive tennis. A member of the United States Tennis Association, GBRCTA features senior, adult, and junior programs with year-round events. In 2009 USTA Southern presented Baton Rouge with the 2009 Best Tennis Town Honorable Mention plaque. The city was cited for the passion and spirit of its tennis players and fans. Contact www .batonrougetennis.com. If you are considering relocating to the Baton Rouge area, you also may want to contact the Baton Rouge Women's Tennis Association, which has various tournaments throughout the year. Contact www.brwta.com.

BREC TENNIS PROGRAMS
www.brec.org
BREC has numerous tennis courts in neighborhoods throughout East Baton Rouge Parish. Two year-round academies for youths under age 12 are held at Independence Park and Highland Park Center. Adults can sign up for cardio tennis, adult fun tournaments, and leagues. For fees at these tennis centers and more information, contact the BREC Tennis Department at (225) 272-9200, ext. 549.

HIGHLAND PARK CENTER
14024 Highland Rd.
(225) 766-0247

INDEPENDENCE PARK CENTER
7505 Independence
(225) 923-2792

YMCA LAMAR TENNIS CENTER
8100 YMCA Plaza Dr.
(225) 612-2420

Programs here include wheelchair tennis and a junior tennis program. Membership is not required for a lesson, although there is an added fee for nonmembers. The center has 10 hard courts and 10 soft courts. Membership per person is $40 to join and $46 per month. Family membership is $50 to join and $74 per month. Nonmembers attending with a member pay $5.

LOUISIANA STATE PARKS

www.crt.state.la.us/parks
Louisiana state parks, located in every region of the state, are very well managed and maintained. Parks and historic sites are under the direction of the Louisiana Office of State Parks. Every park has special programs relating to its ecosystem and Louisiana's diverse natural beauty. The parks vary in size and facilities, but most contain upgraded campsites. Attractive cabins are often reserved a year in advance, so they can be difficult to obtain. However park officials say you can call at the last minute because they often get cancellations. For reservations call (877) CAMP-N-LA (877) 226-7652. Several parks within an easy drive of Baton Rouge make excellent one-day outings. Hours of operation are 6 a.m. to 9 p.m. Sunday through Thursday and until 10 p.m. Friday, Saturday, and days preceding holidays. Entrance fees are $1 per person; free for seniors age 62 and older and children age 3 and under. Some fees apply for rentals or special services.

BAYOU SIGNETT STATE PARK
7777 Westbank Expressway, Westwego
(504) 736-7140, (888) 677-2296
Just a 30-minute drive across the Mississippi River from New Orleans, Bayou Signett State Park puts you into an ecosystem that gives you a chance to view plants, trees, and wildlife from both swamps and marshland. Both salt and freshwater fishing are available because of the park's location. Visitors can enjoy boating, canoeing, picnicking, and playgrounds. There's a 1-mile nature trail and a well-supervised wave pool in summer. The park has 98 premium campsites. From Baton Rouge, take I-10 east (by southeast) to the Huey P. Long

Bridge in New Orleans and cross the Mississippi River to the Westbank Expressway and the park.

LAKE FAUSSE POINTE STATE PARK
5400 Levee Rd., St. Martinville
(337) 229-4764 or (888) 677-7200
Lake Fausse Pointe State Park occupies a 6,000-acre site that was once part of the Atchafalaya Basin. The area was once the home site of the Chitimacha Indians. A boat launch gives visitors easy access to the labyrinth of waterways that winds through the basin. The visitor complex features a boat dock with kayak, canoe, and boat rentals with paddles and life jackets. Programs and activities at the nature center help you learn more about the environment. There are three nature trails and a 7-mile canoe trail. The park has 16 deluxe cabins, 33 improved campsites, 17 premium campsites, five unimproved campsites, and a primitive camping area. From Baton Rouge take I-10 west to Exit 115 to Henderson, heading south on La. 342. The park is about 19 miles down the road on the right.

TICKFAW STATE PARK
27225 Patterson Rd., Springfield
(2225) 294-5020, (888) 981-2020
Tickfaw State Park makes an excellent day trip for families. Visitors can experience the sights and sounds of a cypress and tupelo swamp, hardwood forests, and the Tickfaw River. Bike, stroll, or skate the interconnecting park roadways. Rent a canoe and paddle along the Tickfaw. Raised boardwalks are perfect for birding. Nature presentations at the education pavilions appeal to children and adults alike. You also can join a nighttime program or go night hiking. The park has 14 deluxe cabins, 30 improved campsites, and 20 unimproved campsites. From Baton Rouge take I-12 east to the Albany Springfield exit. Travel 2 miles south on La. 43, merge with La. 42, and continue 1 mile to the center of Springfield. Turn west on La. 1037 and travel 6 miles to Patterson Road (across from Woodland Baptist Church). Then drive south 1.2 miles to the park entrance.

Walk the 6-mile trail at Port Hudson State Historic Site, U.S. 61 about 20 minutes north of downtown Baton Rouge. The trail winds through a lush hardwood forest that was once part of Port Hudson's Civil War battlefield. Signs along the way relate information about the battle. A quarter-mile section along a raised boardwalk gives you an idea of the density of the woods. Open daily. Admission is $2 per person and free to youths age 12 and under and seniors 62 and older. (225) 654-3775.

NATONAL PARKS

JEAN LAFITTE NATIONAL HISTORICAL PARK AND PRESERVE
419 Decatur St., New Orleans
www.nps.gov/jela
The six sites of Jean Lafitte National Historical Park and Preserve represent a treasure trove of south Louisiana's historical and cultural riches. The sites include: French Quarter Visitor Center; Chalmette Battlefield, where the Battle of New Orleans took place; Barataria Preserve, the area where Jean Lafitte and his crew once encamped; Wetlands Acadian Cultural Center in Houma; Prairie Acadian Cultural Center in Eunice; and Acadian Cultural Center in Lafayette. These units interpret the diverse cultural mix and history of south Louisiana. Easiest sites to visit from Baton Rouge on a one-day outing are the French Quarter, Chalmette Battlefield, and Barataria Preserve in New Orleans and the Acadian Cultural Center in Lafayette. Depending on the time you have, you can spend a few hours at each site or stretch your stay to a full day. National park rangers conduct special programs at each site. Take a walking tour through the French Quarter in New Orleans or a boat ride along the Vermilion River at the Acadian Center in Lafayette. Visit Barataria in the spring when wild Louisiana irises are in full bloom. To visit any of these sites, check out full details on the U.S. government Web site.

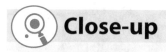 **Close-up**

Atchafalaya Basin Like No Other Place

Baton Rouge sits on the eastern side of the Atchafalaya National Heritage Area, one of America's unique regions. Situated in south-central Louisiana, it is a combination of wetlands and river delta where the Atchafalaya River and Gulf of Mexico come together.

Atchafalaya is a Native American word. In the Choctaw tongue, *hacha* means river and *falala* means long. It translates as Long River. Learning to pronounce it is a challenge, but give it a try. You can say it–like a sneeze: "ah-CHA-fa-LIE-ah."

Designated by an act of Congress in 2006, the Atchafalaya National Heritage Area is made up of 14 parishes in and surrounding the Atchafalaya Basin. "This is one of only 49 heritage areas in the United States," said Debra Credeur, heritage area director. She said the national designation officially recognizes the Atchafalaya region because of its significant resources that are important to the nation. Credeur's office operates within the Louisiana Department of Culture, Recreation, and Tourism under the direction of Louisiana's Lt. Governor. Credeur said one of her office's mandates is to create a management plan for all the parishes to come together to increase visitation yet all the while preserving and conserving the historic and natural resources and the culture of the region. The dynamic system of waterways and geology reveals a land that is both fragile and awesome. "This is a living culture, not just a historic culture," said Credeur. "The food ways, the customs, and the traditions here are connected very closely with the land and the water."

"The Atchafalaya Basin or Atchafalaya Swamp refers to a nine-parish region within the larger National Heritage Area," said Credeur. She said when visitors see the area, they often comment, "It's like a foreign country."

Characterized by a maze of bayous and waterways, the Atchafalaya Swamp is the largest river swamp in the United States. The ecology teems with life. The swamp is a habitat for more than 85 species of fish, crawfish, and other crustaceans. Some 60 species of reptiles and amphibians, along with 270 species of birds, live in the area, including bald eagles, herons, egrets, ibis, cranes, and an array of migratory wildfowl. Other "critters" include alligators, deer, beaver, and black bear. It's no wonder that birders and photographers are drawn to the basin.

The few roads that cross the core area of the Atchafalaya Swamp follow the tops of levees. I-10 crosses the basin on elevated pillars from Maringouin to Henderson. It is a continuous 18.2-mile bridge. About 30 miles west of Baton Rouge, you can take the Atchafalaya Welcome Center exit on I-10 at Butte LaRose. This is not your ordinary state-run rest stop. It's a showcase for the basin. Resembling a southern Louisiana home, the center features a deep raised gallery that surrounds the building on three sides. The interior features high ceilings with exposed beams. Be ready for a surprise. The center also serves as a cultural museum. There's an educational theater with a video presentation on the basin. You can't help but laugh at the animatronics exhibit with a talking Cajun turtle, raccoon, alligator, and bird telling you about their home. The center has racks and racks of tourist brochures about traveling in Louisiana. Patient travel counselors are extremely knowledgeable about the Atchafalaya area. They help visitors with maps and information on whom to contact about swamp tours and nearby towns. The entire facility is designed to be convenient for travelers. There's ample parking for cars and recreational vehicles. There is a separate parking facility for commercial truckers. Contact the center at (337) 228-1095. For more information visit www.atchafalaya.org.

OUTFITTERS

BASS PRO SHOPS
I-12 and Range Ave., Denham Springs
(225) 271-3100
www.basspro.com
With 163,000 square feet, this is one of the largest Bass Pro Shops in the South. Featuring a bayou theme, Bass Pro has all the equipment and gear an outdoors enthusiast could want. There's an aquarium, boat showroom, wildlife mounts, and more. Displays capture the spirit of the local area's heritage. Look for photographs, wildlife exhibits, and artifacts from local hunters. The Islamorada Fish Company restaurant is attracting crowds.

CABELA'S
2200 West Cabela's Parkway, Gonzales
(225) 743-3400
www.cabelas.com
Cabela's, situated just off I-10 at exit 177, is one of America's leading sports outfitters. You'll find everything you need for fishing, hunting, and camping. There's outdoor gear and clothing for men, women, and children. The store includes pet accessories and home décor items with sports themes. The store features a huge aquarium and excellent restaurant with sandwiches, grilled items, and a kids' menu. RV parking is available.

WALKING AND BIKING TRAILS

While people frequently walk and cycle in Baton Rouge neighborhoods, these activities are best enjoyed in parks. Many city streets are heavily trafficked, and only a few are designated with bike paths. The BREC parks in East Baton Rouge Parish include 25.77 miles of walking and running trails and tracks. Eleven parks have hard-surface walk paths, and seven feature nature trails. There are special facility walking paths at Bluebonnet Swamp Nature Center, 1053 North Oak Hills Parkway. Cyclists are welcome to ride the Baton Rouge velodrome operated by BREC. It is a 333-meter smooth concrete track, one of only 15 in the United States. It is located at the Perkins Road Extreme Sports Park, which opens in spring 2010. Other park features include a BMX (bicycle motocross) track, skateboard facility, and rock-climbing wall. A walking and bike trail circles the entire park. Call Jason Hoggatt for information at (225) 218-0918. Off-road cycling is available at the Comite River/ Kerry Stamey Mountain Biking Trail. For more details, contact the BREC Web site, www.brec.org.

BATON ROUGE BIKE CLUB
www.batonrougebikeclub.com
The Baton Rouge Bike Club has Saturday rides. The ride starts at Goodwood Park, near the intersection of Goodwood Blvd. and Jefferson Hwy. The ride takes participants down to the scenic LSU area, around the City Park lakes, to the levee at Skip Bertman Ave., then through downtown Baton Rouge, stopping for coffee at Red Stick Farmers Market. The ride is about 25–30 miles at about 15–19 mph. There are also Saturday outlying area rides that have routes from 20–60 miles. On Sunday the rides meet at the fire station on La. 966, south of St. Francisville. Ride lengths are 50–70 miles; speed 18–22 mph. Dues are $5 per year, singles, and $10, family. Helmets are required. The public is welcome.

SPECTATOR SPORTS

Baton Rougeans just love their sports. Spectator sports at Louisiana State University and Southern University dominate the scene. The teams, the players, and the coaches are major topics of conversation and often become national and international celebrities. Sporting events bring thousands of visitors into town, packing restaurants and hotels on game weekends. Flags in team colors fly from vehicles as avid fans head toward the games. Lavish tailgate parties for football, baseball, and basketball last two or three days. Additional sports that draw crowds include track and field, tennis, soccer, swimming, and gymnastics. Baton Rouge Community College, established in 1995, has a budding athletic program with men's and women's basketball and baseball. In addition to collegiate sports, Baton Rouge plays host to local, regional, and national high school and junior high events. A number of BREC park facilities serve as venues for these sports events. Families traveling with their young athletes are always welcomed, and adult fans can expect a warm reception. Tickets? Well, if it's a big game, you'd better get that ticket well in advance.

COLLEGE SPORTS

BATON ROUGE COMMUNITY COLLEGE
201 Community College Dr.
(225) 216-8166 (Athletic Department)
www.mybrcc.edu
Established in 1995 as a two-year college, Baton Rouge Community College has a young athletic department. Currently men's and women's basketball teams play at the Bonne Santé Wellness Center on the campus. The baseball team, which hosts tournaments every weekend in summer, plays at BREC's Pete Goldsby Field next to Memorial Stadium. For information and tickets, call the athletic department phone number.

LSU SPORTS FACILITIES
Athletic Administration Building
Nicholson Drive at North Stadium Dr.
(225) 578-8001
www.lsusports.net
Purple and gold are the main colors in and around LSU, especially on game days. Fall Saturdays turn the campus into one of the most renowned environments in college football. Tiger Stadium is an intimidating facility on the west side of the campus. With some 92,000 fans filling every possible seat, it's no wonder that the stadium is nicknamed Death Valley. Get to the stadium early for pregame festivities, including the entrance of mascot Mike the Tiger in his specially escorted traveling cage. There's a brief security check. Alcohol, weapons, and umbrellas are not allowed in the stadium.

The Maravich Center, named after LSU's famed basketball star Pete Maravich, seats up to 13,250 fans. LSU has often produced premier players—Bob Petit, Maravich, and Shaquille O'Neal all made the NBA's 50th anniversary all-time team. When the men's basketball team clinched its 10th SEC title in 2009, it achieved a unique honor. LSU became the first school to win double-digit SEC championships in football, baseball, and men's basketball. The Maravich Center, nicknamed The Dome, is also home to women's basketball, gymnastics, and volleyball. The facility, with comfortable purple-and-gold seats, also serves as a venue for traveling concerts, shows, and major local events.

Alex Box Stadium, the new state-of-the-art baseball field, opened in 2009 to cheers and a big crowd. From LSU's first SEC title in 1939 to the 2009 championship at the College World Series, the LSU Tigers have continued to chalk up great moments. Replacing the former historic Alex Box, the stadium features natural grass, a 10-foot fence, and suites.

Bernie Moore Track and Field Stadium, which seats 5,680 fans, features an exceptional all-weather track. The field has played host to numerous elite track and field competitions. Located just north of the field is the Carl Maddox Field House, designed for indoor track and field events. Just beyond the field house, the Natatorium has a 50-meter pool and championship diving pool. It seats 2,200 spectators. Not to be undone, the W.T. "Dub" Tennis Stadium is home to men's and women's tennis. The facility, nicknamed The Dub, has six varsity courts and six practice courts. Viewing stands can seat 550 fans.

Additional LSU sports facilities include the Soccer Complex, with hybrid Bermuda grass and seating for 1,500 spectators, and the new Tiger Park, home of LSU softball, which has 587 chair-back seats.

All fans, regardless of age, need a ticket to enter Tiger Stadium for all football games. For all other sporting events, fans age three and above need a ticket. The Main Ticket Office is on the first floor of the Athletic Administration Building. A photo ID is required to pick up tickets. The PMAC Ticket Office is on the south side of the Maravich Assembly Center on the upper level and is open 90 minutes before the event. The Alex Box Ticket Office is on the southwest corner of Alex Box Stadium behind home plate and is open two hours before the event.

The LSU Athletics Web site, www.lsusports.net, is comprehensive and contains details on teams, event schedules, tickets, parking, and more.

To appreciate the passion of LSU fans, consider the LSU football family's annual National Signing Day party. More than 3,000 fans usually attend the daylong event on the first Wednesday of February. They wear Mardi Gras beads, tailgate, and talk football while future Tiger players fax in letters of intent.

SOUTHERN UNIVERSITY SPORTS FACILITIES
Harding Boulevard and Scenic Hwy. (U.S. 61)
(225) 359-9328
www.gojagsports.cstv.com

Southern University fans proudly wear the distinctive Columbia blue and gold colors. Teams at the historically black university are the Southern Jaguars. They participate in NCAA intercollegiate athletics and Division 1 of the Southwestern Athletic Conference. Football season may last only 11 or 12 weeks, but avid fans stay true year-round. SU's loyal fans follow the team on the road and have become known as the Jaguar Nation. Home games are a barbecue-and-tailgating family event, with reunions and a music festival throughout the afternoon. Part of the fun is seeing SU's Jaguar Band, nicknamed the Human Jukebox. The band has appeared in TV commercials and participated in presidential inaugurations, the Rose Bowl Parade in Pasadena, California, and in Super Bowl halftime shows.

Football games are played in Ace W. Mumford Stadium, a 29,000-seat facility. A new complex at the north end of the stadium features the latest technology and comforts, including additional seats, suites, weight rooms, meeting rooms for coaches and athletes, and new lockers for football and track athletes. SU's football teams have produced numerous legends.

The Jaguars track and field athletes also use Mumford Stadium. These outstanding athletes lately have been coached in track and field and cross country by SWAC Hall of Famer Johnny Thomas. World-class long jumper Brian Johnson is an assistant coach and still competes when his schedule allows. Also playing in the stadium are SU's women's soccer team and Southern Laboratory High School.

The F.G. Clark Activity Center is the home of the Southern men's and women's basketball teams. Southern's basketball greats include former point guard Avery Johnson, who helped lead the San Antonio Spurs to an NBA title and came close to another one while coaching the Dallas Mavericks. Today he works as an ESPN analyst. Bob Love was the Chicago Bulls' all-time leading scorer until a player named Jordan came along. The lady Jaguars have more than held their own—Jacklyn Winfield, the SWAC Player of the Year in 2002, is the only SWAC player to have been drafted into the WNBA. Current SU women's coach Sandy Pugh led the Jaguars to SWAC titles in 2002, 2004, and 2006.

Baseball fans can watch the Jaguars play at Lee-Hinds field. The baseball improvement program includes an upgrade with a locker room/office facility beyond the left field wall. Current coach Roger Cador has won 13 of the school's 25 conference baseball titles. Two emerging stars in the major leagues—San Francisco Giants outfielder Fred Lewis and Milwaukee Brewers second baseman Rickie Weeks—played together in 2002 at Southern. The university's otherJaguars teams include golf, tennis, volleyball, softball, and women's bowling.

Tickets to Southern University sports events are available at the ticket office, 7722 Scenic Hwy. (the old City National Bank Building). Call (225) 359-9328, Monday through Friday, 9 a.m. to 3 p.m. They also are available game day from noon to halftime. You also may purchase tickets through Ticketmaster. For additional information on teams, event schedules, and more, visit the Web site, www.gojagsports.cstv.com.

i Alcohol and weapons are not allowed in LSU and Southern University's sports facilities. Backpacks and purses are searched by security guards at ticket gates. Also, umbrellas are not allowed into the facilities.

VENUES IN CITY

Baton Rouge has two other sports stadiums that are operated by BREC and available to the public.

MEMORIAL STADIUM
1702 Foss St.
(225) 766-5209
www.brec.org
Memorial Stadium is adjacent to I-10 near the Governor's Mansion. The stadium seats 21,500 and is used by high schools and BREC for football games. It's also available for major special events. The facility has two lighted baseball diamonds.

i Sports fans wear comfortable but stylish outfits to games in Baton Rouge. Often jackets, shirts, and hats are in their favorite team's colors. You'll also see people in dressy casual clothing if they are attending parties before or after games.

OLYMPIA STADIUM
7122 Perkins Rd.
(225) 766-5209
www.brec.org
Olympia Stadium, located in Perkins Road Park, is used by high school and BREC tackle football teams. The stadium seats 6,000 spectators. The facility also has soccer fields and baseball diamonds. For other sports activities, see the Parks and Recreation chapter.

KIDSTUFF

There's no doubt that Baton Rouge is a family-friendly city. Activities often center on family life—spending a day at the zoo, attending a football game, or participating in a church festival. Families on vacation can feel comfortable joining in the fun. *Baton Rouge Parents* magazine is an excellent source for family activities. Published monthly, the magazine carries helpful articles, such as a column with dads advising dads. The monthly calendar lists events for both adults and kids, including festivals, free classes at libraries, and family fun and fitness events. You can check the calendar at www.brparents.com. Other sources include the listing of events in the *Advocate*'s Fun section each Friday and the Baton Rouge Convention and Visitor's Bureau Web site, www.visitbatonrouge.com.

Price Code

The price ratings are for an adult admission fee during the summer high season. Keep in mind that many attractions offer discounts for children, seniors, and military personnel.

$	Less than $5
$$	$ 5 to $10
$$$	$ 11 to $20
$$$$	More than $20

BLUE BAYOU WATER PARK AND
DIXIE LANDIN' $$$$
Highland Road and Perkins Road East
(225) 753-3333
www.bluebayou.com
Blue Bayou Water Park and Dixie Landin' is a cross between a modern, high-tech water playground and an old-fashioned amusement park. While it's only open from Memorial Day weekend through Labor Day weekend, the park is a major family destination. Dixie Landin' contains 26 rides, including the Ragin' Cajun, a giant steel looping roller coaster. The Kiddie Section features small rides for the young ones. Gasoline Alley gives kids the chance to drive mom and dad around in a Model T. Blue Bayou Water Park has more than 20 water attractions. Try the six-story Mad Moccasin slide that twists and turns in complete darkness, or ride the Conja, the world's largest in-line water slide. Concessions feature traditional theme park goodies, from cotton candy and funnel cakes to hot dogs, pizza, and more. Live concerts on Saturdays during the summer. Get $5 off the daily admission price when you bring a Coke can.

BREC'S BLUEBONNET SWAMP
NATURE CENTER $
10503 North Oak Hills Parkway
(225) 757-8905
www.bsnconline.net
Bluebonnet Swamp Nature Center is a 101-acre facility that includes 1.3 miles of walking trails through a cypress swamp and a magnolia-beech forest. The center also features a 9,500-square-foot Nature Center with live animal exhibits. Youngsters have a blast here learning and interacting with live animals. Staff members are friendly and extremely helpful. Sign up for the Swamp Night Hike and discover why the Wise Ol' Owl isn't so wise and why being blind as a bat is a good thing. Wear long pants and closed-toe shoes and bring insect repellent. Newcomers to the community may want to sign up their toddler (age one to five) for the four-week toddler program teaching kids about plants and animals. Cost for toddler program is $40 parish residents and $48, non-parish residents. Regular Nature Center hours are Tuesday through Saturday, 9 a.m. to 5 p.m. and Sunday, noon to 5 p.m. Trails close at 4:15 p.m.

BREC'S BATON ROUGE ZOO $$

3601 Thomas Rd.

(225) 775-3877

www.brzoo.org

Let's face it: kids love zoos. BREC's Baton Rouge Zoo is no exception. In this happy, safe environment, a kid can giggle at the antics of monkeys, wonder at the strength of elephants, and talk to the parrots. A trip here is a learning adventure, starting with the Globe Fountain at the entrance. Made of a solid block of granite, the one-ton globe constantly turns while floating on a bed of water. By putting their hands on the globe, kids can turn to different continents and literally stop the world. It's the beginning of a geography lesson and introduction to animal conservation. The zoo is home to tigers, cheetahs, llamas, black bears, giraffes, black rhinos, flamingos, and more. For little ones the Safari Playground is a perfect place to burn pent-up energy, and the Cypress Bayou Railroad gives everyone a sit-down tour of the facility. A picnic area is a great place for lunch, and the gift shop has affordable toys, books, jewelry, and statuary. Pets, shoes with wheels (Rollerblades), skateboards, and bicycles are prohibited. Child must be accompanied by an adult. Open daily 9:30 a.m. to 4 p.m. Grounds close at 5 p.m.

i Animal lovers can get eye-to-eye with hoof-stock at the Global Wildlife Center, 26389 La. 40 in Folsom, about 55 miles east of Baton Rouge. The 900-acre free-roaming preserve offers guided wagon tours where guests can feed giraffes from large plastic containers or cups, wiggle a camel's hump, or feel the woolly fur of bison. There's a picnic area, a snack area, and a large shop filled with a variety of excellent gift items. Contact (985) 796-3585 or www .globalwildlife.com. $$$

ENCHANTED MANSION DOLL MUSEUM $

190 Lee Drive

(225) 769-0005

www.enchantedmansion.org

Enchanting just begins to describe the charm of Enchanted Mansion. Visitors walk through this dreamy Victorian life-sized dollhouse to view rare and antique dolls as well as contemporary favorites and one-of-a-kind dolls created by skilled artists. Displays are created for kid-sized viewing, but there's plenty of appeal for adults. Set aside the time to thoroughly enjoy the setting. Be sure to visit Ted. E. Bear's playroom. The gift shop carries the largest collection of Lee Middleton dolls in the area. Other dolls are from Seymour-Mann, Delton, Madame Alexander, and Adora. The shop also has additional accessories and wardrobes for your doll. On Thursdays you can enjoy tea in the party room. Enchanted Mansion is open Thursday through Saturday, 10 a.m. to 5 p.m. The sole purpose of the museum is to benefit the handicapped. There is no fee for handicapped visitors.

i The Mayor-President of East Baton Rouge Parish always announces the official day and date for Halloween trick-and-treating, usually October 31. The hours are always 6 to 8 p.m.

LOUISIANA ARTS AND SCIENCE MUSEUM AND PLANETARIUM $$

100 River Rd.

(225) 344-5272

www.lasm.org

The Louisiana Arts and Science Museum and Planetarium offers something for the entire family. It's famous for hosting major exhibitions and art displays. Innovative programs capture kids' attention for hours. The number one attraction for the young crowd is the mummy. The Ancient Egypt Gallery focuses on the Ptolemaic period. In the first room kids learn about the ancient Egyptians' religion. The final room is about the Egyptians' belief in the afterlife and their funeral practices. Displays explain the research, including a CT scan at St. Elizabeth Hospital, which revealed the mummy to be a male who appeared to have dried out naturally in hot, dry environmental conditions. Other LASM programs include Discovery Depot for toddlers, featuring educational toys, and Science Station for kids ages 7 to twelve with activities that make science and math fun. In the Planetarium's Solar System Gallery, kids can weigh themselves on the moon and learn how the planets got their names. The ceiling has an orrery—a giant solar system model 40 feet across illustrating the orbital rotation of the planets. Sky shows and large-format shows are featured in the ExxonMobile Space Theater. Children under age three are not allowed in the theater. Available to adults and children is the show *The Zulu Patrol: Under the Weather*. LASM is open Tuesday through Friday 10 a.m. to 4 p.m., Saturday 10 a.m. to 8 p.m., and Sunday 1 to 5 p.m. Show hours vary, so it's best to call ahead. Especially nice is the LASM gift shop, which is filled with quality educational and fun items. See the Attractions chapter.

MIKE THE TIGER CAGE AT LSU   FREE
Stadium Drive, LSU campus
(225) 578-0628
www.mikethetiger.com

Mike the Tiger's new habitat is 15,000 square feet in size with lush plantings, a large live oak tree, a beautiful waterfall, and a stream issuing from a rocky backdrop overflowing with plants and trees. The habitat has an Italianate tower backdrop and a campanile that creates a visual bridge to the architectural theme of the LSU campus. Children and adults love stopping by the habitat and getting an up-close view of the big guy. Mike VI is a Bengal/Siberian mix and has remarkable markings. He was born in 2005 and was flown to LSU in 2007. By 2009 he weighed 420 pounds. His veterinarian reports he is confident, interactive, and friendly to people. You may see him lounging in his stream early in the day. Late in the afternoon, Mike likes to play with a large boomer ball especially made in purple just for him. Check out Mike's Web site to hear him roar.

i Throughout the year, the East Baton Rouge Parish Library offers Storytime, which is scheduled weekly throughout the library system. Storytime provides an excellent opportunity to introduce children to books. For a schedule go to www .ebr.lib.la.us/programs/calendar.htm or go to the main library at 7711 Goodwood Blvd. (225) 231-3740.

SKATE GALAXY $$
12828 Jefferson Hwy.
(225) 756-2424
www.skategalaxy.com

Skate Galaxy is an indoor roller skating haven with plenty of options. Go for casual skating or a more serious workout. You won't be bored. Stretch your muscles with rock climbing and other skills at Laser Tag. Galaxy has an awesome arcade, food court, pro shop, and an adult viewing balcony with TV. Hours are seasonal. Closed Mondays. Skate rentals are $2.

UNIVERSITY LAKE   FREE
901 Stanford Ave.
(225) 272-9200
www.brec.org

For a simple daytime outing that costs nothing, take the kids to University Lake by the LSU campus. This natural setting is beautiful any time of year. It's home to ducks, geese, and other wild creatures. Wild pelicans drop in for a visit from time to time. There's a temptation to feed the waterfowl, but bread, corn, popcorn, and table scraps can actually harm them. These birds naturally seek and feed on foods such as aquatic plants, natural grains, and invertebrates. Instead of food, bring a camera. The lake is a good place to teach kids basic photography skills. Next to the lake is the Baton Rouge Beach operated by BREC. The entire area around the lake isn't technically part of the park, but in practice it ends up working out that way. There's plenty of space to walk, jog, or watch your kids run and jump a bit.

USS *KIDD* AND VETERANS MEMORIAL $$
305 South River Rd.
(225) 342-1942
www.usskidd.com

Visit this museum and learn why the pirate's Jolly Roger flag is flown above the USS *Kidd*. The USS *Kidd*, situated on the Mississippi River, is a fully restored World War II destroyer. It is named for Admiral Isaac Campbell Kidd, who was commander of the USS *Arizona*. During the Battle of Pearl Harbor, he was the first U.S. Flag officer to lose his life in World War II. The museum honors all male and female veterans who have served the country. Youngsters and parents can tour the boat, view sleeping quarters and the kitchen, and see the gun placements. Arrangements can be made for families and organized groups to camp overnight on the ship. The cost is $21 (adult and child) per person. A child must be at least six years old, and all children must be accompanied by an adult. The museum contains a superb ship model exhibit, artifacts, Hall of Honor, Louisiana Memorial Plaza, and a gift shop with Louisiana souvenirs. Open 9 a.m. to 5 p.m. daily. See the Attractions chapter.

ANNUAL EVENTS AND FESTIVALS

Louisiana has more than 400 festivals every year. Events and festivals remind us why we love living here and why we love sharing our gatherings with others. Certain events are seasonal or linked to local history. Some carry us through tough times. Like the rest of the state, Baton Rouge parties throughout the year. From zany carnival parades to solemn events, Baton Rouge marks each occasion with style.

Many events take place in fall, but planners schedule their events around Southern University and LSU's home football game dates. Winter is short in south Louisiana, and calendars stay filled from Thanksgiving through Christmas, a time for family reunions and festivals tied to the rural south past. Thousands of twinkling lights entwine trees downtown and in neighborhoods. Chilly, damp days can arrive in January, but after Twelfth Night (January 6), it's time for Mardi Gras preparations with formal balls and parades to follow. Cold weather never stops a good Mardi Gras party or parade. People simply throw a warm wrap over their fanciful costumes and head out for the fun. Spring is glorious in Baton Rouge with flowering trees and shrubs. It's a grand time for garden pilgrimages and outdoor festivals.

Although the following list is extensive, it doesn't include every event held in the city or nearby towns. I've listed a few of my favorites and longtime events that consistently take place year after year. For a more thorough month-to-month listing, check out the Baton Rouge Convention and Visitors Bureau Web site, www.visitbatonrouge.com. The site includes both one-time and annual events, including festivals, concerts, fundraisers, and more. A comprehensive monthly list appears in *Country Roads* magazine, and a weekly calendar is run in the *Advocate*'s Fun section on www.2theadvocate.com. We also suggest checking the official Louisiana tourism Web site, www.louisianatravel.com.

JANUARY

TWELFTH NIGHT
Twelfth Night (January 6) marks the beginning of Mardi Gras season, the dates for which vary because it is tied to the Christian liturgical calendar. Some families still observe Epiphany (the arrival of the magi) with private parties. It's also a time for attending concerts and plays. Private Mardi Gras balls, which involve detailed planning, start early in the month and run through the season.

FEBRUARY

MARDI GRAS
February is the height of Mardi Gras season with parades, balls, and parties taking place throughout Louisiana. Many Baton Rougeans are invited by friends and relatives to participate in Mardi Gras events in other cities. In turn they often host houseguests here in the Capital City. See the Close-up on Mardi Gras.

MARCH

AUDUBON PILGRIMAGE
St. Francisville
(225) 635-6330
www.audubonpilgrimage.info
Audubon Pilgrimage commemorates the summer John James Audubon spent in St. Francisville and painted many of his bird folios. The town is the garden spot of Louisiana's English Plantation country. Visitors tour historic homes and gardens, many of which are privately owned. Activities include living history demonstrations, cemetery

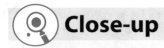 **Close-up**

Mardi Gras

When most Louisiana visitors think about Mardi Gras, they think about wild times in New Orleans. Certainly the city's extravagant parties and parades get huge media attention. However the celebration can be as simple as a festive at-home party. Mardi Gras has been observed for a long time in Louisiana. When French-Canadian explorer Pierre le Moyne, Sieur d'Iberville, and his men were exploring the Mississippi River, they camped for one night, March 3, 1699, at the river's first large bend. In his journal, Iberville noted they were two leagues from the mouth on a point to the right of the river. In tribute to the Carnival holiday being celebrated in France, Iberville named the spot Pointe du Mardi Gras and the adjoining channel Bayoue du Mardi Gras. Some years later in 1743, Governor Marquis de Vaudreuil presented an elegant Carnival ball.

Mardi Gras season is a time of feasting preceding Ash Wednesday, the start of a 40-day period of fasting prior to Easter. In Europe the feasting celebration came to be called Carnival. In France, the pre-lenten event became known as Mardi Gras—Fat Tuesday. The Catholic Church established the moveable dates for Mardi Gras when it developed the formula for the date of Easter, which may occur as early as March 22 or as late as April 25. Mardi Gras is then scheduled 47 days before Easter. Mardi Gras can be as early as February 3 or as late as March 9.

In Louisiana, the spring celebration has spread throughout the state. In towns big and small, community groups and clubs (called *krewes*) organize Mardi Gras parades. Many events benefit local charities. For some the season seems too decadent. However one only had to attend a Mardi Gras parade following Hurricane Katrina to understand that the ancient holiday is still tied to friendship, hope, and renewal.

In Baton Rouge Mardi Gras parades and parties are both traditional and zany. Most krewes host formal balls, which are invitation-only events. Other krewes sponsor parades, which tend to be family-oriented. They attract large crowds in both downtown and in neighborhoods. Parades and floats carry out themes based on anything from Mozart's music to Egyptian mummies. Some themes are harsh political satires. Parade riders wear costumes and masks while carrying out their duties. Parade crowds are experts at catching glimmering strings of plastic beads. To

---

tales, an antiques show and sale, and night festivities. Local men, women, and children dress in authentic 1820s clothing.

BATON ROUGE SPRING GARDEN SHOW
John M. Parker Coliseum, LSU
(225) 578-2158
www.lsu.edu/departments/horticulture
This is a gardener's dream opportunity to get new ideas on landscaping and plant care from some of the region's leading horticultural experts. Sponsored by the LSU Department of Horticulture, the two-day event features exhibits by local and regional nurseries, vendors, and garden societies. You'll find an amazing selection of trees,

shrubs, herbs, ferns, succulents, and more. LSU AgCenter representatives conduct a Plant Health Clinic. Kids can learn about seed planting and insects. Pick up a new garden accessory or two. It's also a good place to hook up with a garden club member interested in sharing your hobby.

i March is typically the season for home tours and garden pilgrimages in south Louisiana. Azaleas, dogwoods, iris, and daffodils turn private and public gardens into magical settings. Tour dates and schedules are listed in local newspapers and magazines. Also contact the Baton Rouge Convention and Visitors Bureau for information, (225) 383-1825 or (800) 527-6843.

catch a rider's attention you'll hear parade watchers yell, "Throw me somethin', Mistah." The more beads you can catch, the better. Tip: wear comfortable clothing and shoes, and carry a sturdy bag to lug your beads home.

Baton Rouge krewes that parade include:

Krewe of Artemis: an all-female krewe parading downtown.

Krewe of Jupiter: a great Mardi Gras crew that rolls through downtown.

Krewe of Orion: a Mardi Gras parade that has been running since 1998.

Krewe of Poseidon: a new krewe that held its first parade in 2009 with the theme of Sovereign of the Seas.

Krewe of Mutts: a yearly dog parade where people dress their dogs up and have a Mardi Gras fling.

Krewe of Southdown: a great parade of adults, teens, and kids running through the Southdown neighborhood near LSU.

Spanish Town Parade is the most irreverant of the season. The parade rolls through Spanish Town, the original old city within the shadow of the Louisiana State Capitol. The political satire theme is usually taken from current events, and all politicians and their cronies are fair game. There are some 70 floats, marching bands, and tons of beads. An Alcohol-Free Zone is designated from the north side of Convention Street and between Fifth and Seventh Streets.

Other krewes that do not parade are Krewe of Achilles, Krewe of Apollo, Krewe of Desk and Derrick, Krewe of Iduna, Krewe le Bon Temps, Krewe of Lyonnesse (a children's krewe), Karnival Krewe de Louisiane, Krewe Mystique de la Capitale, Krewe of Romany, and Krewe of Tucumcari, the oldest krewe in the city.

If planning a visit to the Baton Rouge region during Mardi Gras, make your hotel reservations early. Visit the Convention and Visitors Bureau Web site: www.visitbatonrouge.com. The *Advocate* and local magazines usually run parade schedules and maps the week prior to parades.

HABITAT HOME & GARDEN SHOW
Baton Rouge RiverCenter
(225) 769-7696
www.capitalregionba.com
Sponsored by the Capital Region Builders Association, the Habitat Home & Garden Show features some 200 exhibitors with the latest technology and energy-efficient concepts in home design. Bring your plans, photos, and drawings. Don't forget your dreams.

LAGNIAPPE DULCIMER FÊTE
West Baton Rouge Museum, Port Allen
845 North Jefferson Ave.
(225) 753-7917
www.lagniappedulcimer.org

This acoustic folk music festival features workshops and concerts. Programs include mountain dulcimer, hammered dulcimer, mandolin, autoharp, ukulele, sacred harp, harmonica, and fiddle. Participating instructors are from as far away as Illinois, Missouri, North Carolina, Tennessee, and Virginia.

ST. PATRICK'S DAY PARADE
(225) 925-8295
www.paradegroup.com
Baton Rouge sheds its football colors for the "wearing o' the green" for the annual St. Patrick's Day Parade. The parade rolls through streets near City Park and through the Perkins Road Overpass area. Families gather along the roads to catch

green and white beads tossed by participants riding floats decked out in shamrocks, harps, and other symbols of the Emerald Isle.

APRIL

AUDUBON COUNTRY BIRDFEST
5720 Commerce St., St. Francisville
(800) 488-6502
www.audubonbirdfest.com
Birders flock to the Audubon Country Birdfest in the West Feliciana area where John James Audubon created numerous bird paintings. Headquartered at the St. Francisville Inn, the fest features birding trips to various locations and canoe trips to Cat Island.

i America's Wetland Birding Trail weaves through Louisiana and includes the Baton Rouge area. Nearby trail sites include Cat Island National Wildlife Refuge near St. Francisville and Centenary State Historic Site at Jackson. So get out your walking shoes and binoculars and join the fun.

BATON ROUGE BLUES WEEK
Downtown, Mid City, North Baton Rouge
(225) 383-0968
www.louisianasmusic.com
www.batonrougebluesfestival.org
Featured concerts take place in Manship Theatre, Teddy's Juke Joint, Boudreaux & Thibodeaux, and Chelsea's. Past performers include Irma Thomas, Henry Butler, Tab Benoit, Chris Thomas King, Tabby Thomas and Friends, Kenny Acosta, Big Al and the Heavyweights, and the Dixie Rose Acoustic Circle. Take in Sunday in the Park sessions in Lafayette Park and programs and enjoy some "blues food," especially creamy red beans and rice, and crispy fried chicken. Locally produced radio shows and folk-life seminars round out the week's offerings.

INTERNATIONAL HERITAGE CELEBRATION
Baton Rouge RiverCenter, River Road
(225) 930-0901
www.brcwa.com

Presented by the Baton Rouge Association for World Affairs, this event salutes the people of nations around the world. Enjoy the parade of nations, craft demonstrations, music, dance, storytelling, educational booths, and international foods.

KITE FEST LOUISIANE
West Baton Rouge Soccer Complex, Port Allen
(225) 344-2920
www.westbatonrouge.net
This family-oriented, three-day festival at the West Baton Rouge Soccer Complex in Port Allen includes home-built and professional kite-flying exhibitions, sport team ballets, children's kite-flying workshops, children's candy drops, and classic sounds by Jude. Food booths offer Louisiana cuisine, including gumbo, jambalaya, and seafood po' boys. Friday is designated as Student Day.

LOUISIANA EARTH DAY FESTIVAL
RiverCenter area, River Road
www.laearthday.org
Every spring day, Baton Rouge residents turn out to celebrate the Earth, its complexities, and its bounties. Louisiana Earth Day activities include interactive education and exhibits. There's fun for kids and adults, including music and food.

PONCHATOULA STRAWBERRY FESTIVAL
La. 22, off U.S. 51, Ponchatoula
www.lastrawberryfestival.com
Ponchatoula, about 55 miles east of Baton Rouge, is the Strawberry Capital of Louisiana. In the spring people look forward to the Ponchatoula Strawberry Festival, when juicy berries are consumed in mass quantities. There's a strawberry-eating contest, baking contest, talent contest, sack race, and a big parade. Local bands entertain the crowds. The most popular drink? Strawberry daiquiris, of course.

RED STICK ANIMATION FESTIVAL
Shaw Center for the Arts
100 Lafayette St.
(225) 578-0595
www.redstickfestival.org

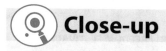

Close-up

Angola Prison Rodeo: A Story of Guts and Glory

Angola, about 59 miles north of Baton Rouge, is the Louisiana State Penitentiary and the largest maximum security prison in the United States. Located on an 18,000-acre property in West Feliciana Parish, the prison is surrounded on three sides by the Mississippi River.

The Angola Rodeo, the longest running prison rodeo in the nation, takes place one weekend in April and every Sunday in October. Huge crowds drive to the prison to see some of the toughest rodeo contestants in the country. Inmates participate in events that far surpass what you see on regular circuits. In the Bareback Riding event, riders are expected to keep one hand in the air and must stay on the horse for eight seconds to qualify. Convict Poker is the ultimate poker game. Four inmate cowboys sit at a table in the middle of the arena playing a friendly game of poker. Suddenly a wild bull is released with the sole purpose of unseating the poker players. The last man remaining seated is the winner. The last event of the rodeo is Guts and Glory. A chit (poker chip) is tied to the meanest Brahma bull available. The object is to get close enough to the bull to snatch the chit.

Organized in 1965, the rodeo was first staged for the entertainment of prisoners and employees. As years passed, it grew in size, adding events and sponsorships. Official Professional Rodeo Cowboys Association rules were adopted in 1972. Angola arranges with professional rodeo stock contractors to provide the rodeo stock. Also professional rodeo clowns are always present in the arena to ensure inmate safety.

A special feature is the Hobbycraft space. Many visitors attend the event to just browse and shop in the Hobbycraft area. Items are created by inmates for this full-blown arts and crafts festival. Bring your appetite. Inmates cook and serve some delicious festival goodies, including blooming onions, boiled peanuts, hot boudin, cracklins, and pecan pralines. Proceeds from the Angola Prison Rodeo cover rodeo expenses and supplement the Louisiana State Penitentiary Inmate Welfare Fund, which provides for inmate educational and recreational supplies.

To reach Angola from Baton Rouge, travel north on U.S. 61 to St. Francisville. About 2 miles north of town, go past the West Feliciana High School and turn left onto La. 66 using the turning lane provided. The 20-mile-long highway ends at the penitentiary's front gate. No food, drink, cell phones, or cameras are allowed through the rodeo entrance gate. When entering the grounds of a penal institution in Louisiana, you consent to a search of your person, property, and vehicle. No weapons, ammunition, alcohol, or drugs are allowed on prison property. All purses, diaper bags, belt pouches, and other bags will be searched before you enter the rodeo grounds. No food items or ice chests are allowed. All vehicles must be locked.

While at Angola, visit the Angola Museum just outside the prison's main entrance. The museum is an official parish tourism site. It contains well-designed, thoughtful displays on Angola's history, prisoner life, famous prisoners, various artifacts, and Louisiana's original electric chair. For information on the Angola Prison Rodeo, check out www.angolarodeo.com. For more details visit www.angolamuseum.com and www.corrections.state.la.us/lsp.

In addition to the Shaw Center for the Arts, the Old State Capitol and the Louisiana Art and Science Museum serve as venues for this lively contemporary festival. Expect free screenings of classic animated films, films from the festival competition, and the popular cartoon-a-palooza.

Animation experts and representatives conduct workshops for aspiring animation enthusiasts.

SPRING AND JAZZ FEST AT DENHAM SPRINGS ANTIQUE VILLAGE
228 North Range Ave.
www.denhamspringsantiquedistrict.com

Denham Springs throws out the welcome mat for the Antique Village festival, which is growing bigger every year. The small town retains its old-time appeal, and it attracts families with a day of fun and antiques shopping. There's a dog fashion show, car show, art, antiques shopping, and food. Activities center around the Train Station Depot. Past performers have included the Ed Perkins Jazz Group, jazz guitarist Robert Holden, and the Deal Breakers.

MAY

FEST FOR ALL
Downtown Baton Rouge
(225) 344-8558
www.artsbr.org
A two-day extravaganza of culture, Fest For All is an art lover's dream day. People pour into downtown to view and buy works from 75 artists. They meander along tree-shaded North Boulevard and check out handcrafted jewelry, pottery, oil paintings, collages, and woven pieces. It's a good time to meet and mix with artists. Many gladly explain their craft and how they came about creating one-of-a-kind pieces. Historic sites, such as the Old State Capitol, and downtown churches provide spaces for performers. You can enjoy contemporary and classic dance groups, and musicians playing everything from symphonic works to jazz. The children's tent is set up for creative explorations and laughter.

JAMBALAYA FESTIVAL
Gonzales Civic Center, Gonzales
(225) 647-2937
www.jambalayafestival.org
Jambalaya, one of Louisiana's signature dishes, is a mixture of rice, meats, or seafood and seasonings often cooked in a big black cast-iron pot outdoors. It has even been celebrated in song. You'll never see as much of it cooked or eaten as you will at the Jambalaya Festival. There are two days of world championship cooking, stage shows, music, and carnival rides. Bring your dancing shoes.

JUNE

JUNETEENTH FREEDOM FESTIVAL
River Road African American Museum, Donaldsonville
(225) 474-5553
www.africanamericanmuseum.org
This event, sponsored by the River Road African American Museum, celebrates the end of slavery in the United States. It also observes the struggle of African Americans to achieve civil rights. The three-day festival features historical exhibits, African dancers, live music, a talent show, arts and crafts, a kids' tent, family reunions, and a health fair.

JULY

ART MELT
Shaw Center for the Arts
100 Lafayette St., downtown
www.artmelt.org
Take in the state's largest juried art show showcasing Louisiana's artists. Start at the Brunner Gallery for a visual uplift, then head for other downtown venues for a tour of the other senses—sound, smell, and taste. Art Melt is for the hip crowd that likes a touch of sophistication, and it appeals to young professionals and to the well-traveled crowd.

DONALDSONVILLE FIREWORKS AND FAIS DO DO
Crescent Park, Donaldsonville
(225) 323-4970
www.donaldsonvilleddd.org
A fais do do is a Cajun dance party. The colloquial French term is similar to "beddy bye" and was used when Cajun mothers urged their babies to sleep so that parents could enjoy a dance. What better time to participate in a community dance than the Fourth of July? Donaldsonville combines the tradition with fireworks, contests, and holiday entertainment.

FELICIANA HUMMINGBIRD CELEBRATION
Rosedown Plantation State Historic Site
12501 La. 10, St. Francisville
(800) 488-6502
www.audubonbirdfest.com
Wee tiny hummingbirds settle in for the summer months in the Baton Rouge region. Most depart for the long trip to Mexico in the fall, but a few stay in the area through the winter. Rosedown, one of the state's treasured antebellum mansions, is the setting for the Hummingbird Celebration in July. Participants can learn how to weigh, measure, and band the birds. Discover more about hummers at lectures and pick up ideas for planting hummingbird-friendly plants.

STAR-SPANGLED CELEBRATION
USS *Kidd* and Veterans Memorial
River Road, downtown
(225) 342-1942
Baton Rouge families gather early in the day for the Star-Spangled Celebration on July Fourth. Streets and plazas are packed near the USS *Kidd*, the World War II Fletcher destroyer docked at the museum. It's usually sunny and hot, so everyone wears casual summer clothing. Food and beverage booths keep folks cooled off. People vie for the best viewing spaces atop the Mississippi River levee. A major part of the entertainment is a mock air attack on the *Kidd* as Air National Guard takes to the sky above the boat. Later the Baton Rouge Concert Band strikes up a medley of patriotic songs and marches, ending with the bombastic *1812 Overture*. The booming cannon sounds within the band signals the beginning of a spectacular fireworks show over the Mississippi River.

AUGUST

WHITE LINEN NIGHT
Ferdinand Street, St. Francisville
(225) 635-3873
www.stfrancisvillefestivals.com

Romantics read about the dramatic "long hot summer," but south Louisiana residents live it. In Baton Rouge activities slow down. It's time for cool menus, cool drinks, and cool clothing. White linen suits and dresses came into fashion long before modern fabrics, but now we don light duds in cool colors. With a nod to their ancestors' summertime garb, residents of St. Francisville enjoy a night in late August to "take in the air," strolling the streets, visiting with friends and visitors, shopping for arts and antiques, and enjoying music. It's a relaxed way to pass a good time.

SEPTEMBER

The weather remains hot in Baton Rouge through September, and few annual events take place this month, since families are settling in for the school year. It's also the beginning of football season, not only for the landmark universities but for high school teams as well. Organizations and individuals check their calendars and try not to plan social obligations on their favorite teams' game days. Few if any annual events are planned this month.

OCTOBER

AWESOME ART IN AUTUMN GARDENS FESTIVAL
Houmas House Plantation
40136 La. 942, Burnside
(225) 473-7841
www.houmashouse.com
One of the most magnificent gardens in Louisiana can be enjoyed in its fall glory during this festival. Stroll at your leisure and enjoy fine art, folk art, and literary and performing arts intertwined with history and nature. The event gives people a chance to admire the numerous semitropical plants that thrive in Louisiana's warm climate. Enjoy the spectacular fountains and garden sculptures.

BIZTECH EXPO
Baton Rouge RiverCenter
(225) 928-1700
www.businessreport.com

Louisiana's largest business and technology trade show, BizTech is a two-day business-to-business event for leading businesses as well as entrepreneurs. More than 200 exhibitors participate in the two-day event, which includes a CEO Forum and updates by experts on the regional and national economies.

BOO AT THE ZOO
BREC's Baton Rouge Zoo
3601 Thomas Rd.
(225) 775-3877
www.brzoo.org
A merry, not scary, trick-or-treating extravaganza, Boo at the Zoo has become a Halloween tradition for families. Let the kids dress up in their favorite costumes. Get snapshots with the animals. Treat stations are set up in different sections of the zoo. There's a Hay Maze and a Boo Den, too.

GREATER BATON ROUGE STATE FAIR
Airline Highway Park, Fairgrounds
(225) 755-3247
www.gbrsf.com
Organized by the all-volunteer Fair Board, the Baton Rouge State Fair stretches over a week with carnival rides and special youth activities. There are lawn tractor races, magicians, clowns, and pony rides. In the Farm Experience, children can watch chickens hatch and learn about raising animals. Live music entertainment includes country, rock, blues, soul, and swamp pop. Buster Brown Day is especially planned for physically and mentally challenged children. Proceeds go toward worthy causes.

LOUISIANA BOOK FESTIVAL
Louisiana State Capitol Grounds
Spanish Town Rd. at North Fourth St.
(225) 755-3247
www.louisianabookfestival.org
Sponsored by the Louisiana State Library, the free festival opens a grand window into the world of writing and reading. Spend the day with Louisiana's book lovers and books. More than 190 poets, writers, and scholars take part in readings, book talks, and panel discussions held

in the Louisiana State Library, the State Capitol, and the State Museum. Get your cherished books autographed by a favorite author. Tents are set up for young readers, book browsing and signing, book-related arts, food, and beverages. The day ends with the Baton Rouge Symphony's performance of *The Sound of Books*, with music selections from movies that originated from books.

THE MYRTLES HALLOWEEN EXTRAVAGANZA
Off U.S. 61 in St. Francisville
(225) 635-6277
www.myrtlesplantation.com
Experience the true meaning of Halloween at The Myrtles, the antebellum home that's been called America's Most Haunted House. The event starts at 7 p.m., and evening shadows lend mystery to the atmosphere of this fascinating home. Guides dress in costumes for the event, and the gift shop stays open. Refreshments and libations are served in the original courtyard.

SUGARFEST
West Baton Rouge Museum, Port Allen
845 North Jefferson Ave.
(225) 336-2422
www.westbatonrougemuseum.org
This is a sweet celebration of the sugar cane harvest and the culture of sugar cane plantations. Tour the museum grounds and view authentic plantation cabins, a shotgun house, and the 1830 Aillet House. Watch a mule-driven cane grinder in action. Chew on fresh sugar cane samples, and let the kids ride the sugar train. They also can take part in historic hands-on activities, such as wash day (scrubbing laundry the old-fashioned way). Live music performances include such groups as the Fabulous Bagasse Boyz and the Storyville Stompers. Check out the sweets contest, cake walk, and sugary treats.

YELLOW LEAF ARTS FESTIVAL
Parker Park, St. Francisville
(225) 635-3665
www.stfrancisvillefestivals.com

The Yellow Leaf Arts Festival showcases the artists of West Feliciana Parish and their friends. It's a good place to look for pottery, mixed media, sculpture, photography, jewelry, and paintings. Be sure to check out the birdhouse. This gathering of Southern bohemians includes yoga classes, poetry, and string band music.

NOVEMBER

WHITE LIGHT NIGHT
Mid City Art and Design District
(225) 924-6437
www.midcitymerchants.com
See the latest in art trends and help start the holiday season. Plan an evening excursion along the Government Street corridor to hunt for unusual Christmas gifts. Pop into Elizabethan Gallery or Caffery Gallery for original art. Stop by Fleur De Lis for a pizza or Doe's Eat Place for a steak. Some 30 shops and restaurants participate. A shuttle service helps you travel between locations.

DECEMBER

BATON ROUGE FESTIVAL OF LIGHTS
Galvez Plaza and North Blvd.
(225) 389-5520
www.downtownbatonrouge.org
People turn out the first of December for a festive evening, which kicks off the Christmas season in downtown Baton Rouge. Just before dusk, people of all ages stroll in the three plazas between the RiverCenter and Old State Capitol. Attractions include school groups singing Christmas carols, art displays, and booths offering everything from shimmering gifts to cookies and hot chocolate. In Galvez Plaza, a band playing traditional melodies awaits the moment when the city's mayor officially turns on the lights of a giant Christmas tree. It also signals the lighting of myriad twinkling lights strung along trees and shrubs on North Boulevard. As the sun sets on the west side of the Mississippi, fireworks burst into the sky above the skyline—it's a magical evening.

BATON ROUGE SYMPHONY AT HOUMAS HOUSE PLANTATION
40136, La. 942, Burnside
(2225) 473-9380
www.houmashouse.com
Houmas House Plantation and Gardens and the Baton Rouge Symphony invite people to start the Christmas season with the superlative sounds of traditional carols and other holiday music underneath magnificent live oaks. The concert takes place in the late afternoon. Enjoy the music and the garden setting as the soft colors of dusk heighten the mansion's beauty.

i The lighting of Christmas Eve bonfires along the Mississippi River levees in St. James Parish fascinate visitors. According to legend the fires are built by local residents to light the way for Papa Noel. The custom is thought to have been brought to Louisiana by French Marist priests sometime after the Civil War. The fires can be seen by driving along River Road in the towns of Gramercy and Lutcher south of Baton Rouge. In keeping with the tradition,some homes in the rural countryside light bonfires during private parties, signaling the warmth and joy of the season.

CHRISTMAS IN THE COUNTRY
Throughout St. Francisville
(225) 635-3873
www.stfrancisvillefestivals.com
Christmas in the Country brightens the spirit with English Plantation Country's earliest holiday traditions. Stroll along Ferdinand Street browsing for gifts, and listen to school choirs in historic churches. At the gazebo in Parker Park, join folks enjoying the sounds of the Main Street Band and the Angola Inmate Traveling Band. View the Live Nativity at the First Baptist Church, or attend the Community Sing-Along in the Methodist Church on Royal Street. Children's activities include train rides, games, pony rides, and clowns. Take the Library Tour of Homes, decorated for the season.

In this part of the world, magnolia leaves, pine branches, nuts, and fresh fruit are often used to decorate for Christmas.

DOWNTOWN CHRISTMAS PARADE
Downtown Baton Rouge
(225) 766-2282
www.christmasinbr.com
Sponsored by the Baton Rouge Kiwanis, the Christmas Parade delights children. Thousands gather along the downtown parade route to view holiday floats, marching bands, horses, and walking groups. It's usually nippy enough for folks to bundle up in warm gear and welcome Santa as he waves to one and all.

RURAL LIFE CHRISTMAS
LSU Rural Life Museum
Essen at I-10
http://rurallife.lsu.edu
Living history re-enactors, wearing simple garments from the 1800s, welcome visitors to a traditional Louisiana Christmas on the farm. Watch demonstrations of farm crafts and domestic skills. Storytellers are part of the scene, and musical groups entertain. Browse for exceptional hand-crafted pieces by Louisiana artisans in the gift shop.

DAY TRIPS

Some visitors picture Louisiana as the land of swamps and bayous. Others think of people sitting around speaking Cajun French, eating platters of boiled crawfish. Some may look for cities with unusual shops, sophisticated dining, and a nightlife that never ends. Well, they're right. To find all this and more, you need to explore. Baton Rouge is the ideal hub for day trips.

Head west and drive across the striking Atchafalaya Basin to view one of America's vast untamed natural heritage areas. In Lafayette view a world-class contemporary art museum. Driving east, antiques buffs can look for untold treasures in Ponchatoula or Denham Springs. Drives south of town lead to dramatic antebellum mansions and swamp tours. North leads to communities settled by English colonists, Civil War battlefields, and hills perfect for hiking and biking.

BREAUX BRIDGE AND ST. MARTINVILLE

There's a good reason that Breaux Bridge is called the Crawfish Capital of the World. People here pay tribute to the crustacean with flourish. You'll find crawfish cooked every possible way and shops with porcelain platters and serving plates—even water glasses—decorated with bright red crawfish.

Less than 50 miles west of Baton Rouge via I-10, the town takes pride in its Acadian heritage. Its name started with Acadian pioneer Firmin Breaux, who in 1771 built a footbridge across Bayou Teche to have easy passage for his family and neighbors. The town received its official founding in 1829 when Scholastique Picou Breaux, a determined Acadian woman, drew up plans for the city and started selling lots to other settlers.

Restaurants here were among the first to offer crawfish openly on their menus, so be sure to try the crawfish étouffée, the dish that was invented in Breaux Bridge. **Crawfish Town USA** (2825 Grand Point Hwy., 337-667-6148, www.crawfishtown.com) has a huge menu, including steaks, ribs, and seafood cooked every which way. **Mulate's** (325 Mills Ave., 800-854-9149, www.mulates.com), the "original Cajun restaurant," serves Cajun food for lunch and dinner daily. Peo-

ple drive for miles for the nightly live Cajun music and dancing. Then there's **Cafe Des Amis** (140 East Bridge St., 337-332-5273, www.cafedesamis.com), which kicks Acadian cooking up two or three notches and offers a Sunday zydeco brunch with music and dancing around the tables.

The **Breaux Bridge Crawfish Festival** takes place the first weekend in May. Sample the crawfish pies or crawfish burrito. More than 30 groups perform on three stages over three days. Past performers have included Lil Nathan and the Zydeco Big Timers and Feu Follet. For sweets and a surprise, try **The Coffee Break** (109 North Main, 337-442-6607) for specialty coffees, freezes, and sometimes an impromptu jam session by local musicians.

Historic buildings downtown contain boutiques and nifty shops. Search for handcrafted items, fine porcelains, costume jewelry, and antique musical instruments. **Lucullus** (107 North Main, 337-332-2625) specializes in exceptional 18th-century culinary antiques. **Janell's Gifts** (200 East Bridge St., 337-332-5409) is loaded with a mixture of antique furniture, pictures, mirrors, and lamps. **Trading and Flag** (202 Guilbeau St., 337-332-2427, www.bbtradingandflag.com) is a good place to look for accordions, flags, and souvenirs.

About 10 minutes from town is **Lake Martin**, a wondrous small lake within Cypress Island Preserve, which contains an enormous number of birds and animals. The southern half of the lake is leased to the Nature Preserve. You'll learn to tread lightly and not disturb the wildlife in this primitive area—it's not for campouts. Bring your cameras. Birds include the roseate spoonbill, great egret, and barred owl. Animals include alligators, nutria, and turtles.

St. Martinville, on La. 347 south of Breaux Bridge and Lafayette, is a storybook town. Tales of romance and hardship give it an inescapable poetic aura. Start your visit in Town Square and at the **St. Martinville Tourist Information Center** (215 Evangeline Blvd., 337-394-2233). Ask about brochures and details on local sights.

Inspired by the plight of the Acadians, Henry Wadsworth Longfellow wrote his fictional epic poem, "Evangeline," and the story is forever linked to St. Martinville. Across from the Information Center along Bayou Teche is the ancient **Evangeline Oak**, where descendants claim Emmeline Labiche landed at the end of her long trip from Nova Scotia. Legend tells that it was here that she learned of her lover's betrothal to another. Local musicians often gather here to greet locals and tourists. In February the town sponsors Calling All Lovers, a reception in honor of couples who were married or engaged beneath the Evangeline Oak.

On the square visit **St. Martin de Tours Catholic Church**, the Mother Church of the Acadians. Established in 1765, it is one of the oldest Catholic churches in Louisiana. The present church was erected in 1844. Tours are given in English and French. To the side and slightly to the rear of the church is the Evangeline Monument. The production company that filmed the epic movie *Evangeline* donated the statue to the town in 1929. The star of that film, Dolores del Rio, supposedly posed for the statue.

To the left of the Evangeline Oak is the **St. Martinville Cultural Heritage Center**, which houses the **African American Museum and the Museum of the Acadian Memorial** (121 South New Market St., 337-394-2258). The African American Museum interprets the history of slavery, and a 26-foot mural highlights the accomplishments of St. Martinville's free people of color. The Aca-

dian Memorial honors the 3,000 Acadian exiles from Nova Scotia who found refuge in Louisiana. On the third Saturday of the month, the museum sponsors a festival highlighting Cajun traditions and music, wooden boats, theater, and storytelling and stages a re-enactment of the arrival of the Acadians on Bayou Teche.

Located just north of St. Martinville on La. 31 is **Longfellow-Evangeline State Historic Site**. While touring the home built by the wealthy Creole planter Pierre Olivier Duclozel de Vezin in 1830, you see influences of Creole, French, and Caribbean styles in the Raised Creole Cottage architecture. Simple furnishings and everyday utensils reflect the lifestyle of early European colonists. Also on the site is a reproduction of an 1800 Acadian farmstead with an outdoor kitchen, bread oven, slave quarters, and barn. In the pasture are cattle typical of those raised by Creole and Acadians of that time. Costumed interpreters give tours in French and English.

Other attractions in St. Martinville include the lovely **Duchamp Opera House and Mercantile** (200 South Main St., 337-394-6104, www.duchamp-operahouse.com), restored to its 1830 beauty, where you can attend special events and shop for antiques, gifts, and regional art. **The Petit Paris Museum**, to the left of St. Martin de Tours Church, houses an interpretive Mardi Gras costume exhibit and a small gift shop. St. Martinville may not be known for its restaurants, but you should still drop by **Josephine's Creole Restaurant,** 830 S. Main St., for a lunch plate of chicken or shrimp stew. **Danna's Bakery,** 207 E. Bridge St., is a good place to pick up pecan macaroons or thumbprint cookies to munch on the banks of Bayou Teche.

Accommodations are limited in St. Martinville, but the **Old Castillo Hotel** (220 Evangeline Blvd., 800-621-3017), is quaint and historical. **Bienvenue House B&B** (421 North Main St., Parks, 337-394-9100) is another lovely choice. In Breaux Bridge, bed-and-breakfast establishments range from rustic cabins to raised cottages with sophisticated décor. We suggest **Maison Madeleine at Lake Martin** (105 John D. Hebert Drive, 337-332-4555). Also at Breaux Bridge is **Cajun**

Palms RV Resort, a new and extremely well-designed haven for campers (1055 North Barn Rd., 337-667-7772). It features deluxe RV spots, 20 delightful themed cabins, recreation rooms, a swimming pool, and more. For more information on Breaux Bridge, contact www.tourismbreaux bridge.com. For more information on St. Martinville, check out www.stmartinville.org. These sites also list swamp tours available in the area.

i For an afternoon jaunt to the Atchafalaya Basin, visit McGee's Landing, 1337 Henderson Levee Rd., Henderson, (337) 228-2384. McGee's offers guided Atchafalaya Swamp tours in the basin. The landing, resembling a rambling fishing camp, also is a bar and restaurant offering Cajun and Creole food. Local bands play live music on Sunday from 12:30 to 3:30 p.m.

GONZALES AND DONALDSONVILLE

The Ascension Parish straddles the Mississippi River just south of Baton Rouge. The parish has two interesting cities: Gonzales on the east side of the river, and Donaldsonville on the west side. Original inhabitants were the Houmas and Chitimacha tribes. The earliest European settlers were mostly Spanish and Canary Islanders, but the population quickly became a cultural gumbo of many ethnic groups. Within its 300 square miles, the parish contains thriving petrochemical plants, swamps, woodlands, farms, long-established neighborhoods, and new upscale suburban subdivisions. Plan an easy trip to tour an antebellum plantation, shop at an outlet, or give your muscles a workout by playing a game of tennis or golf.

Tanger Outlet Center at I-10 and La. 30 is a spacious area with plenty of parking. The center features more than 60 brand-name shops. For the most part the shops cater to the casual lifestyle of local residents. It's a great place to pick up top-quality jeans, sharp-looking shirts, and sneakers. Wise shoppers head for stores such as Gap, Bass, Levi's Outlet, Jones New York, Liz Claiborne,

and Kasper. If you're looking to dazzle, stop by Zale's the Diamond Store or Ultra Diamonds. If you're ready for a break, head to Cracker Barrel for chicken and dumplings, or Chili's for a big, juicy hamburger.

Feeling ready for a grand fling? Drive south along La. 44 to La. 942 and turn right to **Houmas House Plantation and Gardens** (40136 La. 942, 225-473-9380, www.houmashouse.com) to view one of the most dramatic mansions on the Mississippi River. Owner Kevin Kelly, entrepreneur and preservationist, has turned Houmas House into a spectacular showplace. Pick up tickets in the gift shop packed with unusual gifts. Then take your time walking through a series of gardens beneath magnificent oaks and stop by one of the twin garconierres, now the turtle bar. Enjoy a lemonade or something stronger before meeting your guide and entering through the front door. A massive wall mural by artist Craig Black depicts a sugar cane field filled with animals and birds. Parlors are filled with antiques from several eras, and sparkling chandeliers illuminate porcelains, silverware, and paintings. Climb the striking spiral stairway and walk onto the front gallery, where you can imagine what life was like in the 1850s. Before leaving, you will have ample time to browse in the gift shop. Lunch is served in Cafe Burnside. If you take an early evening tour, you can stay for dinner in the signature restaurant, Latil's Landing.

Bocage Plantation (39050 La. 942, 225-588-8000, www.bocageplantation.com) is a Louisiana jewel. Smaller and more intimate than Houmas House, it too offers a close-up view of a planter's life. Bocage Plantation began as a Creole cottage, built in 1801 by Emanuel Marius Pons Bringier as a wedding gift for his daughter Francoise and her husband Christophe Colomb, a French refugee and descendant of Christopher Columbus. The original house appears to have burned down, and a new structure designed by architect James Dakin was built in 1837. Now the house has been meticulously restored by Dr. Marion Rundell, a native of Pineville. Modern technology has been incorporated in the renovation to allow Bocage to survive for centuries. Rooms are filled with antique furniture, including rare Louisiana pieces from Dr. Rundell's private collection. Special lighting has been installed to spotlight original works of art. The setting is beautiful but not overwhelming. Tours can be arranged Thursday through Sunday, noon to 5 p.m. Rooms are available for bed-and-breakfast beginning at $200.

Not far from these plantation homes is **The Cabin Restaurant** (5405 La. 44, 225-473-3007, www.thecabinrestaurant.com). In contrast to the lavish mansions, the restaurant is built from slave dwellings from Monroe Plantation. Visitors sit beneath the cypress ceiling and view old farm implements and tools. Meals are simple fare—try the meat loaf or seafood platter. The cornbread is downright good.

On any day trip you can divide your day between Gonzales and Donaldsonville. The latter town is still seeking a return to its pre–Civil War era. Donaldsonville, on the west bank of the Mississippi River, is a treasure trove for history buffs who seek sites less traveled. The town is named after landowner William Donaldson. In 1806 Donaldson commissioned architect and planner Barthelemy Lafon to plan a new town. It served briefly as the Louisiana capital (1830–31) after New Orleans was deemed "too noisy." However after one year the legislators decided to return to New Orleans. The Donaldsonville Historic District covers about 50 blocks, with some 640 buildings dating mainly from the period of 1865–1933. The district includes residences, commercial and public buildings, five churches, and three cemeteries. View shotgun houses, cottages, and bungalows as well as neighborhood stores. The **Romanesque Revival Courthouse** is on Houmas Street. **The Lemann Store**, located at 314 Mississippi St., may well be the finest Italianate commercial building in any Mississippi River town north of New Orleans. The store houses a local museum with photographs and artifacts revealing life in years gone by. Nearby on the Mississippi River you can visit the site of Fort Butler, a Federal garrison attacked by Confederate troops on June 28, 1863. After fierce fighting and shelling by a Union gunboat, *Princess Royal*, the Confederate troops lost this battle. However the shelling severely damaged the town; today nothing remains of

the fort, but you can read the historical marker on this site.

Of special interest is the **River Road African American Museum** (406 Charles St., 225-474-5553, www.africanamericanmuseum.org). Founded by Kathe Hambrick, the museum contains thoughtful exhibits on the hundreds of free people of color who received their freedom in Ascension Parish or who moved there after receiving their freedom. Other displays focus on the African influence on Louisiana cuisine, as well as black doctors, inventors, and folk artists and the rural roots of jazz. For example, Joe King Oliver was born in Abend, about a mile downriver from Donaldsonville. Plas Johnson, who played the slinking intro to Henry Mancini's "Pink Panther" theme, is also a Donaldsonville native. The museum sponsors the **Juneteenth Freedom Festival** in June. See the Annual Events chapter.

If you're in Donaldsonville at lunch, stop by the **Grapevine Cafe and Gallery** (211 Railroad Ave., 225-473-8463, www.grapevinecafeandgallery.com) The menu includes excellent Creole and Cajun food in an art gallery setting. **Cypress Cafe** (206 Railroad Ave., 225-473-0010) serves seafood and steaks Monday through Wednesday, lunch only; and Thursday through Saturday, lunch and dinner. **Cafe LaFourche** (817 Bayou Rd., 225-473-7451, www.cafelafourche.com) serves creative cuisine such as shrimp, oysters, and scallops with green and black olives in a rich marinara sauce.

Donaldsonville also has bed-and-breakfast inns. **BitterSweet Plantation B&B** (404 Claiborne Ave., 225-473-1232) is luxuriously furnished with period antiques from the 1890s. **Cabahnosse B&B** (602 Railroad Ave., 225-474 5050 or 717-1069 after hours) has 1850s restored suites with sitting rooms and baths. A delightful antiques shop is downstairs. **The Victorian Inn on the Avenue** (117 Railroad Ave., 225-473-1876) features five themed suites and Victorian furnishings.

For more on Ascension Parish and its city of Gonzales, contact www.ascensiontourism.com or call (888) 775-7990. Also for more information on the Donaldsonville area, visit www.tour donaldsonville.org.

i Learn more about Gonzales at the Tee Joe Gonzales Museum, 217 W. Main St., (225) 647-9552. Home of the city's founding father, it's located on its original site on the New River. Artifacts and memorabilia focus on the area's first settlers. Tours are available for groups of 20 to 25 people by appointment.

HAMMOND AND PONCHATOULA

For a day of antiques shopping and just being nosy, strike out for Tangipahoa Parish and the towns of Hammond and Ponchatoula. Hammond was named for Peer Hammond, a Swedish immigrant and sailor who settled the area around 1818 and sold masts and charcoal to the maritime industry. The town sits at the crossroads of I-12 and I-55. About 15 miles south lies Port Manchac, which provides access via Lake Pontchartrain to the Gulf of Mexico. Modern Hammond is a major transportation hub, and it acts as a distribution point for Walmart and other businesses. The city is the home of Southeastern Louisiana University and is a stop on Amtrak's City of New Orleans route.

Plan on spending some time exploring the downtown Hammond area, which contains a mix of late 19th- and early 20th-century architecture. In 1980, the area was named a historic district in the National Register of Historic Places. The designation sparked a revival of downtown shops, restaurants, bars, and mixed-use apartments. Among the restorations was the old Columbia Theatre, which attracts regional and national talent.

Baton Rouge residents on a day's outing often plan a lunch or dinner trip to **Jacmel Inn** (903 East Morris Ave., 985-542-0043), known for its innovative dishes; you might want to try the scallop appetizer on risotto. Other popular restaurants are **Tope Là** (104 North Cate St., 985-542-7600, www.topela.com), with Louisiana and contemporary cuisine; **Trey Yuen** (2100 Morrison Blvd., 985-345-6789, www.treyyuen.com), featuring fine Chinese dining in a palace setting; and **Kirin's** (223 South Cate St., 985-542-8888, www.kirinjapanesecuisine.com), serving outstanding Japanese dishes.

A more recent addition is the **Tangipahoa African-American Heritage Museum** (1600 Phoenix Square, 985-542-4259, www.africanamericanheritagemuseum.com), with displays on African-American achievements and genealogy. If you're in Hammond in March, take on the **Smokin' Blues and Barbecue Challenge.** In November and December make a beeline for the **Louisiana Renaissance Festival**, off U.S. 190, with jousting tournaments, swordplay, and medieval royalty.

Ponchatoula, about 5 miles south of Hammond via I-55, is a small town with big titles. It's known as the Strawberry Capital of the World and America's Antique City. You'll certainly agree with the first nickname if you visit during the **Ponchatoula Strawberry Festival,** when huge crowds turn out for the parade, strawberry eating contest, baking contest, and music. See the Annual Events chapter.

In the early 1900s the strawberry industry boomed with the development of refrigerated railcars. New varieties of strawberries and the formation of strawberry growers' associations added to the developing industry. One result of the era's burgeoning economy was the construction of impressive brick buildings along Ponchatoula's main street. Many are now landmark structures containing businesses. The historic brick buildings that line the area are a perfect match for antiques dealers who have opened numerous shops in the city. Visitors can find anything from Tiffany lamps to massive oak desks, from porcelain teacups to old butter churns. While there are some exquisitely fine antiques here, most shops are filled with collectibles and items from estate sales; it's a road show treasure hunter's haven. The old train depot is now the **Ponchatoula Country Store** with vendor booths. It's a good spot for picking up a jar of Ponchatoula strawberry jam and hand-sewn children's clothing.

In front of the old depot is a large cage and pond, home of Ol' Hardhide, the town's pet alligator. Across the way is the Strawberry Train, which is a steam engine and single car that is roped off in a way that children can climb into the engine and car. There are several good cafes in town, but for something other than regional food, try the **Taste of Bavaria Restaurant and Bakery** (14476 La. 22, 985-386-3634). Their German cold meats, hot German potato salad, sauerkraut, and schnitzel are excellent. You also can buy breads or desserts to munch on later in the day.

If you're hankering to find out more about alligators, then stop at **Kliebert's Alligator and Turtle Farm** (1264 West Yellow Water Rd., off La. 22, 985-345-3617). A commercial establishment, Kliebert's is a serious business. Guides will show you gators from 3 to 17 feet long and explain gators' eating habits. Most people walk away very impressed by the 50-year-old pond where the largest gators are kept. Tour fees are $6 for adults, $4 for seniors, and $3 for children. Contact www.tangitourism.com or (800) 617-4506.

JACKSON AND CLINTON

Jackson and Clinton are small towns on La. 10 in East Feliciana Parish. About 30 miles north of Baton Rouge, they make a quick trip for anyone who wants to see how rural southern towns looked in the early 1900s. Stop and talk to residents—you'll meet Americans with old-fashioned values who love to show off their towns and talk about plans for the future.

Feliciana is a Spanish word for "Happy Land," and the name is said to have its origin from Felicite, wife of Don Bernardo de Galvez, the governor of Spanish Louisiana. Jackson was founded in 1815 as the seat of justice for Feliciana Parish, before the parish was divided into East and West in 1824. The town was originally called Bear Corners for the many wild black bears crossing nearby Thompson Creek. It eventually took its name from General Andrew Jackson, who supposedly camped there with his troops on a return trip north following the Battle of New Orleans. The town's historic district of 124 structures is on the National Register of Historic Places.

Jackson was the first location of the College of Louisiana, 1825–45, and the Methodist-affiliated Centenary College, 1845–1908. Visit

Centenary State Historic Site (3522 College St., 225-634-7925) and learn how students (all male) studied foreign languages, the classics, and astronomy. Walk the spacious grounds and visit two remaining structures, an 1837 dormitory and the 1898 professor's cottage. The former features exhibits on early Louisiana education, a student dorm room, a hospital room circa 1862, and a classroom. Wounded Confederate soldiers were sent to the Centenary-turned-hospital from Port Hudson battlefield in 1863, and some 75 graves are in the Civil War–period cemetery. The historic site often participates in heritage festivals with living history programs, and it is open 9 a.m. to 5 p.m. daily. Fee is $2 for adults and free for seniors and children under age 13.

Stop by the **Republic of West Florida Historical Museum** on College Street (3405 East College St., 225-634-7925) to view military, aircraft, scientific, and musical artifacts. Be sure to ask about the day Charles "Lucky" Lindbergh landed his plane in a Feliciana field. The museum is a "must" stop for kids and adults who love model railroads because the **Greater Baton Rouge Model Railroaders Club** is housed here. Children smile from ear to ear as they watch trains race through miniature worlds. There's a spectacular outdoor garden railroad layout, and it would take a real Scrooge not to love the Railroaders Christmas Open House. Other Jackson attractions include the **Old Feliciana Courthouse** (1752 High St.); and **Feliciana Cellars Winery** (1848 Charter St., 225-634-7982), with wines and gifts. Driving into Jackson on La. 951, you will see the dramatic Greek Revival building that houses the Eastern Louisiana Mental Health System, formerly the East Louisiana State Hospital. Under tight security, it is not open to the general public. There is a local movement to preserve the integrity of this building, which dates from the mid-1800s.

Accommodations in Jackson include **Milbank Historic House** (3045 Bank St., 225-634-5901), with elegant antiques and full breakfast and **Old Centenary Inn** (1740 Bank St., 225-634-5050), with eight furnished in-period rooms and continental breakfast. Dining is limited in the area, but there are several convenience stores where you can pick up snacks.

Clinton, settled in 1824, is a blend of the old South of yesteryear and small-town fun. You will see some 30 examples of Greek Revival, Victorian, and Carolina I styles of architecture. The East Feliciana Parish Courthouse (225-683-5145), built in 1840, is the oldest still in operation today. It combines with **Lawyer's Row** (225-683-8753) to form a National Historic Landmark. The site was the film location for the 1950s William Faulkner classic, *The Long Hot Summer*. More recently the 2005 film *The Dukes of Hazzard* was filmed in and around Clinton. The HBO hit series *True Blood* is also shooting scenes in the town. You'll quickly understand why the town has such appeal for movie producers and directors. It's an authentic setting.

Stop for a meal at one of the local cafes, including Josephine's Restaurant, 11302 Bank St, (225) 683-4470, featuring home cooked Ceole food; Feliciana Delights, 12311 Saint Helena St., (225) 683-1420, offering deli sandwiches; and Williams Family Front Porch, 9173 La. 67, (225) 683-1039, Creole and Cajun seafood and steak. **Clinton Community Market,** downtown on Main Street, featuring fresh produce, handcrafted items, live music, and art, is a popular outing the first Saturday of every month. Maps are conveniently available at the market for walking, biking, and driving. On a quick drive about town, you'll see wonderful old churches. Be sure to stop a moment at the old Confederate Cemetery. For complete information contact www.felicianatourism.org or (225) 634-7155 and www.clintonla.com.

i Every Labor Day Weekend in September, Opelousas, north of Lafayette and birthplace of Zydeco legend Clifton Chenier, hosts the Zydeco Festival in Plaisance Zydeco Park. Fans gather to hear such performers as Feufollet and Lil Nathan and the Zydeco Big Timers. Activities include workshops, jam sessions, and lessons. Stick around for the Squeeze Box Contest and the Big Dance Contest in front of the Main Stage. Check it out at www.zydeco.org.

LAFAYETTE

Lafayette, about 55 miles west of Baton Rouge via I-10, puts you in the heart of Acadian country. It's one of the most unusual drives in America: Along the way you travel along an 18.2-mile stretch of elevated highway known as the Atchafalaya Swamp Freeway. As it goes over the Atchafalaya River and adjacent swamps, you'll see the amazing beauty of Louisiana's wetlands. Early morning and evening sunlight and shadows create spectacular views. State law requires that traffic slow down along this twin-span stretch because traffic accidents can be treacherous. Speed limit for commercial trucks with 10 wheels or more is 55 mph; for all other vehicles it's 60 mph.

Lafayette is in a geographical area of forests and prairies interlaced with bayous, swamps, and marshes. The first inhabitants were the Attakapas Indians. The exact date when the first Europeans reached the area is not known. Historians record that a few trappers, traders, and ranchers were present prior to the Spanish occupation of 1766. The greatest cultural impact on Lafayette was the migration of French-speaking Catholic Acadians from French Canada. Expelled by the British in 1755, the exiles ended up in various locations. Some settled along the eastern seaboard, but most fled to New Orleans. There they were met with hostile attitudes of early French settlers, so they settled in the wetlands and prairies of south central and southwestern Louisiana. In 1821 Jean Mouton donated land for a Catholic Church, and the parish of St. John the Evangelist of Vermilion was created. The settlement grew, and the town of Vermilionville was renamed Lafayette in 1884 in honor of the Marquis de Lafayette.

Stop by the **Lafayette Visitors Center** (1400 Northwest Evangeline Throughway, U.S 49 South, 800-543-5340) to pick up a town map and ask about the Lafayette Museum Loop and current activities. Check out the **Acadiana Center for the Arts** (101 West Vermilion St., 337-233-7060, www.acadianacenterforthearts.org), a downtown facility for both visual and performing arts. In the wake of hurricanes Katrina and Rita, the center is currently adding a 20,000-square-foot facility that will include a 300-seat theater and atrium housing cafes and restaurants. Stop at the antebellum **Alexandre Mouton House** (1122 Lafayette St., 337-234-2208), home of Louisiana's first Democratic governor, and the **Cathedral of St. John the Evangelist** (914 St. John St. 337-232-1322, www.saintjohncathedral.org), built in a German-Romanesque style. Then head to the University of Louisiana at Lafayette and view the Paul and Lulu Hillard University Art Museum, a handsome contemporary building with perfect spaces for showing outstanding changing exhibitions as well as regional art.

The city has two outdoor living history museums. **Acadian Village** (200 Greenleaf Drive, 337-233-4077, www.acadianvillage.org), on the southeast edge of town, is a folk-life museum with a general store, schoolhouse, chapel, and original steep-roofed Acadian houses; buy a ticket and pick up a guide sheet describing the structures. The cottages were moved to the site from throughout Acadiana. They are furnished with everyday Cajun household items, many dating from the 1800s. One of the structures was the birthplace of Acadian state senator Dudley J. "Couzin Dud" LeBlanc, who in the 1940s and 1950s made millions selling his "Miracle Elixir": Hadacol. The Acadian Village is a project of the Lafayette Association for Retarded Citizens. During the Noel Acadian Village each Christmas season, the entire village is illuminated with thousands of twinkling lights. **Vermilionville** (300 Fisher Rd., 337-233-4077, www.vermilionville .org) portrays the cultures of the Cajuns, Creoles, and Native Americans between 1765 and 1890. Restored buildings and cottages replicate an early Acadian town. Programs include craft demonstrations, lectures on Acadian life, and storytelling. A Cajun music jam session is held every Saturday afternoon. For lunch, try the chicken and sausage gumbo. There's an excellent gift shop and boat rides on the Vermilion River during warm months.

Get to Lafayette early enough for breakfast at **Hub City Diner** (www.hubcitydiner .com, 1412 South College), a 1950s diner where locals eat. For dinner go to **Randol's Restau-** rant and Dance Hall (2320 Kaliste Saloom Rd., 800-962-2586, www.randol.com), or **Prejean's** (3480 Northeast Evangeline Throughway, 337-896-3247, www.prejeans.com). Afterwards head to the **Blue Moon Saloon** (215 East Convent St., 877-766-2583, www.bluemoonpresents.com) to rub elbows with the locals and dance the night away; the Blue Moon is also a hostel if you want to stay the night.

Lafayette is a spirited city with outstanding festivals. Especially outstanding is **Festival International de Louisiane,** held every April. The focus is on the music and art of French-speaking people from around the world. Traditionally Festival International features more than 100 performances in five days (visit www .festivalinternational.com). Equally exciting is the **Festival Acadiens et Creoles** (www.festivalsaca-diens.com), held in Gerard Park downtown during the second weekend in October. While there, festival-goers waltz and two-step to the rhythms of accordions, fiddles, and triangles. Information on Lafayette and the surrounding towns is available from the **Lafayette Convention and Visitors Commission** (800-543-5340, www.lafayette .travel).

NEW IBERIA

Iberia Parish likes to tell visitors it's "too hot to pass up." Well, it's impossible to argue the point considering this is the home of TABASCO, the world's most famous hot sauce. New Iberia, the parish seat, has a distinctive heritage and sense of belonging. The town was founded in 1779 on the banks of Bayou Teche by a group of Spaniards from Malaga. It is the only town to be founded by Spaniards during Louisiana's colonial era. Soon the pioneers were doing business with their Acadian neighbors; the town's location on the Teche gave it an advantage for transporting goods by keel boats, flatboats, and schooners. You can still see diesel-powered towboats pushing barges along the bayou.

Eventually owners of local plantations subdivided their land, and lots were sold as the town began to grow. Throughout the Civil War the

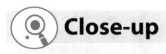

Close-up

Swamp Tours: Rare Habitats and Critters

The beauty of Louisiana's bayous, marshes, and lakes needs to be experienced firsthand to fully comprehend these environments' unique features. The wetlands are habitats for rare and endangered species. At the same time they sustain people who have lived and worked here for centuries. Visitors are encouraged to bring their cameras and their inquisitive minds on tours to learn about this unique part of the United States. Many people expect to see alligators in the wild, and there are thousands of gators in Louisiana. People need to know that the gators hibernate in winter because they are warm weather creatures. However, you will see numerous birds, including herons and ducks, year-round. View the sunlight filtering through trees laced with Spanish moss. You'll understand the songs and stories written about the waterways once you watch the sunlight dance off the shimmering water. It's best to plan a day's outing if you plan to take a swamp or airboat tour. It takes anywhere from 30 minutes to two hours to reach most tours from Baton Rouge. Most tour boats with expert guides go out once in the morning and once in the afternoon. Tours are usually several hours long. Always call ahead for reservations and to check on weather conditions. In the summer insect repellent and sunscreen are musts. Included here are contacts for well-known tours. For more visit the Louisiana Tourism Web site at www.louisianatravel.com.

Airboat Tours by Arthur Matherne
4262 U.S. 90, Des Allemands
(985) 758-5531
www.airboattours.com

Annie Miller's Son's Swamp Tours
4038 Bayou Black Rd., Houma
(985) 868-4758, (800) 341-5441
www.annie-miller.com

The Atchafalaya Experience
Leave from Atchafalaya Welcome Center
Exit 121 off I-10
(337) 277-4726, (337) 233-7816
http://theatchafalyaexperience.com

Cajun Country Swamp Tours
1321 Rookery Rd., Lake Martin, Breaux Bridge
(337) 319-0010 or (337) 332-6365
www.cajuncountryswamptours.com

Cajun Jack's Swamp Tours
112 Main St., Patterson
(800) 256-2931
www.cajunjack.com

A Cajun Man's Swamp Cruise
Bob's Bayou Black Marina
Marina Drive, Gibson
(985) 868-4625
www.cajunman.com

Champagne's Swamp Tours
Rookery Road, Lake Martin, Breaux Bridge
(337) 230-4068
www.champagnesswamptours.com

Honey Island Swamp Tour
41490 Crawford Landing Rd., Slidell
(985) 641-1769
www.honeyislandswamp.com

McGee's Landing
1337 Coffeetown Rd., Henderson
(337) 228-2384
www.mcgeeslanding.com

Munson's Swamp Tours
979 Bull Run Rd., Schriever
(985) 851-3569
www.munsonswamptours.com

Torres Cajun Swamp Tours
105 Torres Rd., La. 307, Kraemer
(985) 633-7739
www.torresswamptours.net

Teche country fell prey to the foraging of both Confederate and Federal troops; New Iberia was occupied briefly by Union forces in April and May of 1863 during the Teche campaign. During the 1880s and 1890s, the town was home to five brick companies and three rice mills. The Little Bayou Oil Field opened in 1917, and a semi-professional baseball team came to New Iberia in 1920. In 1934, the town's team became a charter member of the Evangeline Club, where it became a member of the Evangeline League and a farm club of the St. Louis Cardinals. It furnished a host of players to St. Louis, including Mel Parnel, Red Monger, and Terry Fox.

Parades and festivals have always appealed to New Iberians—carnival krewes plan lavish balls and parades. The annual **Sugarcane Festival and Fair** in September is a three-day blowout. Local residents and visitors gather for a Fais Do Do in Bouligny Plaza on Main Street on both Friday and Saturday nights. Among the past performers for these nights of dancing are zydeco musicians Gino Delafosse and Rockin' Dopsie. New Iberia also is home to the South's largest source of quality religious articles, the **Rosary House,** 200 Ann St. (337) 364-5401, that draws visitors, to buy hand-made rosaries, devotional candles, statues and medals.

Shadows-on-the-Teche (317 East Main St., www.shadowsontheteche.org, 337-369-6446) is an exquisite plantation home, and its gardens on Bayou Teche are a major attraction. Property of the National Trust for Historic Preservation, the mansion contains original furnishings and 17,000 papers from the original owners and their descendants.

If Main Street seems familiar, you may have read about it in one of James Lee Burke's *Dave Robicheaux* novels. The fictionalized version of New Iberia plays a prominent part in these stories. The Main Street that Burke describes as "the most beautiful in the country" is just part of the attraction of New Iberia. One of his novels, *In the Electric Mist of the Confederate Army,* was turned into a movie and filmed in the area. Burke himself still spends part of the year in New Iberia. To rub shoulders with locals, dine at **Lagniappe Two** (204 East Main St., 337-

365-9419) or **Clementine Dining & Spirits** (113 East Main St., 337-560-1007).

It's really fun to tour **Conrad Rice Mill** (307 Ann St., 800-551-3245, www.conradricemill.com), the oldest rice mill in America. Now owned by Mike Davis, the mill is a rare surviving example of a factory using a belt-drive power transmission. Walk next door into the mill store where you can buy the mill's specialty Konrico rice products, spices, cookbooks, and more. Schedule your itinerary so you can visit the **TABASCO Factory** at Avery Island. There you can learn about the history and bottling and packaging of the famous pepper sauce. Make sure to spend time in the colorful company store; in addition to sauces, you'll find cookbooks, aprons, dishes, and glassware. For those who have never been to the area, **Rip Van Winkle Gardens,** 5505 Rip Van Winkle Road, is always a surprise. The 25-acre site landscaped with semi-tropical plants is situated atop a salt dome. Recently a local resident said, "Lunch at Rip Van Winkle Gardens while looking out at Lake Peigneur says it all." He's talking about the Victorian mansion on the site built by 19th-century actor James Jefferson, who portrayed Rip Van Winkle on stage. View the film that tells how the lake disappeared into a salt mine when an oil company accidentally drilled through the earth into the mine below. The lake refilled and today is a tranquil site. **Cafe Jefferson,** with scenic lake views, is open daily. Call (337) 359-8525. Dramatic? Yes. Beautiful? Yes. And it's all part of New Iberia.

Visit www.cityofnewiberia.com and www.iberiatravel.com, or call (888) 942-3742 for more information.

NEW ORLEANS

Only 80 miles from Baton Rouge, New Orleans makes a grand day trip. Area residents travel to the Big Easy for dining and shopping as well as attending cultural and sporting events. Following Hurricane Katrina, a number of New Orleans residents moved to the Baton Rouge region, so the trip has become a daily commute for some. As a result of growth in communities throughout the entire area, the Baton Rouge–New Orleans I-10 corridor stays busy continually. Traffic can be snarled in both cities during morning and evening rush hours. From time to time accidents can slow traffic to a turtle's pace. If you have a particular deadline to meet, add a half hour to your estimated driving time.

i When visiting New Orleans, go ahead and indulge in some of the city's famous food traditions. Try the crispy puffed-up pommes souffle at Galatoire's, Bananas Foster at Brennans, the sugary beignets at Coffee Call, and a pecan waffle at the Camellia Grill. If you dare, order a Sazarac, the official cocktail of New Orleans made with rye whiskey and Herbsaint liqueur.

The **French Quarter**, facing a large crescent on the Mississippi River, is a good place to start. Walk to Jackson Square, originally the Place d'Armes, which is the heart of the city. In 1851 the drill ground was revamped into a landscaped park and renamed for Andrew Jackson, hero of the Battle of New Orleans. Centering the park is the landmark equestrian statue of Jackson riding his horse rearing on his hind legs. Bordered by St. Ann, St. Peter, and Chartres Streets, the square is flanked by the Pontalba Buildings with shops and restaurants on the street level. St. Louis Cathedral, facing the square, is flanked by the Cabildo and Presbytere, units of the Louisiana State Museum. If your party gets separated, the square is a good place to meet. The **Louisiana Welcome Center** (529 St. Ann, 504-566-5661) is the best place to get free maps, self-guided walking tours, and information from friendly, well-informed tourism counselors. It's open daily 9 a.m. to 5 p.m.

There's so much to see and do in New Orleans, so it's best to have a game plan before you start. Make a list of "must-see" places. Consider your interests—art, music, food, shopping—and center your visit on the most important. Remember, there are hundreds of outstanding restaurants offering fantastic menus, and places to hear the sounds of world-class musicians throughout town. Write

down a list of things to do indoors in case you hit a rainy day (not unusual in this sub-tropical climate).

To really absorb the feel of New Orleans, get beyond the French Quarter into the neighborhoods. Take a streetcar ride along St. Charles Avenue to view the magnificent Queen Anne and Victorian mansions located throughout the Garden District, the university section, and Uptown. Head to the Arts District and Julia Street to find the Contemporary Arts Center, the Ogden Museum of Southern Art, and the National World War II Museum, and view incredible galleries. Magazine Street, which extends through several neighborhoods, is lined with a typical New Orleans mix of restaurants, art galleries, grocery stores, barbers, taverns, bookstores, pottery shops, and antiques shops. Head out on Esplanade to City Park with its winding paths, ancient oaks, Sculpture Garden, and the New Orleans Museum of Art.

Enjoy the city like a New Orleans native. Start with a breakfast or brunch at **Stanley** (547 St. Ann, 504-587-0093) in Jackson Square, and then visit the **Historic New Orleans Collection** (533 Royal St., 504-523-4662) with authentic documents, prints, and artifacts on New Orleans and Louisiana in a collection of historic buildings and courtyards. Get a Pimm's Cup, a refreshing cocktail with Pimm's gin, 7-Up soda, lemon, and cucumber, to go at Napoleon House on your way to Canal Street. Visit the newly restored **Roosevelt Hotel** (123 Barrone St., 504-648-1200), now part of the Waldorf Astoria Collection, and have a small plate at chef John Besh's new Italian restaurant, Domenica, in the lobby. Enjoy a Sazarac cocktail in the lobby bar if you have the constitution for it. Ride the Canal Street streetcar line to Carrolton and get off at the **New Orleans Museum of Art** (1 Collin Diboll Circle, 504-488-2631, www.noma.org). Check out the lake to the right of the museum and walk through the Sydney and Walda Besthoff Sculpture Garden. Have a light dinner at **Ralph's On the Park** (900 City Park Ave.), and watch the sun set on the gates of City Park. Take a cab back down Esplanade to catch the early jazz show at **Preservation Hall** (726 St. Peter St., 504-522-2841, www.preservationhall

.com). Afterwards head to Frenchmen Street and visit DBA, Cafe Negril, Spotted Cat, or the Apple Barrel for music and drinks.

For a family itinerary spend an afternoon at **Audubon Zoo** in Audubon Park or combine a trip to the **Aquarium of the Americas** at the foot of Canal Street and the **Insectarium** in the old Custom House just blocks away on Canal Street (www.auduboninstitute.com, 800-774-7394). Let the kids run and jump in the grassy space at **Woldenberg Park** while you sit and watch the traffic on the Mississippi River. Fantastic floats and costumes entertain the entire family at **Blaine Kern's Mardi Gras Museum** (1380 Port of New Orleans, 800-362-8213, www.mardigrasworld .com), the largest creators of parade floats in the world.

If all of this is too much for one day, then see attractions that best fit your time and save the rest for another day. The secret of any good day trip to New Orleans is to enjoy just enough to leave with happy memories. If you decide to visit during Mardi Gras or one of the city's famous festivals—Jazz Fest, Voodoo Experience, French Quarter Festival, Satchmo Festival, Essence Festival, or Christmas in New Orleans—make plans early. For information, a hotel guide, and an official Visitors Guide, visit the New Orleans Convention and Visitors Bureau Web sites (www .neworleanscvb.com, www.neworleansonline .com, 800-543-6652).

i In the era before superstores, Louisianians got their discount imports from the pirates of Barataria, a unit of today's Jean Lafitte National Park. The word *Barataria* comes from the Spanish word for "cheap," and at the time, it also implied "ill-gotten."

ST. FRANCISVILLE

Baton Rougeans often drive to St. Francisville on day trips; for some it's a daily commute because they've chosen to make this quaint town home. It's often the first place locals recommend for

a day trip into Plantation Country. Established in 1809, St. Francisville sits on a narrow ridge overlooking the Mississippi River. It was the commercial and cultural center of the surrounding countryside settled by mostly English and Scottish planters. An earlier settlement, Bayou Sara, was established in the early 1790s, and it was at one time the largest shipping port on the Mississippi River between New Orleans and Memphis. However repeated flooding destroyed Bayou Sara, and nothing exists of it today. A few of its structures were hauled up the hill into St. Francisville in the 1920s.

Historic plantations and Queen Anne homes, along with beautiful gardens and intriguing shops, make the town a major tourist destination. Efforts by the West Feliciana Historical Society and a vibrant Main Street program help preserve the charm and cultural economy of the town. Make the Historical Society office on Ferdinand Street your first stop. You can pick up a simple driving/walking map and brochures on attractions and bed-and-breakfast inns. Pick up a bit of friendly local gossip and tips on the best things to see and do in the area. Restored plantations are open daily for tours. They include: **Afton Villa Gardens** (9247 U.S. 61), site of the Barrow family home that burned in 1863, which is open seasonally; **Butler Greenwood Plantation** (8345 U.S. 62), a 1790s plantation that features its original parlor and is still occupied by the original family; **Catalpa Plantation** (9508 U.S. 61) has been a family-owned plantation since the 1600s and is open by reservation; and **Cottage Plantation** (10528 Cottage Lane) is the area's oldest plantation and most complete complex. Andrew Jackson slept here after the victory at the Battle of New Orleans. Other plantations include: the **Greenwood Plantation** (6838 Highland Rd.), a reconstructed Greek Revival built from the ruins of the 1830s mansion that burned in 1960; **The Myrtles Plantation** (7747 U.S. 61), which is furnished with French antiques and surrounded with intrigue; the **Audubon State Historic Site, Oakley House** (11788 La. 965), with daily guided tours and special living history programs; and **Rosedown Plantation State Historic Site** (2501 La. 10), a beautifully restored 1835 plantation mansion with 90 percent of its original furnishings, 28 acres of formal gardens, and 12 historical outbuildings.

Many drive to St. Francisville to grab some lunch and shop. You can split a gigantic muffaletta sandwich two or four ways at **Magnolia Cafe** (5687 Commerce St.), or go for the gourmet breakfast buffet at the **St. Francisville Inn & Restaurant** (5720 Commerce St.). **The Oxbow** (7193 U.S. 61) is a fine dining restaurant featuring steaks and seafood. **The Carriage House** (7747 U.S. 61) serves regional cuisine, such as grilled shrimp with hush puppies and white chocolate bread pudding, in a delightful setting looking out on the original courtyard at the Myrtles Plantation Home. Finally, **Birdman Books and Coffees** (5695 Commerce St.) is a cozy nook for espresso, sweet treats, and good books.

It's nearly impossible to pick out one shop over another in St. Francisville. Most are found on Ferdinand Street, Royal Street, and Commerce Street. Browsers looking for a special gift or a one-of-a-kind treasure have numerous choices. Do stop in at **Grandmother's Buttons** (9814 Royal St.) to view the amazing button collection on display in the old bank vault.

St. Francisville is a treasure trove of bed-and-breakfasts. Some are quaint, and others are grand and elegant. For a list of choices, check with the Historical Society Office on Ferdinand Street. Also ask about annual festivals, including the Audubon Pilgrimage in spring, Audubon Country Birdfest in April, Angola Prison Rodeo, and Christmas in the Country. See the Annual Events and Festivals chapter.

There are two sites unique to the St. Francisville area. **The Angola Prison Museum** (see Close-up in Annual Events chapter), located outside the gates of the Louisiana State Penitentiary, presents displays on prison history, life, and challenges. History buffs should not miss the **Port Hudson State Historic Site,** located on U.S. 61 between St. Francisville and Baton Rouge. The Civil War battlefield here was the site of the longest siege in U.S. military history, and it was the first time African-American soldiers served in battle fighting for the Federal Army. The museum has excellent displays, and the interpretive rangers are well versed in details of the battle. For more information, check out www.stfrancisville .us or call (888) 307-8244 for details on touring plantation homes and bed-and-breakfast inns.

WEEKEND TRIPS

In addition to many day trips from Baton Rouge, there are a number of destinations within range of the city that make great weekend getaways. Heading east, many residents enjoy both long and short holidays along the sparkling white-sand beaches in Mississippi, Alabama, and the coastal towns of the Florida Panhandle. In addition to serious fishing and boating, you can take in a little golf and see first-class entertainment in casino resorts. Heading west, I-10 is a direct route to western Louisiana, east Texas, and the myriad attractions in the Houston/Galveston area. From Lafayette, you can drive north on I-49 to the green rolling hills of Louisiana's piney woods country and the Ark-La-Tex area of Shreveport. Travelers find U.S. 61 has much less traffic. It's a relaxing trip, and you can enjoy the scenery and historic sights of Natchez, Vicksburg, and the Mississippi Delta country. The highways are well maintained and patrolled. It's a good idea to stop at the welcome centers as you enter a new state. Louisiana welcome centers offer free cups of steaming hot Community Coffee; in Mississippi's welcome center, you can get free soda. The centers are excellent sources for up-to-date maps, brochures, and discount coupons for travelers on the road.

BILOXI AND GULFPORT

The drive from Baton Rouge to Biloxi and stunning Beach Boulevard takes about two and a half hours. Leave on a Friday afternoon or early Saturday morning, and you can easily spend two full days enjoying the casual atmosphere along this stretch of the Gulf Coast. Once home to the Biloxi Indians and later to French colonists, the Mississippi Gulf Coast has changed hands countless times over the centuries. Traces of Spanish rule can be seen at the **Old Spanish Fort** in Pascagoula, built in 1718.

The blend of cultures, the demands of coastal living, and a pioneer spirit have much to do with the incredible resilience of local residents. The region sustained terrible damage from Hurricane Camille in 1969 and Hurricane Katrina in 2005, but the area is rebounding once again. Certainly many of the grand old mansions that lined Beach Boulevard (U.S. 90) are gone, but 26 miles of soft white sand are as beautiful as ever. The chain of barrier islands limits the amount of strong waves racing to the beaches, making the gentle waters great for water-based sports, kite flying,

and splashing in the Gulf. **Pass Christian** and **Long Beach**, just west of the Gulfport/Biloxi area, are residential areas offering quieter, tranquil sections of beaches for sunbathing or romantic walks. New condos are popping up, and hotels and motels can be found along the beach as well as major roads and I-10 exits. For those seeking excitement, casino resorts are back in business.

Standing stalwart and strong at Beach Boulevard and Porter Avenue, the **Biloxi Lighthouse** makes a great photo. Several pullovers along the beach are available for taking photos and beach strolling. Several areas are protected nesting areas for least terns, an endangered bird species. These beautiful birds and seagulls also make great photos.

Make lodging reservations before leaving for the Mississippi Coast. The area has more than 12,000 rooms, but they fill fast during the summer and on holidays. **Beau Rivage Resort and Casino** (888-567-6667) and **Hard Rock Hotel & Casino** (228-374-7625) are excellent full-service hotels on the beach. Ask for gulf-view rooms if seeing the water is a must. A number of popular chain hotels, including Comfort Inn, Days Inn,

Courtyard Marriott, and Best Western, are located on Beach Boulevard and in town. For more information, access the **Mississippi Hotel and Lodging Association** Web site at: www.mshla.com.

Dining is a big part of any weekend getaway, and the Biloxi/Gulfport area has just about any cuisine you could want. Certainly the casinos have both upscale restaurants and lavish buffets. Seafood is as fresh as it can be and comes prepared in myriad ways. You can also find restaurants specializing in southern cooking and ethnic dishes. An absolute institution is **Mary Mahoney's** (116 Rue Magnolia, 228-374-0163). One of the oldest houses in America, this brick French house survived Hurricanes Camille and Katrina despite water that rose almost all the way up to the ceiling. Their seafood and Creole dishes are as rewarding as the atmosphere.

Take a break from the beach and visit **Beauvoir** (2244 Beach Blvd., 228-388-4400), the retirement estate of Confederate President Jefferson Davis, who acquired it in 1877. Authentically restored following Hurricane Katrina, the raised cottage–style residence is one of the few antebellum homes left on Beach Boulevard. Tour the mansion and learn about what happened to the Davis family following the Civil War. Beauvoir is designated as both a Mississippi Historical Landmark and a National Historic Landmark.

Don't be surprised if you feel like a kid again after visiting a children's attraction on the coast. **Lynn Meadows Discovery Center** (246 Dolan Ave., 228-897-6039) is one of the nation's Top 50 Children's Museums with sensational things to do; start at the top of the building and work your way down the delightful spiral path. **The Center for Marine Education and Research** (101 Dolphin Lane, 228-896-9182) is the newest attraction on the Mississippi Gulf Coast and features interactive exhibits. During the warm months, the entire family can slip and slide at **Gulf Islands Waterpark** (I-10 at exit Hwy 49 north, 228-604-4045) with 18 acres of fun.

Work in a trip to **Ship Island**, one of the nation's remarkable barrier islands. **Ship Island Excursions** (228-864-1014, www.msshipisland .com) offers daily passenger ferry service to West

Ship Island and Fort Massachusetts (circa 1848). Part of Gulf Islands National Seashore, the island is about 10 miles offshore from the Gulfport Small Craft Harbor. It sings to those who love swimming and shelling. Bring plenty of sunscreen—the sun can be fierce, especially in the summer. Food service and chair and umbrella rentals are available on the island. Watch for dolphins on the hourlong cruise out to the island. Ship Island Excursions operates March through October.

Serious anglers will probably spend their entire weekend getaway in a boat. If you want to venture out to the offshore oil rigs for red snapper, grouper, amberjack, or bluefish, or skiff-fish for speckled trout and reds at Chandeleur Island, then contact the **Mississippi Charter Boat Captain's Association**, www.mscharterboats.org. Tours are also available on two-masted schooners.

Art lovers may want to extend their journey a few miles to Ocean Springs, Mississippi, where they can visit the **Walter Anderson Museum of Art** (510 Washington Ave., 228-872-3164) and view the incredible murals of this 20th-century artist and the works of his brothers: Peter Anderson, founder of Shearwater Pottery; and James McConnell Anderson, painter and ceramist. A short drive away at **Shearwater Pottery** (102 Shearwater Drive, 228-875-7320), you can visit

ℹ️ From time to time, the sky above Biloxi is filled with really big birds—the planes that fly from Keesler Air Force Base. The base was dedicated August 25, 1941, as Keesler Army Airfield in honor of 2nd Lieutenant Samuel Reeves Keesler Jr., a Mississippi native and distinguished aerial gunner killed in action in France during World War I. The Air Force plays a strong role in the community, as does the NASA John C. Stennis Space Center (800-237-1821) on the Louisiana/Mississippi border. Visitors can tour the StennisSphere featuring space exhibits on space exploration, science, and geography. Shuttle buses leave from the Mississippi Welcome Center at exit 2 on I-10. Tours take place Wednesday through Sunday, 10 a.m. to 2 p.m.

the Anderson family's specialty shop and art gallery.

For brochures, maps, and activities in Biloxi, Gulfport, and nearby communities, contact the **Mississippi Gulf Coast Convention and Visitors Bureau**, www.gulfcoast.org, (888) 467-4853.

GULF SHORES, ORANGE BEACH, AND PENSACOLA

Alabama's Gulf Coast is a natural choice for a weekend trip. The Gulf Shores and Orange Beach area is about a four-and-a-half-hour drive east of Baton Rouge. The Spanish were the first to camp out here. The first Indian village in America visited by an explorer was located near the present-day site of Shellbanks Baptist Church on Fort Morgan Road in Gulf Shores, where a member of Hernando de Soto's party encountered a member of the local Indian tribe, the Achuse. Travelers have been "discovering" the area ever since.

Situated at the mouth of Mobile Bay, Gulf Shores, Alabama, is literally a second home for many south Louisianans. The long stretch of wide, soft, white sand beaches and water sports make it a great destination for relaxing. You can be as lazy as you like or get up early to pack in two days of activities both offshore and inland. In addition to a long list of casual cafes and funky nightspots, the area also has sleek, upscale shopping areas, condos, and restaurants. Definitely don't limit your fun to the beach—extend your travels just across the border to Florida and the Pensacola area.

The weather is glorious in spring and fall; January and February can be damp and chilly, but don't count winter out along the coast. Summer is always busy with tourists, but it's also furiously hot. Make lodging reservations early, especially on holidays. Lifeguards carefully patrol the beaches and remind people to watch beach safety flags. Green flags mean calm conditions, while red flags act as a warning to keep out of the water, as high surf and strong conditions are dangerous. In addition rip tides occur frequently along these beaches and can be extremely dangerous.

Aim for a three-day weekend, but if you leave Baton Rouge early Friday afternoon, you can pack in a lot of fun. After checking into your Orange Beach abode for the weekend, check out the **Flora-Bama Lounge and Oyster Bar** (17401 Perdido Key Dr., 850-492-0611). This local institution is dizzy and different with a mix of salvaged buildings, nutty decorations, and live music in the evenings. This rite-of-passage hangout straddles the Alabama-Florida border and is famous for zany events, including the International Mullet Toss in spring, when twenty-something patrons gather on the beach to toss slippery mullets across the state line. Wear a bathing suit if you go. Later aim for dinner at **Cobalt** (28099 Perdido Beach Blvd., 251-923-5300, www.cobaltrestaurant.net), with picture windows overlooking Perdido Pass. Menu favorites include Spanish paella and stone hearth pizzas.

Start Saturday with breakfast in your condo, or stop at **Tacky Jack's** (27206 Safe Harbor Dr., 251-981-4144) for a Belgian waffle. Morning half-day fishing excursions with **Distraction Charters**' Captain Troy Friday leave as early as 6:30 a.m., starting at Zeke's Landing in Orange Beach. Start later around 9 a.m., and pick up a kayak at **Ike's Beach Rentals** to paddle the brackish waters of Little Lagoon, a half-mile-wide stretch of beach known as West Beach in Gulf Shores. History buffs may prefer a tour of **Fort Morgan,** a U.S. defensive post in the War of 1812, the Civil War, the Spanish American War, World War I, and World War II. The famous command, "Damn the torpedoes! Full speed ahead!" was given here by Union Admiral David Farragut during the battle to take Mobile Bay from the Confederates in 1864. A living history program is conducted during the summer. Fort Morgan can be blazing hot in the summer, so be sure to bring a hat.

Lunch at **King Neptune's** (www.kingneptunesseafoodrestaurant.com), an unassuming family-run restaurant that serves up the best oysters, shrimp, and fresh fish found anywhere on the Gulf. During the afternoon spend several hours relaxing on the beaches or go shopping at **The Wharf**, an upscale resort area with boutique shops such as Barefoot Cottage, Go Fish Clothing

& Jewelry, and White Cabana. If the ocean still calls, take a dolphin-watch cruise (www.dolphin expresscruises.com) on the back bays.

Around 6 p.m., take in a spectacular view at the new **Gulf State Park Pier**, the longest fishing pier in the Gulf of Mexico. The pier's end is a 65-foot octagon extending over a sandbar where fish like cobia, king mackerel, and tarpon live. For dinner, head to **LuLu's at Homeport Marina** (200 East 25th Ave., 251-967-5858), known for its great food and music. Owned by Lucy Buffett, the restaurant serves appetizers, sandwiches, and entrees—try the mahi tacos with blackened fish for a delicious treat, or go for the fried green tomato BLT.

On Sunday get up for a beach stroll, then drive to **Villaggio Grille at the Wharf** (4790 Wharf Parkway) for a champagne brunch. Pick up several desserts at the **Intracoastal Bread and Bottle Co.** next door before starting your return trip to Baton Rouge. Also, just a short car ride away in Pensacola, Florida, the **National Museum of Naval Aviation** (www.naval-air.org) showcases an extensive collection of some 150 aircraft representing every military branch. Earn your wings in the flight simulators or strap in for a wild ride thanks to the Imax theater. The museum is situated on the Pensacola Naval Air Station.

Pensacola, which observed its 450th anniversary in 2009, makes a great destination in itself. You'll want to visit Seville Quarter, Historic Pensacola Village, Pensacola Beach, Perdido Key State Park, Big Lagoon State Park, and Gulf Islands National Seashore. When driving about, you may find yourself back at the Flora-Bama Lounge and one step from Orange Beach, Alabama. If you decide to visit Pensacola first, simply backtrack past the Alabama beaches on your way back to Louisiana.

Excellent information on Alabama's Gulf Coast is available at www.gulfshores.com. The Pensacola Web site, www.visitpensacola.com, is equally well designed and easy to follow.

HOUSTON

Houston's grand metropolitan mix is just that, grand. Big and bold, the huge Texas city can be delightful and frustrating at any given moment. There's so much to do and see, you can squander your getaway time just traveling from one side of the city to the other. The secret is to divide and conquer and to decide what you most want to do. Select lodging that will be reasonably close to where you will be spending your time. If you're going for a shopping spree, then you'll probably be happiest in the Galleria area. If it's theater and concerts you're looking for, then downtown is your best bet. Main Street leads south through the Museum District and the Texas Medical Center and on to Reliant Park. The downtown METRO Rail will get you there quickly and efficiently. There is ample parking around the museums unless there's a blockbuster exhibition in the works.

To reach Houston, follow I-10 west out of Baton Rouge, about 280 miles. Plan on about five hours, including several stops. The earlier you can leave on a Friday, the better. If you reach the Texas border before 5 p.m., stop at the Welcome Center on the Sabine River and ask for a Houston map. Highway traffic will build up the closer you get to the city, but you're in luck—Houston residents tend to flee the city on weekends, so the traffic flow will be opposite your direction. Traffic in the city is much lighter on Saturday and Sunday. When you're ready to return, leave by mid-afternoon and you'll avoid the mass of Houstonians returning from their weekend getaways.

History buffs may want to stop at **San Jacinto Battleground State Historical Site** (2523 Battleground Rd. at LaPorte), east of Houston. On clear days you can see the San Jacinto Monument from I-10. The site marks the decisive battle of the Texas Revolution on April 21, 1836. You can see a short film on Texas history and visit the museum containing documents and artifacts relating to the battle. Nearby is the **Battleship Texas State Historic Site**, the first battleship memorial museum in the United States.

Shoppers gravitate to the **Galleria on Westheimer.** You can literally spend the entire weekend in this complex containing 2.4 million square feet of retail space. Go to Neiman-Marcus, Macy's, Saks, and Nordstroms, shop at the boutiques, and dine at the food court around the ice-skating rink. If you can't leave, stay at one of the Galleria's two Westin Hotels; visit www.simon.com for info. **Rice Village** (www.ricevillageonline.com), established in the 1930s, has some 300 shops in a 16-block area between Kirby and Greenbriar near Rice University. Pop into Half Price Books for reading material, Dromgoole's for writing utensils and paper, or the Houston Numismatic Exchange for coins. **The River Oaks Shopping Center** at West Gray and South Shepherd has top-notch shopping in one of Houston's most prestigious neighborhoods. While there, catch foreign flicks at the 70-year-old **River Oaks Theatre**.

Houston's Museum District contains some of the most fascinating museums in America. **The Houston Museum of Fine Arts** (1001 Bissonnet, 713-639-7554) includes Ima Hogg's collection of Remington paintings, the Beck Collection of impressionists and post-impressionists, and the Strauss Collection of Renaissance and 18th-century art. Major exhibitions draw thousands to the museum. Visit the delightful gift shop and grab a snack in Cafe Express on the lower level. Across the way, walk through the Cullen Sculpture Garden for a serene break. **The Houston Museum of Natural Science** (One Herman Circle Drive, 713-529-4848) intrigues with its exhibit halls on gems and minerals, shells, fossils, and more. Everyone smiles the minute they enter the beautiful Butterfly Center.

Stop and talk with a Houstonian and ask for a few good insider tips. They might tell you to ride a pontoon boat on **Buffalo Bayou** for $7, order a Ninfarita—made with freshly squeezed lime juice—at **Ninfa's** on Navigation St. for $6.95, or catch a game at the **Houston Polo Club**, only minutes from the Galleria, for $25 a ticket. On weekends save money by opting for the twilight tee time and enjoy 18 holes at **Memorial Park Golf Course** for $24.

There are hundreds of restaurants in the city. For local atmosphere try the catfish and grits or the wings and waffles at the **Breakfast Klub** (3711 Travis, 713-528-8561) where lines form early on Saturday morning. Eat authentic Texas barbecue smoked brisket at **Goode Company**

Barbecue (5109 Kirby, 713-522-2530). You'll find a great Tex-Mex menu at **Spanish Flowers** (4701 North Main, 713-869-1706), where the menu includes Mole Poblano and Carne Guisada. To see Houston's professionals at play, visit **Max's Wine Dive** (4720 Washington, 713-880-8737) and order a Texas "Haute" Dog served with venison chili.

For more information visit the **Houston Convention and Visitors Bureau** Web site, www.visithouston.com. Click on "Ask Veronica" to get the right answers to all your questions. For more on museums visit www.houstonmuseumdistrict.org.

> **i** The Coushatta Casino Resort, 777 Coushatta Dr. at Kinder, is north of I-10 via U.S. 165. The premiere gaming destination features six restaurants, 500 rooms, an RV park, and a golf course. The Coushatta Indian Museum spotlights the tribe's pine needle baskets along with additional artifacts. It's open weekdays. Call (800) 584-7263.

LAKE CHARLES

Lake Charles is a sassy city. Residents welcome visitors with casinos and excitement. At the same time they have deep respect for nature and Louisiana's wetlands. Start talking with a local, and the conversation likely will turn to fishing, alligators, or hurricanes. Lake Charles is the principal city in Calcasieu and Cameron Parishes. It's also called Louisiana's Outback. About 30 miles from the Gulf of Mexico, the city sits on the north edge of America's great wetlands. The region has survived Hurricane Audrey in 1957 and Rita in 2005. While working on recovering, the city continues to pursue new ideas and new business. It's a major center for the petrochemical industry, seafood industry, and tourism.

The trip from Baton Rouge takes two and a half hours. If gaming is your destination, then check in at **L'Auberge du Lac Casino** (777 Avenue L'Auberge, 866-580-7444, www.ldlcasino.com). In addition to a complete gaming casino, the L'Auberge Tower has 1,000 rooms with a sophisticated rustic theme and comfy beds. Plan a meal at the Snake River Bar and Grill or the more sporty Jack Daniel's Bar and Grill. Le Cafe has sandwiches and snacks 24 hours. Desserts include gelato and decadent chocolate candy. Work it off at the Contraband Bayou Golf Course or in the cardio fitness center. Take a dip in the adult pool or go for a couples massage at the Spa du Lac. Another option is **Isle of Capri Casino and Hotel** (Westlake Ave., 337-430-2400, http://lake-charles.isleofcapricasinos.com), where you can choose a room in either the Inn at the Lake or the Tower Hotel. Lake Charles has a good selection of hotels and motels and some delightful bed-and-breakfasts in the Charpentier Historic District dating from the city's lumber days at the turn of the 20th century.

Get outdoors. Lake Charles is the jumping-off spot for the world-famous **Creole Nature Trail All-American Road**, 180 miles of bayous, marshlands, and gulf shores. The "trail" travels through thousands of acres of untouched wetlands. The entwining ecosystems are enchanting. A loop—a series of Louisiana roadways—takes you through incredible wildlife refuges. Depending on the season, you'll see ducks, geese, wading birds, and roseate spoonbills. Alligators are always there, but they do hibernate in winter. Just west of Lake Charles, head south on La. 27. As small ponds and bayous appear, cross the Ellender bridge into Cameron Parish, a land of salt marshes and tall grass. Stop in the little town of Hackberry (home of the Hackberry Ramblers) for a quick snack. Then a little further along the way is the **Sabine National Wildlife Refuge**. Park your car at the Wetland Walkway and walk the self-guided loop through a level marsh. Look for swamp rabbits, muskrats, nutria, water snakes, and gators. During February, March, and April, be sure to see migrating warblers. The walk is safe, but keep in mind, this is the critters' home. You never know when a gator or snake will decide to cross the path. Bring your camera. As you reach the Gulf, you'll come to Holly Beach, the community that was wiped out by Hurricane Rita. A few people have returned, but it looks like an RV park. Walk to the beach and wade in the Gulf a bit. The Creole

Nature Trail continues on, but at this point you probably will want to return the way you came. To hike the entire trail takes the better part of a day. Before visiting the byway, check current traveler and weather information at www.creolenaturetrail.org.

Back in Lake Charles, try to fit in a stop at the **Mardi Gras Museum of Imperial Calcasieu** (809 Kirby St., 337-430-0043), which features some 300 dazzling costumes dripping with sequins, beads, and feathers. The town celebrates Mardi Gras with an extended weekend of parades, cooking events, and parties. Other festivals include Contraband Days Pirate Festival in May and the Marshland Festival in August. They all have plenty of Cajun, zydeco, and swamp pop music. For information, contact the Southwest Louisiana/Lake Charles Convention and Visitors Bureau at www.visitlakecharles.com or (800) 264-5521.

NATCHEZ AND VICKSBURG

Natchez and Vicksburg are quintessential Southern towns. Hollywood movies filled with romance and glamour seldom do justice to the beauty and complex history of these two towns. Each is a travel destination in itself. However, if pressed for time, you can visit major sights on a weekend getaway. Extend your time a day or two and you won't be disappointed. Start early on a Friday and drive U.S. 61 north through St. Francisville and Natchez to Vicksburg. The 161-mile trip takes about three hours.

Vicksburg was originally territory of the Nachez tribe. Following the arrival of Europeans, the site was controlled by the French, Spanish, and finally, the Americans. The town was incorporated in 1825 as Vicksburg, named after Newitt Vick, a Methodist minister and conscientious objector of the American Revolution. During the Civil War, the entire town was bombarded during the 46-day Siege of Vicksburg, a significant battle in which the Union gained control of the entire Mississippi River. The siege ended July 4, 1863, when Confederate John C. Pemberton surrendered to General Ulysses S. Grant. **The Vicksburg National Military Park** (601-636-0583, www.nps

.gov/vick), northeast of downtown, is a major attraction. The park entrance and visitor center are on Clay Street (U.S. 90) within a quarter mile of I-20. An excellent audiovisual program explains the campaign and siege. The 16-mile battlefield tour along steep hills puts you in the middle of the action. Red markers designate Confederate lines, and blue markers pertain to Union troops. You will see impressive memorials to the soldiers of both sides who gave their lives here. Along the way you can view the USS *Cairo*, the gunboat that was sunk in the Yazoo River in 1862 and salvaged in the early 1960s. Numerous artifacts, including the personal gear of the crew, are displayed in the USS *Cairo* Museum adjacent to the Vicksburg National Cemetery.

Vicksburg's attractions include the **Vicksburg Battlefield Museum** (601-638-6500, www.vicksburgbattlefield.net), just east of the military park, featuring models of gunboats, a diorama depicting the siege, and the film *Vanishing Glory*. The **Old Court House Museum** (1008 Cherry St., 601-636-0741) contains an eclectic mix of Civil War clothing and artifacts and Indian and pioneer implements. Built in 1858, it's one of the city's most historic structures. On March 12, 1894, the soft drink Coca-Cola was bottled for the first time in Vicksburg by Joseph Biedenharn, who owned a candy shop. **The Biedenharn Coca-Cola Museum** (1107 Washington St., 601-638-6514) displays the equipment used to bottle the soft drink as well as a prized Coca-Cola memorabilia collection. It's a fun place to stop for ice cream, fountain Cokes, Coke floats, and souvenirs.

Vicksburg is home to five casinos, each with its own theme and personality. All have their own hotels with river views and a wide selection of restaurants. They include: **Ameristar Casino** (4116 Washington St., 800-700-7770); **Diamond-Jacks Casino Hotel** (3990 Washington St., 877-711-0677, www.diamondjacks.com); **Horizon Casino Hotel,** (1310 Mulberry St., 601-636-3423); **Rainbow Hotel Casino** (1380 Warrenton Rd., 800-503-3777); and **Riverwalk Hotel Casino** (1046 Warrenton Rd., 866-615-9125).

Accommodations in Vicksburg include familiar chain hotels, casino hotels, and picturesque bed-and-breakfast inns. Restaurants include everything from fast food to fine dining. For exceptional southern gourmet meals, reserve lunch or dinner in the antebellum restaurant **Anchuca (**1010 First St., 601-661-0111). **Walnut Hills Restaurant** (1214 Adams St., 601-638-4910) is famous for its Southern plantation cuisine, especially its fried chicken and desserts. The **Vicksburg Convention and Visitors Bureau** lists it all at www.vicksburgcvb.org.

Natchez is about 60 miles south of Vicksburg. Get there by noon Saturday and you'll have plenty of time to explore the town, shop a bit, and see one of the town's famous mansions. Make the **Natchez Visitors Reception Center,** U.S. 84 and Canal Street, your first stop. See the 20-minute show, *The Natchez Story*, as well as Natchez exhibits. You can get National Park Service information, pick up brochures and maps on the Mississippi, make hotel and bed-and-breakfast reservations, and get tickets for tours at this well-run center. Step outside for a breathtaking view of the Mississippi River.

Natchez is an old town. The mound-building and sun-worshiping Natchez occupied the site for centuries before the French built a fort here in 1716. During the 1700s, control subsequently fell under British and then Spanish rule. By the early 1800s plantations were flourishing, and wealthy planters built magnificent homes in and around the city. Today Natchez has more antebellum structures than any other city of its size in America. The same families have owned some of the properties for more than 150 years. Before adventuring further, start with lunch in the **Carriage House at Stanton Hall** (401 High St., 601-445-5153, www.stantonhall.com), one of the town's most elegant mansions. The restaurant is known for its outstanding fried chicken, fluffy biscuits, homemade desserts, and mint juleps. The mansion, built in the 1850s by a wealthy cotton planter and broker, features Carrara marble mantels, silver-plated hardware, and stunning antiques.

Longwood (140 Lower Woodville Rd., 601-442-5193), on the outskirts of town, is probably the most famous of the town's homes. Planned for Haller Nutt and his wife, Julia, the octagon-shaped house was begun in 1860. The structure was to have 32 rooms, a solarium, and an observatory. The Civil War began in 1861, and all of the craftsmen dropped their hammers and fled north to pick up rifles and bayonets. Nutt and a few workers and slaves completed the basement. The Nutt family, including eight children, moved into the nine completed rooms. Today, the home is maintained, yet unfinished, by the Pilgrimage Garden Club. Open daily 9 a.m. to 4:30 p.m.

Natchez National Historical Park (www.nps.gov/natc/historyculture) maintains two must-see properties. **Melrose Plantation,** on the Melrose-Montbello Parkway and built in 1842–48, is remarkable for its preservation and ornate Victorian and Empire furnishings. National park guides provide accurate and entertaining information. The three-story **William Johnson House** in downtown Natchez illuminates the life of a free man of color in Natchez. Johnson, an African-American barber and diarist, used bricks from buildings destroyed by an 1840 tornado to construct his State Street estate and commercial business area. The family lived in the upper stories, and the first floor was rented out to merchants. Visitors learn about the extensive diary kept by Johnson. It reveals what life was like for free African Americans in the pre–Civil War South.

Downtown Natchez also offers antiques shops, boutiques, and bookstores. You can browse to your heart's content on Saturday, visit more mansions on Sunday, and make the two-hour return to Baton Rouge at your leisure. Check out the **Natchez Convention and Visitors Bureau** Web site, www.visitnatchez.org. For information on spring and fall pilgrimages, home tours, and bed-and-breakfasts, visit natchezpilgrimage.com and www.natchezontheriver.com.

NATCHITOCHES

Natchitoches puts you in another time and place. This town in central Louisiana preserves its past but knows how to make the present lively and fun. From Baton Rouge follow I-10 west to Lafayette where you pick up I-49 north. The drive takes a little over 3 hours, and you definitely need to spend a night or two.

Founded in 1714 by Louis Juchereau de St. Denis, Natchitoches is the oldest permanent settlement within the borders of the 1803 Louisiana Purchase. It started as a French outpost on the Red River and was named after the Indian tribe in the area. Following the Louisiana Purchase, several plantations were built along the Red River. Planters built mansions downriver and fine townhouses in the city. However the course of the river shifted, cutting off its connection to the Mississippi River. The result was beautiful Cane River Lake, with downtown fronting the lake on one side and private homes on the other.

Natchitoches retains a European flavor. At the heart of its National Historic District is Front Street, a brick road where buildings with cast-iron balconies face the landscaped riverfront. You can easily spend an entire day just meandering in this area. Shops here are quaint and a bit unusual. Check out **Georgia's Gift Shop** for Natchitoches and Louisiana gifts, **Les Saisons** for homemade fudge, and **Book Merchant** for regional titles. **Kaffie Frederick General Mercantile** is Louisiana's oldest general store with hardware, housewares, and gifts. **Gingerbread House** on the riverbank and at 520 Keyser Ave. has intriguing gifts and holiday decorations. The Natchitoches Welcome Center also is situated on the riverbank. It's *the* place for information, guides, and maps.

The town has its own distinct food, the Natchitoches meat pie, similar to the Spanish empañada. The folded pastry dough is filled with a spicy ground-meat mixture and fried. The pies are served as appetizers or as a main meal. **Lasyone's Meatpie Restaurant** (622 Second St., 318-352-3353, www.lasyones.com) has been serving the meat pie and other local dishes since 1968. **The Landing Restaurant** (530 Front St., 318-352-1579, www.thelandingrestaurantandbar.com) serves lunch, dinner, and a Sunday champagne brunch. The restaurant is noted for its original sauces over fish, shrimp, and steaks. Another local favorite is **Merci Beaucoups Restaurant** (127 Church St., 318-352-6634) where the Cajun baked potato is loaded and topped with crawfish étouffée. Save room for the bread pudding. The city offers numerous other dining choices, including Mexican, Chinese, and barbecue.

Natchitoches also is a college town. **Northwestern State University** (www.nsula.edu) adds much to the town's culture and entertainment. Check out listings for concerts, dramas, and art shows on the campus. The Louisiana Folk Life Center, located on the campus, sponsors one of the nation's most comprehensive folk festivals with a focus on culture, music, crafts, and more.

The movie *Steel Magnolias* was based on a true story. Filmed entirely in Natchitoches and released in 1989, the film is now a classic. Hospitality abounds here, and you'll no doubt meet a few Natchitoches "magnolias," especially if you stay in one of more than 35 bed-and-breakfast inns. Among those within walking distance of downtown are the **Judge Porter House** (321 Second St., 800-441-8343), a 1912 townhouse filled with handsome antiques; **Levy East Home** (338 Rue Jefferson, 318-352-0662), an elegantly furnished three-story mansion; and Steel Magnolia House (320 Rue Jefferson, 888-346-4095), one of the sites featured in the movie. Hotel and motel rates are very affordable, but they do increase during the city's Christmas season.

Go exploring. **Fort St. Jean Baptiste State Historic Site** (155 Rue Jefferson, 318-357-3101) on Cane River Lake was constructed from original plans of the fort and features interpretive programs and exhibits. A Creole Culture tour takes you to Melrose Plantation and a community known as Isle Brevelle. It was established by descendants of an early Creole family descended from Marie Thereze Coin-Coin, an enslaved woman, and Frenchman Claude Thomas Pierre Metoyer. At Melrose you will see where artist Clementine Hunter lived and painted her colorful primitive paintings. At Isle Brevelle walk into St. Augustine Catholic Church, the first Roman Catholic church established by and for people of color in the United States. The church fair held the second weekend in October celebrates Creole culture. The **Cane River National Historical Park** (www.nps.gov) south of town features two properties, Oakland Plantation and the complex

at Magnolia Plantation, which have numerous original outbuildings and artifacts.

Natchitoches also is known at the City of Lights. From November 21 through New Year, the city's Festival of Lights draws thousands of visitors. Thousands of lights illuminate the town and Cane River Lake. There's music and fireworks every weekend. RVers start rolling into town at least one week before the opening date, and hotel reservations go fast. If you decide to visit during the festival, keep in mind you don't have to be there for opening night festivities. It's amazingly beautiful throughout the season. Contact the Natchitoches Convention and Visitors Commission at www.natchitoches.net or (800) 259-1714.

i Toledo Bend Reservoir, the largest man-made lake in the South, was formed by a dam on the Sabine River, which runs along the western Louisiana border with Texas. Seven public boat launches and multiple private marinas surround the 186,000-acre lake filled with largemouth bass, bream, catfish, and crappies. It can be reached from I-10 in south Louisiana or I-20 in north Louisiana. Louisiana state parks on the reservoir include South Toledo Bend State Park, 120 Bald Eagle Road at Anacoco, (888) 398-4770; and North Toledo Bend State Park, 2907 N. Toledo Park Rd., Zowlle, (888) 677-6400. Contact the Toledo Bend Reservoir and Tourist Center, 150 Texas Hwy., Many, (800) 259-5253, www .srala-toledo.com. Located near the southern end of the lake is Hodges Garden, 1000 Hodges Loop at Florien, with 40 acres of landscaped gardens, a 225-acre bass fishing lake, and miles of hiking and biking trails. Call (800) 354-3523.

SHREVEPORT AND BOSSIER CITY

Shreveport and Bossier City are "Louisiana's Other Side." Situated in the center of the Ark-La-Tex area, the towns share a heritage with Texas and Arkansas. Visitors find a mix of wide-open Texas spirit, spicy Cajun influences, and Arkansas homespun attitudes. The twin cities on the Red River in northwest Louisiana are situated at the crossroads of I-20 and I-49. From Baton Rouge take I-10 west to Lafayette and follow I-49 north. The trip takes about four and a half hours.

The Red River has always been the center of activities here. Shreveport was founded in 1836 by the Shreve Town Company as the meeting point of the river and the Texas Trail. The river was cleared and made navigable for commerce by Captain Henry Miller Shreve. During the Civil War it was a Confederate stronghold and briefly became the Confederate capital. **Barksdale Air Force Base**, which opened in 1933 as Barksdale Army Air Field in Bossier City, is a major military facility. A museum on base displays exhibits on U.S. Air Force history and military aircraft. Call to request a tour, (318) 752-0055.

The advent of riverboat gambling in the mid-1990s spurred revitalization of downtown, which is still the heart of the city. Casino hopping is a sport in Shreveport. Five casinos offer 24-hour action. Each has its own flair and brings in Las Vegas–style entertainment. They include **Sam's Town Hotel & Casino** (315 Clyde Fant Memorial Parkway, 877-429-0711, www.samstownshreve port) in Shreveport, and **DiamondJacks Casino Resort** (711 Diamondjacks Blvd., 318-678-7777, www.diamondjacks.com), **Eldorado Casino Resort Horseshoe Hotel & Casino** (711 Horse-shoe Blvd., 800-895-0711, www.horseshoeboss iercity.com), **Boomtown Casino** (300 Riverside Drive, 318-746-0711, www.boomtownbossier .com), and **Harrah's Louisiana Downs** (8000 East Texas St., 318-752-6500, www.harrahslouisi anadowns.com), a horse track and casino, all in Bossier City. The casino hotels are first class and several have top-notch meeting facilities that cater to groups.

Break away from the slots and gaming tables and explore. There's a lot to see on a two- or three-day visit. The **Robinson Film Center** (617 Texas St., 318-424-9090, www.robinsonfilmcenter .org), in the West Edge Arts District, highlights independent, international, and classic cinema and features Abby Singer's Bistro. The **Stage of Stars Museum** (705 Elvis Presley Ave., 318-220-9434) inside the historic Municipal Auditorium features memorabilia from the heyday of *Louisiana Hayride*, the radio show broadcast from the auditorium from the 1940s to the 1970s. One of the most beloved stars to get his start here was Elvis Presley. A handsome bronze statue of Elvis greets visitors, as well as one of James Burton, a local guitar legend who played on the *Hayride* and in Elvis's band. With a nod to the city's star appeal, Shreveport-Bossier recently launched the first film trail in Louisiana. More than 70 movies have been filmed in the area. Shreveport locations have doubled for Kansas City, Miami, Boston, Paris, and many more. Pick up a brochure in your hotel or at the visitor center to make the tour.

i Shreveport was the home of the world-renowned bluesman Huddie Ledbetter, more commonly known by his stage name, "Leadbelly." This is the man who famously "sang" his way out of state prisons in Texas and Louisiana by composing songs for the sitting governors. He is memorialized in a life-size statue along Texas Street in downtown Shreveport, although his gravesite is northwest of the city at Shiloh Baptist Church near Mooringsport.

Shreveport is beautiful in spring and fall. Visit the **Gardens of the American Rose Center** (8877 Jefferson Paige Rd.) to view thousands of roses blooming in season. At the **R. W. Norton Art Gallery** (4747 Creswell Ave, 318-865-4201), there's a wonderful collection of European and American art. View the subtle colors and detail in Western paintings by Frederic Remington and Charles M. Russell. The **Southern University Museum of Art** (610 Texas St., 318-670-6634) is on Louisiana's African American Trail and features outstanding African masks and sculptures and works by African-American artists.

A Higher Ground: Cheniers

The Creole Nature Trail All-American Road takes you through much of Louisiana's Chenier Plain. *Chenier* is French for oak tree, and the trees are the backbone of Louisiana's cheniers (ridges). According to the Trail's official Web site, www.creole naturetrail.org, the wooded sandy ridges formed thousands of years ago through a combination of silt deposits from shifting river deltas and Gulf of Mexico currents that trapped these deposits, isolating strips of sandy beaches. Over time these isolated or "stranded" beaches became ridges. Hardwood trees—especially live oaks—took root and grew in abundance. Although the highest cheniers are only 10 feet above sea level, this critical extra height made settlement possible. In addition to hunting and fishing, residents raise cattle that graze in the marsh during the winter when the insects are few and then graze on the ridges in summer when insects fill the marsh. Cheniers are vital to Louisiana's Outback because:

- They are a first-line defense against the devastation of tropical storms.

- They help block saltwater intrusion into freshwater marshes.

- They provide habitat for many species of area wildlife.

- They are the first stop in Louisiana's Outback for many migratory birds.

Take the kids to the **Sci-Port: Louisiana's Science Center** (820 Clyde Fant Parkway, 318-424-3466) and giggle with them. The center boasts 90 hands-on exhibits in space science, astronomy, and math. Land a space shuttle at one of the simulators or view the Milky Way. Maybe you'll catch a demonstrator dissecting a shark in BodyWorks. Learn about the Red River's ecosystems and check out the terrariums with frogs, turtles, snakes, and alligators.

Dining and shopping are plentiful in Shreveport and Bossier. The Louisiana Boardwalk in Bossier City has more than 60 shops, including Gap, Guess, Nike, Chico's, and Banana Republic. Bass Pro Shop is the anchor for the center on the Red River. Be sure to check out Chocolate Crocodile for fine chocolates and caramels. Riverfront eateries include the Saltgrass Steak House and Buffalo Wild Wings. Line Avenue has long been popular for finding fine antiques and specialty gifts. **Wine Country Bistro and Bottle Shop** (4801 Line Ave., 318-629-9463) offers excellent food and wines at reasonable prices. Other popular restaurants are **Fertita's Delicatessen** (318-424-5508) and **Columbia Cafe** (3030 Creswell St., 318-425-3862) in a renovated 1932 building and boasting seasonal contemporary cuisine.

Shreveport and Bossier City have great annual festivals, including Mardi Gras parades, the Mudbug Madness Festival on Memorial Day weekend, and Red River Revel in October. For complete information from the **Shreveport/ Bossier Convention and Tourist Bureau**, visit www.shreveport-bossier.org or call (888) 646-8328.

LIVING HERE

In this section we feature specific information for residents or those planning to relocate here. Topics include real estate, education, health care, and much more.

RELOCATION AND REAL ESTATE

Baton Rouge appeals to residents on many levels. A friendly and relaxed atmosphere prevails, and rich traditions create a sense of pride. You'll discover people who are passionate about family, food, and football. Distinctive cultures have created a colorful patchwork of personalities. The blend of Spanish, English, French, German, Italian, African-American, and Asian cultures creates culinary, musical, and artistic traditions like few other places in the country. Southern University and Louisiana State University, both major land grant institutions, provide a healthy academic atmosphere for highly acclaimed scientists and researchers who bring their knowledge and expertise to the community. The Pennington Biomedical Research Center is one of the world's leading nutrition research institutes. It boasts several outstanding business incubators. Baton Rouge is economically diverse and business-friendly. People often visit Baton Rouge for the culture and history, but they return or stay because they have fallen in love with the people and the atmosphere. Local youth often leave to find their fortunes in faraway places, but many return for the gumbo and the aromatic coffee and to reconnect with previous generations who decided to call this home.

The capital region has expanded rapidly following Hurricane Katrina in 2005. There was a boom in the residential and retail sectors. New restaurants and entertainment venues gave a boost to the downtown scene. The nation's 2009 economic downturn slowed the growth a bit, but despite the slump, Baton Rouge's economy has remained relatively stable. Some companies announced layoffs, but others are holding their own and investing in future projects. City-parish government remains committed to a bold vision of the future.

REAL ESTATE

Real estate in the Baton Rouge region continues to hold its own despite conditions in other markets around the country. Sandy Davis, immediate past president of the Greater Baton Rouge Association of Realtors, is confident that low interest rates and the 2009 federal tax incentives have boosted the local market. "We have not seen a huge downturn in the market," said Davis. "The first-time homebuyer's tax credit [$8,000] was a shot in the arm. It kept the market stable."

In addition Davis said the $6,500 credit offered to current homeowners in 2009 let people who were downsizing or seeking new construction get into the market "The other side of the tax credits is that so much of the money goes back into the local pot," said Davis, a realtor with C. J. Brown. It helps keep the economy strong."

Davis said, "We haven't had a lot of foreclosures, and our employment has been somewhat stable. We should be able to continue for the next few years as we have in the past few years. Without any unforeseen downturns the real estate market should be steady as it goes," she said. "One thing people should know—those of us who live in the greater Baton Rouge area are fortunate to have quality homes, and sellers get good value for their homes."

Pat Wattam, realtor with RE/MAX First, said, "Baton Rouge is one of the most affordable cities in the United States. The state's homestead exemption saves on property taxes. We also have a wide price range and diversity of homes.

"You can enjoy the outdoors year-round in Baton Rouge because of the weather," continued Wattam. "You can play tennis, golf, or soccer and enjoy hiking in the Tunica Hills. You also can find a festival or something to do every weekend. Think of the quality of life. You have all the conveniences of a medium city and the setting of a large city."

i Neighborhood streets in Baton Rouge are often named after antebellum plantations that once thrived along the Mississippi River corridor. Other streets are named for 18th-, 19th-, and 20th-century military heroes and politicians.

Real Estate Agents

BURNS & COMPANY
17400 Memorial Ave.
(225) 752-3100
www.burnsandco.com
This locally owned company, established in 1993, assists first-time homebuyers to those seeking landmark properties. Emphasis is placed on cutting-edge technology. The relocation department will arrange for a comprehensive tour of the region.

CENTURY 21 INVESTMENT REALTY
2435 Drusilla Lane
(225) 291-2121
www.c21ir.com
This franchise firm was founded in 1997 and has been the number one Century 21 in the state of Louisiana for the past six years. It assists clients in seeking fine homes and estates, recreational properties, commercial land, and property management in Louisiana and Mississippi.

C. J. BROWN REALTORS (A LATTER & BLUM COMPANY)
4324 Sherwood Forest Blvd.
(225) 292-1000
www.chbrown.com
Established in New Orleans in 1916, this company is the largest full-service brokerage company in the Gulf South. Agents handle all phases of residential and commercial real estate sales and leasing.

COLDWELL BANKER MACKEY
4111 South Sherwood Forest Blvd.
(225) 292-8230
www.coldwellbanker.com
Founded by Marge and Ralph Mackey in 1975, this locally owned company represents buyers and sellers alike. Some 250 trained associates assist clients in residential and commercial needs as well as relocation.

COLDWELL BANKER ONE
5025 Bluebonnet Blvd.
(225) 925-2500
www.coldwellbankerone.com
Founded in 1945, this company affiliated with Coldwell Banker in 2003 and in 2007 became Coldwell Banker Phelps and McKey. It then joined Saurage Realty to become Coldwell Banker One. Agents serve clients in Baton Rouge, Ascension Parish, East Baton Rouge, East Feliciana, Iberville, Livingston, Pointe Coupee, St. Helena, West Baton Rouge, and West Feliciana parishes.

EAST BANK REALTY
2014 South Burnside Ave., Gonzales
(225) 647-5337
www.eastbankrealty.com
East Bank Realty handles both residential and commercial properties. It focuses on keeping abreast of trends, property values, and schools. Agents specialize in Ascension, Livingston, East Baton Rouge, and West Baton Rouge parishes as well as the towns of Saint Amant and Sorrento.

ERA STIRLING PROPERTIES
9247 Bluebonnet Blvd., Suite B
(225) 757-0709
www.erastirling.com
Affiliated with a national real estate company, ERA Stirling helps clients with single and family dwellings as well as condo, townhouse, commercial and industrial, land, lease, and co-op properties. The company maintains a working relationship with Platinum Title and AHS Home Warranty.

KELLER WILLIAMS REALTY–RED STICK PARTNERS
8686 Bluebonnet Blvd.
(225) 768-1800
www.kw.com

Founded in 2000, this franchise company considers service to the client as its primary goal. Agents represent both residential and commercial properties as well as some land.

KELLER WILLIAMS REALTY—RED STICK PLUS
19850 Old Scenic Hwy, Suite 100, Zachary
(225) 570-2900

LATTER & BLUM COMPANIES
10455 Jefferson Hwy, Suite 200
(225) 295-0800
www.latter-blum.com

Latter & Blum, which started in 1916 in New Orleans, is the largest full-service real estate brokerage in the Gulf South. Agents assist clients in Lafayette, Shreveport, Baton Rouge, and the Mississippi Gulf Coast.

M. A. ALLEN REALTY GROUP
1208 South Range Ave., Denham Springs
(225) 665-8654
www.maallen.com

Some 60 agents with this firm are committed to providing professional service to clients round the clock. They specialize in both residential and commercial real estate. The company offers 24-hour phone service.

PRUDENTIAL GARDNER REALTORS
3888 South Sherwood Forest Blvd., Suite T
(225) 296-0500
www.prudentialgardner.com

With roots in New Orleans starting in 1945, this brokerage firm specializes in southeast Louisiana and southern Mississippi. The company takes pride in being a one-stop shop offering comprehensive services.

RE/MAX FIRST
4750 Sherwood Common Blvd.
(225) 291-1234
www.brhomesfirst.com

Associated with one of the most recognized real estate companies in the United States, this franchise company specializes in personal service. The firm does business in Baton Rouge, Gonzales, Maurepas, and Denham Springs.

i *The Park adjacent to the Municipal Building in Baker includes playground equipment donated by entertainer Rosie O'Donnell's Foundation and a Veteran's Plaza built with memorial donations.*

INFORMATION FOR NEWCOMERS

If you are new to the Baton Rouge region, here are some things you should know:

Auto and Driver's License

Permanent residents of Louisiana must obtain a Louisiana driver's license and obtain a plate within 30 days of establishing residency. Drivers with valid out-of-state licenses need only pass the vision exam. First-time drivers must be at least 17 years old to apply for a personal driver's license, and must pass a written test, driving test, and vision exam. The cost is approximately $36.50 for a four-year license, although fees vary from parish to parish. Only cash, cashier's check, or money order is accepted. Contact the Louisiana Office of Motor Vehicles for more information on driver's license and registration, (887) 368-5463. Online renewal can be obtained at www.expresslane.org.

Auto Inspection Stickers

Louisiana residents' vehicles are required to pass annual motor vehicle safety inspections. Individuals with vehicles registered in Ascension, East Baton Rouge, Iberville, Livingston, and West Baton Rouge parishes must be inspected in their parish. The cost is $18. Numerous dealers and service stations throughout the parish conduct automobile inspections. Check "Automobile Inspection Stations" in the Yellow Pages.

Law Enforcement

Law enforcement agencies in East Baton Rouge Parish often rely on the public to report crimes and provide arrests. Residents can call authorities to report suspicious activity or let them know what they might have seen or heard regarding a crime. Those who want to remain anonymous can call Crime Stoppers of Baton Rouge at (225) 344-STOP. If the information provided by a resident leads to an arrest or an indictment, the person can receive a reward of up to $1,000.

In addition to arrests, the law enforcement agencies also work to reduce crime by patrolling streets and providing crime-prevention counseling to the public. On its Web site, http://brgov .com/dept/brpd, the Baton Rouge Police Department suggests residents "stay alert and tuned in to your surroundings" for personal safety. In addition to safety tips, the site provides answers to frequently asked questions about everything from alarm permits to curfew for teenagers. If you want to view the incidences of crime in your neighborhood, visit the department's Crime Statistics page at http://brgov.com/dept/brpd/csr. The statistics are not in real time but are compiled and categorized using standards set by the FBI Uniform Crime Reporting program.

The cities of Baker and Zachary have their own police departments, as do LSU and Southern University. There are also several federal law enforcement agencies in Baton Rouge.

Louisiana State Police is headquartered in Baton Rouge. The statewide law enforcement agency patrols the state's highways and investigates criminal activity.

Voter Registration

To register to vote in Louisiana, you must be a citizen of the United States and a resident of the state, parish, and city in which you want to vote. You also must be at least 17 years old, and 18 years old prior to the next election. You currently cannot be under an order of imprisonment or conviction

of a felony or under a judgment of interdiction for mental incompetence. You may apply at any of the following state offices: Registrar of Voters, Motor Vehicle, Social Services, WIC, Food Stamp, Medicaid, offices serving persons with disabilities, armed forces recruitment centers, or by mail. You must be registered at least 30 days prior to be eligible to vote in the next election. For information contact the office of the Louisiana Secretary of State, (225) 342-4479 or www.soslouisiana.gov.

Economic and Demographic Information

Anyone considering relocation to Baton Rouge or current residents seeking information on the city's economic base and demographics can choose from a number of sources. To start, the Baton Rouge Area Chamber is an excellent source for a wide range of information in a nine-parish area surrounding the city of Baton Rouge. The chamber's Web site not only offers a Business Guide but information that every resident will need from time to time, including a list of resources, from technical assistance providers to other facilities. The site also includes information on quality of life and a list of regional events. Contact the www.brac.org or (225) 381-7125.

Other local agencies and resources can help newcomers with information about licenses and permits, selected laws, advice, and assistance.

i Baton Rouge is located at the convergence of the swamplands and marshes to the south and upland forests to the north. As a result the city has a luxurious tree canopy with most Southeastern trees in evidence.

BATON ROUGE CITY-PARISH
www.brgov.com
Baton Rouge City-Parish government has a comprehensive Web site that offers demographic details. Click on "search" then "demographics" and get info on population, employment, income, housing, and more.

Helpful Numbers (225 Area Code)

Quick Reference
General Emergency 9-1-1
Baton Rouge Police 389-2000
EBR Parish Sheriff 389-5073
State Police 754-8500
Poison Control 800-256-9822

Getting Connected
Energy 800-386-3749
Baton Rouge Water Company 925-2011
EBR Parish Sewer 389-5378
Trash Pickup 778-3800
Recycling 925-3442

Tourism
BR Convention and Visitors Bureau 383-1825
BREC (Recreation and Parks) 272-9200
Capitol Park Welcome Center 219-1200
Louisiana Office of Tourism 342-8100
Louisiana State Parks 342-1111

LOUISIANA ECONOMIC DEVELOPMENT
www.louisianaforward.com
(800) 450-8115, (225) 342-3000

As the State of Louisiana's economic development department, LED serves as an information clearinghouse on economic indicators, parish profiles, demographic statistics, infrastructure and industrial data, and contact information on local economic development assistance. The department provides detailed information for businesses interested in locating and expanding in Louisiana.

LSU OFFICE OF ECONOMIC DEVELOPMENT AND FORECASTING
130 David F. Boyd Hall
(225) 578-5833
www.bus.lsu.edu/centers/ded

A team of internationally recognized professors continually updates information available to the public. Check out the Web site for its published newsletter *LSU Research*, www.research.lsu.edu.

LIBRARIES

The East Baton Rouge Parish library system is the largest public library system in Louisiana. It is exceptional and features attractive, comfortable facilities throughout the parish. It offers a main library, 12 community and regional libraries, and a bookmobile. Each of the libraries provides books, journals, videotapes, audiocassettes, CDs, DVDs, paintings, and sculptures. Patrons also have access to the library's online catalog where they can renew library materials. Computer classes are offered for free. Libraries also offer adult services that include a summer reading program and workshops.

Children's services include story times, arts, crafts, and more. Teenagers can take advantage of Young Adult Services, which provides information for school projects. Financial aid workshops and practice tests for the ACT college entrance exam are offered, as are volunteer math tutors.

Libraries also feature year-round scheduled programs, speakers, workshops, and seminars for people of all ages.

The Main Library (7711 Goodwood Blvd., 225-231-3740) is located near the geographical center of Baton Rouge. For more information visit www.ebr.lib.la.us.

The Louisiana State Library (707 North Fourth St.), in the Capitol Complex area downtown, operates under the state's Department of Culture, Recreation, and Tourism. It contains books, magazines, newspapers, state and federal documents, and audiovisual materials. The Louisiana section houses a comprehensive collection. The library also provides books and magazines in large print for the blind and physically disabled, as well as Braille and recorded formats. The library provides free public access to the Internet and offers an online database of videotapes. Books can be checked out by state employees. The general public can request books through their local branch library. The State Library also sponsors the acclaimed Louisiana Book Festival, free to the public each fall. Call (225) 219-4804.

MEDIA

A city of politicians, educators, and business leaders, Baton Rouge has a population that likes to keep tuned to the latest news. It doesn't take long to discover which newspaper, television show, or radio station you prefer. Like many who live here, you may choose to follow several sources in keeping up with the latest developments.

Louisiana's lively political climate is daily conversation. News is constantly being generated by the Louisiana state government, the City-Parish Council, and federal agencies. Academic and sports activities at Louisiana State University and Southern University, along with entertainment and art, keep people involved. Pick up a copy of *The Advocate* or one of the smaller magazines or newspapers that focus on a particular segment of the population, or tune in to a local TV or radio news program.

Newspaper

THE ADVOCATE
7290 Bluebonnet Blvd.
(225) 383-1111
www.2theadvocate.com

The Advocate, founded by Charles P. Manship in 1925, is published by Capital City Press. The Manship family continues to maintain ownership of the daily newspaper and other media outlets. In addition to local, state, national, and international news, *The Advocate* covers sports, business, and entertainment. Pick up a copy of the Friday edition for the Fun Section's listing of what's happening in and around Baton Rouge. The company's online division, www.2theadvocate.com, maintains a daily update on events.

Magazines

BATON ROUGE 225 MAGAZINE
9029 Jefferson Hwy
(225) 928-1700
www.batonrouge.com
Published by Louisiana Business Inc., *Baton Rouge 225 Magazine* is a savvy monthly magazine that appeals to youthful movers and shakers in the community. Its cutting-edge coverage includes entertainment and style.

BATON ROUGE BUSINESS REPORT
9029 Jefferson Hwy, Suite 300
(225) 928-1700
www.businessreport.com
The *Baton Rouge Business Report*, published every two weeks, is a product of Louisiana Business Inc. This award-winning publication covers Baton Rouge business, political, and community news. It's available at some 80 locations around town, and the newsstand price is $2.25. Also check out www.daily-report.com.

BATON ROUGE PARENTS MAGAZINE
11831 Wentling Ave.
(225) 292-0032
www.brparents.com
This quarterly magazine is an excellent source for parents. Coverage includes latest news on child care, health, safety, and family life. Also included are stories about family-friendly community events and activities.

CITY SOCIAL INC.
4415 South Sherwood Forest Blvd.
(225) 292-0445
www.citysocial.com
This colorful monthly magazine covers people and places from St. Francisville to the north shore of Lake Pontchartrain. Look for articles on social events, community trends, food, fashion, fitness, and health.

COUNTRY ROADS MAGAZINE
728 France St.
(225) 343-3714
www.countryroadsmagazine.com
This monthly magazine reports on cultural life in the Great River Road region between Natchez, Mississippi, and New Orleans. Created in 1983 by publisher Dorcas Brown, it is now produced by Brown's daughter Ashley Fox-Smith and her husband, James Fox-Smith. Country Roads contains an extensive calendar of events (small and large) held throughout the region. Articles include restaurant and accommodation news, day and weekend trips, and profiles of regional artists, crafters, and other personalities. Distributed widely, Country Roads is free and easy to find in shops and stores the first few days of each month.

INREGISTER
9029 Jefferson Hwy
(225) 924-5253
www.inregister.com
Established in 1989, this social magazine covers everything from gala fundraisers to garden parties and fashion. Look for interesting profiles on local personalities. Available at bookstores, newsstands, and drugstores.

Radio Stations

With some 30 radio stations in Baton Rouge, you could stay up all night listening to country and western, jazz, Cajun, zydeco, or classical music. Of course there are always sports and talk shows. Louisiana State University students and Baton Rouge Magnet High School students run the show on their respective FM stations. Radio DJs are always

a good source of inside information and know the latest about local clubs and eateries.

Christian/Gospel
KPAE 91.5 FM
13028 Hwy 190 West, Erwinville
(800) 324-1108
www.soundradio.org

WJFM 88.5 FM
(225) 768-3688
www.jsm.org

WTQT 94.9 FM
1755 Nicholson Drive
(225) 343-1075
www.wtqt.org

WXOK 1460 AM
650 Wooddale Ave.
(225) 499-1460
www.heaven1460.com

Contemporary/Rock
KLSU 91.FM
Hodges Hall, LSU Campus
(225) 578-5578
www.klsuradio.fm

WCDV (SUNNY) 103.3
650 Wooddale Ave.
(225) 499-1033
www.sunny1033.com

WDGL 98.1 FM
929 Government St.
(225) 499-9898
www.eagle981.com

WFMF 102.5 FM
5555 Hilton Ave.
(225) 231-1860
www.wfmf.com

Country
WTGE 107.3 FM
929 Government St.
(225) 388-9898
www.countrylegends1073.com

WYNK 101.5 FM
5555 Hilton Ave.
(225) 488-9965
www.wynk.com

WYPY 100.7 FM
929 Government St.
(225) 388-9898
www.tigercountry1007.com

Hip-Hop
WEMX 94.1 FM
650 Wooddale Ave.
(225) 499-9410
www.max94one.com

Public Radio
WBRH 90.3 FM
Baton Rouge Magnet High
2825 Government St.
(225) 383-3243
www.baton-rouge.com/wbrh

WRKF 89.3 FM
3050 Valley Creek Drive
(225) 231-9448
www.wrkf.org

Oldies/Rhythmic
KBRH 1260 AM
Baton Rouge Magnet High
2825 Government St.
(225) 387-1260

Sports
WIBR (ESPN) 1300 AM
650 Woodale Ave.
(225) 499-1300
www.radiotime.com

Talk/News
WJBO 1150 AM
5555 Hilton Ave.
499-9526
www.wfmf.com

Television
Television in Baton Rouge is lively and competitive. City residents benefit from having stations affiliated with the country's major networks: ABC, CBS, NBC, and FOX. The news teams of these channels are experienced professional journalists who provide thorough and well-balanced news to the community. In addition Baton Rouge is home of WLPB, the Louisiana Public Broadcasting channel that has produced many award-winning topical and educational features. Cox Communications (7401 Florida Blvd., 225-615-2000) offers comprehensive cable service. Satellite service is also available.

WAFB (CHANNEL 9) CBS AFFILIATE
844 Government St.
(225) 383-9999
www.wafb.com

WBRZ (CHANNEL 2) ABC AFFILIATE
1650 Highland Rd.
(225) 387-2222
www.wbrz.com, www.2theadvocate.com

WGMB (FOX 44)
(225) 766-1463
www.fox44.com

WLPB (CHANNEL 27) LOUISIANA PUBLIC BROADCASTING
7860 Anselmo Lane
(800) 272-8161
http://beta.lpb.org

WVLA (CHANNEL 33) NBC AFFILIATE
10000 Perkins Road
(225) 768-9195
www.nbc33tv.com

WORSHIP

Baton Rouge chapels and churches are as varied as its culture. From small wood-frame houses of worship to large, impressive temples, there are numerous places from which to choose.

i The churches in downtown Baton Rouge join in an annual evening Christian carol pilgrimage featuring most of the congregations and their choirs. In addition to their regular services, several of the churches also serve as venues for serious music concerts throughout the year.

Interfaith Cooperation

The leading ecumenical group is the Interfaith Federation of Greater Baton Rouge (3112 Convention St., 225-267-5600). The federation brings together different congregations for service projects and community dialog.

Catholicism

Catholicism in south Louisiana is deeply rooted in French and Spanish influences and remains one of the largest religious influences in the area today. The Catholic Diocese of Baton Rouge is housed at the Catholic Life Center on Acadian Thruway. The Baton Rouge Diocese covers 11 civil parishes. For information about parish churches and schools, visit www.diobr.org. People from various denominations participate in a Stations of the Cross walk on Good Friday each year. The walk is sponsored by St. Joseph's Cathedral and Catholic Community Services. The Cathedral also is the site of a Christmas music concert each year presented by the Baton Rouge Symphony Brass Ensemble.

Catholic and Protestant Churches

To better understand the city's Christian population, as well as the community's religious history, visit the downtown churches. They include St. Joseph's Cathedral (412 North St., 225-387-5928); First United Methodist Church (930 North Blvd., 225-383-4777); First Presbyterian (763 North Blvd., 225-387-0617); St. James Episcopal (205 North Blvd., 225-387-5141); Mount Zion First Baptist Church (356 East Blvd., 383-5401); and First Baptist Church (529 Convention St., 225-343-0397). A number of these churches are historic landmarks.

Some of the area's larger churches include Shiloh Missionary Baptist Church (185 Eddie Robinson Sr. Drive, 225-342-0640); Bethany World Prayer Center (11107 Honore Lane, 225-293-2100); the Healing Place Church (19202 Highland Rd., 225-753-2273); Jefferson Baptist Church (9135 Jefferson Hwy, 225-923-0356); and Istrouma Baptist Church (I-12 and Airline Hwy, 225-926-4800).

Islamic Life

An active Muslim community supports three mosque locations. The Islamic Center has locations at 820 West Chimes St. (225-387-3617) and 285 East Airport Ave. (225-924-0070). There also is the Islamic Complex (740 East Washington St., 225-338-0022). The Atlas Interfaith Foundation (7712 Goodwood Blvd., 225-923-8247) sponsors an annual interfaith sundown dinner during Ramadan, the Islamic holy month. The organization also has sent Louisiana residents on interfaith trips to Turkey.

Jewish Synagogues

Though the Baton Rouge Jewish population is relatively small, it supports two active reform synagogues: Congregation B'nai Israel (3354 Kleinert Ave., 225-343-0111) and Beth Shalom (9111 Jefferson Hwy, 225-924-6773).

Other Choices

The Church of Latter Day Saints and Mormon Temple (10335 Highland Rd., 225-761-9467) serves communities throughout Louisiana. The Religious Society of Friends (Quakers) welcomes visitors to its Sunday service in the Red Shoes building (2330 Government St., 225-665-3560). Unitarian Church (8470 Goodwood Blvd., 225-766-9474) is a progressive church with creative programs for children and adults. The Vietnamese Buddhist temple, Tam Bao Temple (975 Monterrey Blvd., 225-248-8263) has Mindfulness Meditation Hall, which is open for use by anyone seeking a place to meditate. The Church of Scientology Mission of Baton Rouge (9432 Common St., 225-928-7804) offers programs about Dianetics. Hindu temples include Hindu Samaj Temple, 6406 Quin Drive, (225) 753-3000; and Data Temple, 6221 Equity Drive, (225) 769-8671. The Baha'i Faith of Baton Rouge is at 4270 Perkins Road, (225) 769-8671.

EDUCATION AND CHILD CARE

Baton Rouge offers numerous education opportunities. The state's major institutions of higher learning, Louisiana State University and Southern University, draw thousands of students annually. The city also is home to Baton Rouge Community College and a campus of Louisiana Community and Technical College, which offers two-year programs and other types of training.

Parents seeking schools for youngsters from pre-K through 12th grade can choose between numerous private schools and the public school system. This includes all the schools in the entire parish, except for the towns of Central, Zachary, and Baker, which have their own school districts. Child care facilities vary from nationally recognized child care centers to independent early learning schools.

HIGHER EDUCATION

Baton Rouge is home to both of the state's flagship universities, Louisiana State University and Agriculture and Mechanical College, and the main campus of Southern University, the only historically black university system in the United States. The two have a combined student population of nearly 40,000. Baton Rouge Community College has a student population of more than 7,000. These institutions offer an exciting range of educational opportunities, options for postgraduate studies, and continuing education. Area residents participate in cultural and sports events at the universities. The faculties, staffs, and students create a youthful atmosphere in the city, to say nothing of their fresh ideas and new approaches to modern living.

BATON ROUGE COMMUNITY COLLEGE
201 Community College Drive
(225) 216-8000
www.mybrc.edu
Baton Rouge Community College is an open-admissions two-year institution offering academic programs that prepare students for transfer to four-year institutions. Students can acquire associate degrees in such subjects as computer information science, criminal justice,

general studies, liberal arts, and nursing. Certificate programs enable students to renew or establish employable skills that allow them to enter the workforce. The college accepts graduates of a state-approved high school, individuals who have obtained the General Equivalency Diploma (GED), or individuals who are 18 or older. High school students who are at least 16 may be admitted through concurrent enrollment, which allows them to register for a maximum of two college courses simultaneously with their high school courses. The college is accredited by the Commission on Colleges of the Southern Association of Colleges and Schools.

LOUISIANA STATE UNIVERSITY
(225) 578-3202
www.lsu.edu
Louisiana State University and Agriculture and Mechanical College, more commonly known as LSU, has long been recognized for distinctive educational programs that are rooted in the unique cultural history and geography of Louisiana. The state's flagship institution is located on more than 2,000 acres of land south of downtown Baton Rouge and bordered on the west by the Mississippi River. A majority of buildings on the main campus were built between 1925 and 1940. Their Italian Renaissance character is defined by red pan-

tile roofs, overhanging roofs, and honey-colored stucco. Grounds landscaped with oaks, magnolias, azaleas, and native plantings are recognized nationally for their artistic appeal.

The university is accredited by the Commission on Colleges of the Southern Association of Colleges and Schools to award bachelor's, master's, doctoral, and professional degrees. LSU is one of only 21 universities nationwide designated as a land-grant, sea-grant, and space-grant institution. The university achieved top tier ranking in *U.S. News & World Report*'s Best National Universities 2009 list. Also in 2009 the LSU Robert S. Reich School of Landscape Architecture was ranked among the top five schools in the nation by *DesignIntelligence,* the leading journal of design professionals.

LSU is the only public university in Louisiana designated as having very high research activity by the Carnegie Foundation for the Advancement of Teaching, the highest ranking awarded to doctorate-granting institutions. LSU's schools and degree programs are increasingly landing near the top of national rankings. The Flores MBA program of the E. J. Ourso College of Business has been ranked in the nation's top 10 by the *Wall Street Journal* among schools that draw corporate recruiters regionally.

In 2008 LSU was one of only two universities in the nation to produce the combination of a Truman Scholar, four Goldwater Scholars, and a *USA Today* All-USA College Academic First Team member. In addition four LSU students have also been selected as Presidential Management Fellows. LSU's list of prominent alumni and former students is long indeed. Included are Eduardo Aguire Jr., appointed U.S. Ambassador to Spain in 2005; Dr. James Andrews, world-renowned orthopedic surgeon and founder of the American Sports Medicine Institute; James Carville, author, media personality, and chief political strategist for President Bill Clinton's 1992 campaign; Bill Conti, Academy Award–winning composer who has written theme music for television programs and movies, including *Rocky* and its sequels; Mary Landrieu, first female U.S. senator from Louisiana; Steven Soderbergh, Academy Award–winning director for film,

including *Sex, Lies and Videotape, Erin Brokovich*, and the *Ocean's Eleven* franchise; and Shaquille O'Neal, four-time NBA Champion, three-time NBA MVP, and center for the Cleveland Cavaliers.

LSU is equally famous for its Tigers athletic teams, with the football team taking two BCS championships and the baseball team winning six national championships in Omaha. Women's basketball, field and track, and gymnastics continually place among the tops in the country. LSU's spirit extends far beyond the playing field. Walk across the campus, stop by the Student Union, and mingle with the students and faculty. You'll find a sense of discovery and enthusiasm is generated here that sticks with people for the rest of their lives. To send mail to the campus, address a specific department, such as "Office of Admissions, Louisiana State University, 70803.

OUR LADY OF THE LAKE COLLEGE
7434 Perkins Rd.
(225) 768-1700
www.ololcollege-edu.org
Our Lady of the Lake College evolved from the founding of Our Lady of the Lake School of Nursing, established in 1923 by the Franciscan Missionaries of Our Lady. Accredited by the Southern Association of Colleges and Schools, the college confers master's, bachelor's, and associate's degrees in 21 academic areas and offers 8 technical programs through the Health Career Institute. In 2009 the college restructured its degree programs to include a new bachelor of arts program in liberal studies. Human medicine and forensic science degree programs were redesigned as concentrations within a revised bachelor's degree in biology. The college currently occupies nine buildings near the intersection of Essen Lane and Perkins Road, near Our Lady of the Lake Regional Medical Center in South Baton Rouge.

SOUTHERN UNIVERSITY
(225) 771-1512
www.sus.edu
The Southern University and Agriculture and Mechanical College System has become the only historically black university system in America. The

school opened its doors in 1880 in New Orleans with 12 students, five faculty, and a budget totaling $10,000. In 1914 the university was relocated to Baton Rouge. The same year, a public law school also was opened at this site. Today the Southern system offers 86 baccalaureate degree programs, 23 associate degrees, and 12 certificate programs. Although most programs are offered at the undergraduate level, the university currently offers 26 master's degrees, one post master, one professional, and five doctoral degree programs. The University Law Center (SULC) graduates the majority of Louisiana's African-American lawyers.

Southern University provides opportunities for students to do internships and summer assignments in industry and the federal government. Southern also is home to the Timbuktu Academy, a national model program for mentoring students in science, math, engineering, and technology.

The Southern sports teams, the Jaguars, have thrilled fans for years. Among notable athletes who attended Southern are Mel Blount, Pro Football Hall of Fame defensive back for the Pittsburgh Steelers; Harold Carmichael, an NFL player and four-time Pro-Bowler who played 14 years for the Philadelphia Eagles and Dallas Cowboys; Willie Davenport, two-time gold medalist of the U.S. Olympic Track Team; and Rodney Milburn, track and field gold medalist at the 1972 Munich Olympic Games.

Other notable alumni include: Alvin Batiste, renowned jazz artist and educator; Isiah Carey, television news reporter; Randy Jackson, musician, record producer, and *American Idol* judge; Branford Marsalis, jazz saxophonist; and Melvin "Kip" Holden, mayor of Baton Rouge.

Along with athletes, the Southern University Human Jukebox marching band has been invited to participate in the Rose Parade in Pasadena, California; presidential inauguration ceremonies; and several Super Bowl halftime presentations. The band has appeared in television commercials and was once named the number one marching band in the United States by *USA Today*.

Visit the campus and its historic buildings. You will find enthusiastic students boldly meeting the challenges of today. To send mail, address items to specific departments such as Office of Admissions, Southern University, Baton Rouge, 70813.

UNIVERSITY OF PHOENIX
2431 South Acadian Thruway
(225) 927-4443
www.phoenix.edu
University of Phoenix began at San Jose University in California and opened its first campus in 1976 in Phoenix, Arizona. It now has campuses in 40 states. Specializing in online programs, Phoenix offers bachelor's, master's, and doctoral degrees as well as certificates. Students do some course work at the Baton Rouge campus as well as online studies. Visit the Web site and use the Campus Finder to learn more about the Baton Rouge location.

VOCATIONAL AND TECHNICAL COLLEGES AND SCHOOLS

DELTA COLLEGE OF ARTS AND TECHNOLOGY
7380 Exchange Place
(225) 927-9096
www.deltacollege.com/batonrouge
Delta College offers associate degrees and certificates in numerous fields, including practical nursing, medical assistant, medical office administration, business office administration, and graphic design. Day and evening classes are available. The school is accredited by Accrediting Commission of Career Schools and Colleges of Technology.

ITI TECHNICAL COLLEGE
13944 Airline Hwy.
(225) 752-4233
http://iticollege.edu
This technical school offers two-year associate's degrees in instrumentation and control systems, electrical technology, technical drafting, electronics technology, office administration, and more. Certificates include industrial instrumentation, electrical technology, air conditioning, electronics technology, and office administration. The school offers placement assistance and free remedial studies.

LOUISIANA CULINARY INSTITUTE
10550 Airline Hwy.
(225) 769-8792,
(225) 769-8820
http://louisianaculinary.com
Founded by E. Keith Rush in 2003, Louisiana Culinary Institute offers a 16-month associate's degree in Advanced Culinary Arts or Advanced Baking Pastry. Students can become certified in as many as five different areas of culinary arts and professional cooking. The institute is located in a new 28,500-square-foot facility with up-to-date classrooms, three demonstration labs, a restaurant kitchen, a project kitchen, a bakery demonstration, and an amphitheater with a residential kitchen.

LOUISIANA TECHNICAL COLLEGE
3250 Acadian Thruway East
(225) 359-9201
www.region2.ltc.edu
This technical school is governed by the Board of Supervisors and Board of Regents. Programs include accounting technology, air conditioning and refrigeration, automotive technology, barber styling, cosmetology, emergency medical technician, practical nursing, welding, drafting and design, and culinary arts occupations.

MEDICAL TRAINING COLLEGE
10525 Plaza Americana Dr.
(225) 926-5820
www.mtcbr
Licensed by the Louisiana State Board of Regents, the Medical Training College offers programs in dental assistant, massage therapy, medical assistant, and medical office specialist.

REMINGTON COLLEGE
10551 Coursey Blvd.
(225) 236-3200
www.remingtoncollege.edu
Remington confers an associate of science degree in business administration, computer and network administration, and criminal justice. Diplomas are available in electronic technology, medical assisting, medical insurance and coding, and pharmacy technician. The college has day and evening training sessions and a career services department.

PUBLIC SCHOOLS

EAST BATON ROUGE PARISH SCHOOL SYSTEM
1050 South Foster Dr.
(225) 922-5400
www.ebrpss.k12.la.us
East Baton Rouge Parish School System has 83 schools, several pre-K centers, and 11 nationally recognized blue ribbon schools. Programs offered include adult continuing education for students age 17 and up who are not enrolled in K–12 schools, with adult review of basic math, reading, and language and preparation for GED, ACT, SAT, and school entrance exams. Additionally the system includes three charter schools, English as a second language, extended day at selected sites, magnet schools, identified exceptional students in pre-K through 12th grades, and talented K–12 students in visual arts, theater, and music. The East Baton Rouge Laboratory Academy 9–12, supported by the Institute for Student Achievement, is a college preparatory school. Programs include extended instructional weeks and extended day for instruction.

Students are required to wear uniforms in all elementary schools (plain white top with a collar and navy bottoms) and in all middle schools (plain navy top with a collar and khaki bottoms). Pre-K students must be 4 years old on or before September 30 of the year entering school. Kindergarten students must be 5 years old on or before September 30 of the year entering school. To register a student in the East Baton Rouge Parish School System, parents need a withdrawal slip from their child's previous school, inoculation records, the student's Social Security number, and proof of present address.

For information on programs involving exceptional students, contact Exceptional Student Services, (225) 929-8600. For school ratings visit www.localschooldirectory.com/district-schools/017/east-baton-rouge-parish-school-board-district/la.

i For a number of years, the French language has been taught in public schools. More recently, immersion programs in French and Spanish have been made available to public school students. Middle and high schools offer instruction in French, Spanish, Latin, German, Russian, and Japanese at designated schools.

CENTRAL COMMUNITY SCHOOL SYSTEM
13421 Hooper Rd., Suite 6
(225) 262-1919
www.centralcss.org, www.centralgov.com
The Central Community School District was created in 2006 and is considered one of the fastest growing school systems in Louisiana. Schools include Bellingrath, Tanglewood, Central Intermediate, Central Middle, and Central High School. The enrollment has increased from 2,500 students to an expected 3,800 students for the 2009–10 school year. Students of Central achieved a high level of performance on the state's accountability tests in spring 2009. Eighty-eight percent of the students in fourth grade and 81 percent of eighth graders met promotional standards on state accountability tests.

CITY OF BAKER SCHOOL SYSTEM
3033 Ray Weiland Dr.
(225) 774-5795
http://bakerschools.org
The Baker School System includes three elementary schools, one middle school, and Baker High School. Combined with private schools, the area is known for families deeply concerned about their children's education. Baker High School is known for its wrestling team and its strong band program. Baker schools also have formed strong partnerships with area businesses. For ratings, visit www.localschooldirectory.com.

ZACHARY SCHOOL SYSTEM
4656 Main St., Zachary
(225) 658-4969
http://zacharyschools.org

The Zachary school district became independent from the East Baton Rouge Parish school district in 2004. The system includes Copperville, Northwestern Elementary, Zachary Elementary, Northwestern Middle School, and Zachary High School.

PRIVATE SCHOOLS AND ACADEMIES

BATON ROUGE LUTHERAN SCHOOL
10925 Florida Blvd.
(225) 272-1288
www.brlutheranschool.org
The Baton Rouge Lutheran School offers a curriculum for grades pre-K through 8 that meet or exceed Louisiana state standards. Traditional elementary classes offer math, science, English, art, music, and computer. All enrichment courses are not included for every grade level. No special education courses are offered, but the school will work with some selected students with special needs. Mandatory interview with parents and students.

CATHOLIC HIGH SCHOOL
855 Heatherstone Dr.
(225) 383-0397
www.catholichigh.org
Founded in 1894 by the Brothers of the Sacred Heart, Catholic High School continues as an independent, Catholic, all-male college preparatory high school accredited by the Southern Association of Colleges and Schools. Academic studies follow a traditional curriculum honors program, which includes a minimum of at least 12 honors courses with a cumulative grade-point average of 3.5. Electives range from fine arts and foreign language to business and computer education. Athletics include a broad range of sports from football to golf.

CATHOLIC SCHOOLS DIOCESE OF BATON ROUGE
1800 South Acadian Thruway
(225) 336-8735
www.diobr.org/schools-all
With south Louisiana's strong ties to the Catholic Church, it's understandable that East Baton

Close-up

LIGO Opens Windows onto the Cosmos

Scientists and researchers at Baton Rouge universities create an enriching environment that attracts the curious and inventive to work and study in the city. Fortunately sometimes residents and visitors get to see some of their projects. A major project conducting research beneficial to the fields of astronomy and physics is the Laser Interferometer Gravitational-Wave Observatory, known as LIGO. Nestled in the forests north of Livingston, just east of Baton Rouge, LIGO exists for the purpose of measuring cosmic gravitational waves for scientific research. Studies here may throw open an entirely new window onto the universe.

Though it is operated by Cal Tech, LIGO is funded by the National Science Foundation. It sits on land leased from Louisiana State University. Joseph Giaime, LSU professor, is director of the observatory. The program has multiple ties with LSU, Southern University, and Tulane University in New Orleans. A number of graduate students work at LIGO as part of their doctoral projects.

LIGO's Science Education Center (SEC) gives people a chance to better understand the facility's function. They participate in hands-on experiments, made up of items used in everyday life. About 5,000 students and 3,600 teachers visit LIGO each year.

William Katzman, SEC program leader, said LIGO invites visitors to Science Saturday, held the third Saturday of each month from 1 to 5 p.m. The program is far different from activities offered at many tourist attractions. It opens windows into the universe—both fun and educational. A big chunk of the learning is done hands-on in the Exhibit Hall.

"We have over 40 different exhibits," said Katzman. Kids and adults are urged to "play" with exhibits dealing with areas of physics including: light, waves, interference, gravity, resonance, oscillations, feedback, and astronomy. "On Science Saturdays we sometimes make liquid nitrogen ice cream," said Katzman. "We show you how to enjoy science while waiting for dinner. We have a giant Slinky and cameras that allow you to see an experiment with the infrared light you give off."

There's even a model-sized interferometer to help people better understand how LIGO works. One element along the center's front exterior is a series of 122 inline aluminum pendulums that represent a sine wave when in motion.

Rouge Parish has a large number of Catholic schools. Roman Catholic schools in the Diocese of Baton Rouge promote religious education programs for students, parents, and faculty. Programs include a department of special education and a department of child nutrition. All of the schools are accredited by the State of Louisiana. Privately owned schools include Sacred Heart Academy and Catholic High. Contact Baton Rouge Catholic Schools, Catholic Life Center, P.O. Box 2028, Baton Rouge LA 70821.

DUNHAM SCHOOL
11111 Roy Emerson Dr.
(225) 767-7097
www.dunhamschool.org
An independent, interdenominational Christian school, Dunham School has about 700 students and offers rigorous academic instruction in the framework of Christian education. Programs include chapel, some Bible studies, a variety of sports, and fine arts.

LIGO measures gravitational waves using two 4-kilometer (2-mile) long tubes in the shape of an L. The tubes are fitted with a series of mirrors that sense gravitational waves. A single laser beam is shot and split into the two tubes of the L. As the beams are shot back and forth, the distance between where they cross is measured. This helps sense and measure the presence of gravitational waves. If no passing gravitational waves are affecting the beams, they will hit one another. If they are being affected by gravitational waves, they won't touch.

Gravitational waves are ripples in the fabric of space and time produced by violent events in the distant universe, such as the collision of two black holes or shock waves from the cores of supernova explosions. Gravitational waves are emitted by accelerating masses, much as electromagnetic waves are produced by accelerating charges. These ripples in space-time fabric travel toward Earth bringing with them information about their cataclysmic origins, as well as invaluable clues as to the nature of gravity.

Albert Einstein predicted the existence of these gravitational waves, which change the shape of space-time, in his 1916 general theory of relativity. Only now in the 21st century has technology advanced to enable their detection and study by science.

"Sometimes we take people on a tour of the control room where the interferometer is operated remotely," said Katzman. "Also at times we take people to the top of a hill where they can see the arms of the instrument."

LIGO has a sister observatory located 2,000 miles away in Hanford, Washington. The two widely separated installations operate in unison as a single observatory. These two sites were selected from 19 that were proposed across 17 states. The observatory is available for use by the world scientific community and is a vital member in a developing global network of gravitational wave observance.

Before making a visit, Katzman recommends you check the LIGO Web site, http://ligo-la .caltech.edu/sec/sechome.html, or call (225) 686-3100.

i All four public school systems in East Baton Rouge Parish offer free bus service. Also many private school students receive free bus service. For student transportation information, call East Baton Rouge (225-226-3784); Baker (225-620-1521); Central (225-262-5495); or Zachary (225-654-9994).

Gables offers small class sizes in grades 1 through 12. The academy provides specialty work with students not functioning in mainstream school environments, including dyslexic students. Activities include baseball, basketball, and cheer squad. This well-established school provides tutorial assistance as needed and makes learning a positive experience.

GABLES ACADEMY
1533 Jefferson Hwy
(225) 752-9231
www.gablesacademy.com

ST. JOSEPH'S ACADEMY
3015 Broussard St.
(225) 333-7207
www.sjabr.org

St. Joseph's Academy is an all-girls privately owned Catholic high school founded by the Sisters of St. Joseph of Medaille. The academy is a college preparatory school, and its curriculum is built on traditional academic studies and a technology immersion program. The school has been recognized three times as a Blue Ribbon School of Excellence by the U.S. Department of Education. In 2002 the Academy was recognized as a school of technology excellence by the U.S. Department of Education. The school offers a wide range of athletics. The sports teams, known as the Red Stickers, have been very successful in volleyball, swimming, and cross-country. Current leadership is Sister Adele Lambert, CSJ, president, and Linda Harvison, the first lay principal in the history of the academy.

EPISCOPAL SYSTEM

Baton Rouge has multiple elementary Episcopal Church day schools, many of which feed into Episcopal High School. They include: St. James, www.stjameseds.org; Trinity Episcopal, www.trinitybr.org; and St. Luke's Episcopal, www.lukesbr.org.

EPISCOPAL HIGH SCHOOL
3200 Woodland Ridge Blvd.
(225) 753-3180
www.ehsbr.org
Operated by the Diocese of the Episcopal Church of Louisiana, Episcopal High School of Baton Rouge is one of the leading independent schools in Baton Rouge with a student–teacher ratio of 11 to 1. Established as a challenging college preparatory school, it serves students in grades pre-K through 12. Episcopal works within the framework of a fully accredited college entrance curriculum. The primary goal is to develop honest, intellectually curious, and academically disciplined students. French and English instruction starts in pre-K. Advanced placement and honors courses are included.

PARKVIEW BAPTIST
5750 Parkview Church Rd.
(225) 291-2500
www.parkviewbaptist.com
Parkview Baptist offers a Christian education in grades K through 12, with more than 1,000 students. Students have an average of 24 on the ACT test, above the national average of 21.1. Some honors and advanced placement courses are offered. Students participate in a variety of sports, the arts, and community projects. The elementary school hosts the ACSI District Spelling Bee, Math Olympics, and National Geographic Geography Bee.

REDEMPTORIST HIGH SCHOOL
4000 St. Gerard Ave.
(225) 357-4555
www.rhsbr.org
Redemptorist, a private co-ed high school, is a Diocesan regional high school designed to meet students' needs in academic excellence, spiritual growth, and moral development. It offers a comprehensive traditional curriculum. The school is widely known for an exceptional football team through the years. The faculty includes laymen and laywomen, one priest, and one Redemptioner Brother.

RUNNELS
16255 South Harrells Ferry Rd.
(225) 751-2193
www.runnels.org
Runnels, founded in 1965, is one of the oldest independent schools in Baton Rouge. It offers classes in grades pre-K through 12. Courses at every grade level are designed to stimulate and challenge. The core curriculum includes traditional classes, while electives include drama, art, photography, computer, psychology, human geography, environmental science, foreign languages, string orchestra, chorus, harp, and band. High school students choose from more than 70 credit courses, including the most Advanced Placement courses in town. Students and faculty participate over the Internet in Louisiana Vir-

tual School, expanding the number of for-credit courses offered to Runnels students. The preschool campus is located at 6455 Jefferson Hwy.

VICTORY ACADEMY
3953 North Flannery Rd.
(225) 272-8339
www.victoryacademybr.org
Victory Academy offers a Christ-centered education with fewer than 400 students in grades pre-K through 8. Traditional classes are taught along with Bible courses. Sports activities include basketball, volleyball, football, and cheerleading. The school is affiliated with Victory Harvest Church.

UNIVERSITY LAB SCHOOLS

LSU LAB SCHOOL
45 Dalrymple Dr.
(225) 578-3221
www.uhigh.lsu.edu
Louisiana State University Lab School on the LSU campus is within the LSU College of Education. It offers classes in grades K through 12. The high school is the first International Baccalaureate Diploma Program school in Louisiana. All instructors have master's degrees or a doctorate. It is recognized as a School of Academic Distinction.

SOUTHERN LAB SCHOOL
129 Swan St.
(225) 771-3490
www.sulab.subr.edu
Southern University Lab School on the university campus is operated within the College of Education and offers classes in pre-K through 12th grade. The high school offers some honors classes.

STATE SCHOOLS IN BATON ROUGE

LOUISIANA SCHOOL FOR THE DEAF
2888 Brightside
(225) 769-8160
www.lalsd.org

LOUISIANA SCHOOL FOR THE VISUALLY IMPAIRED
2888 Brightside
(225) 757-3482
www.lsvi.org
Both of these schools are now on the same campus, a primarily residential site with some day students. They provide services for students ages 3 through 21. The School for the Deaf teaches sign language and lip reading. Teachers and staff are fluent in sign language. Braille is a major component of the instruction at the School for the Visually Impaired. Students are familiarized with computer aids such as Window-Eyes.

CHILD CARE CENTERS

Many early education and child care centers in Baton Rouge offer field trips, meals, and activities that are both fun and educational. They include centers offered by church-affiliated schools, independent centers, schools associated with public education, and nationally recognized brand-name franchises. I strongly encourage parents to personally inspect the child care schools and centers in which they are interested, visit the schools, and interview the personnel. The schools can be found in every region of East Baton Rouge Parish. The listing here provides a sampling of your choices. You can consult the Yellow Pages for a complete listing of day care centers in the city. You also can research all the possible licensed day care centers at www.dss.state.la.us. Scroll down to the left and click on DSS for business, then click on East Baton Rouge Parish.

ALFRED G. RAYNER LEARNING CENTER
9111 Jefferson Hwy.
(225) 924-6772
www.bethshalomsynagogue.org
This school, located in Beth Shalom synagogue, has an open-admission policy, and is regarded as one of the top preschools in Baton Rouge. The school takes children from three months to six years old and follows an active Montessori-style training. Hours are 7:30 a.m. to 6 p.m.

BATON ROUGE LUTHERAN SCHOOL
10925 Florida Blvd.
(225) 275-9517
www.brlutheranschool.org
Baton Rouge Lutheran School has day care for infants to age two. Hours are 7 a.m. to 6 p.m. No mother's day out program. Mandatory interview with parents and students.

BETHANY CHRISTIAN SCHOOL
13855 Plank Rd.
(225) 774-0133
www.bethanychristianschool.com
No children are accepted younger than three. Pre-K ages three to four. No mother's day out program. Hours are 7:30 a.m. to 6 p.m., full day, and 8 to 11:45 a.m., half day.

BROADMOOR PRESBYTERIAN SCHOOL
9340 Florida Blvd.
(225) 926-3421
www.broadmoorpresbyterian.org
Broadmoor Presbyterian has a mother's day out program and takes ages six months to three years old. Hours are from 9 a.m. to 2 p.m. or 8:30 a.m. to 3 p.m. Hours for the pre-K program for ages three to five are 9 a.m. to noon with extended lunch or an extended day, 8:30 a.m. to 3 p.m.

BROADMOOR UNITED METHODIST CHILDREN'S LEARNING CENTER
102 Molly Lea Drive
(225) 926-5243
http://broadmoor-umc.org
Broadmoor Methodist Learning Center takes children ages four months to four years. Hours for ages four months to two years are 8 a.m. to 4 p.m. For ages three to four, hours are extended to 3:45 p.m. No mother's day out program.

COUNTRY DAY SCHOOL OF BATON ROUGE
4455 North Blvd.
(225) 928-4042

3743 Silverside
(225) 767-5259

7424 Highland Rd.
(225) 766-1159
www.countrydayschoolbr.com
The North Boulevard school is the largest of three Country Day Schools in Baton Rouge. The school houses an infant care, preschool, and elementary program. On Silverside Drive the school has an early childhood program for infant through pre-kindergarten. The Highland location also has an early childhood program. Preschools are open 7:30 a.m. to 5:30 p.m., Monday through Friday.

EARLY LEARNING CENTER
930 North Blvd.
(225) 387-4229
www.firstmethodist.org
Regarded as one of the top preschools in Baton Rouge, the center takes children three months through kindergarten. A standard curriculum is offered, and hours are 7:30 a.m. to 5:30 p.m. No mother's day out.

ÉLAN VITAL MONTESSORI SCHOOL
522 Perkins Rd.
(225) 767-6620
www.elanvitalmontessori.org
This school offers half-day classes, 8:30 a.m. to 11 a.m., and full-day 8:30 a.m. to 3 p.m. Early childhood primary is three to six years. Elementary school is offered for grades 1 to 3. Children must be potty trained.

KINDER CARE LEARNING CENTERS
4435 Floynell Dr.
(225) 293-6599

11349 Greenwell Springs Rd.
(225) 273-0932

7315 South Picardy Ave.
(225) 769-0805

1188 O'Neal Lane
(225) 272-4210
www.kindercare.com

LA PRINTANIERE MONTESSORI SCHOOL
5064 Perkins Rd.
(225) 769-2255
www.laprintaniere.com
Children accepted starting with age three (must be potty trained). Classes run through grade 5. Half-day hours are 8:30 to 11 a.m. Full-day hours are 8:30 a.m. to 2:30 p.m.

LSU CHILD DEVELOPMENT LABORATORY PRESCHOOLS
107 Tower Drive, LSU
(225) 578-1707
www.preschool.huec.lsu.edu

This school operates within the LSU School of Human Ecology. It is a half-day program for three- and four-year-olds from 8 a.m. to noon. Teachers follow a play-based curriculum and present an in-depth investigation in topics of interest to children. The school will work out afternoons with other day care programs.

PARKVIEW BAPTIST PRESCHOOL
5750 Parkview Church Rd.
(225) 293-9447
www.parkviewpreschool.com

Children accepted from six weeks to pre-K. Programs and training designed for specific age groups. Hours are 7 a.m. to 6 pm. A half-day program for ages three to five is 9 a.m. to 1 p.m. with naps. No mother's day out.

UNIVERSITY BAPTIST CHILD DEVELOPMENT CENTER
5775 Highland Rd.
(225) 766-9524
www.ubc-br.org
The center accepts children six weeks to age three, Monday through Friday. Arrangements can be made for a Monday-Wednesday-Friday or Tuesday-Thursday program.

UNIVERSITY METHODIST PRESCHOOL OF EXCELLENCE
350 Dalrymple Drive
(225) 344-0345
www.universitymethodist.org
The school accepts children from three months up to age six for a transitional kindergarten. Hours are 7:15 a.m. to 5:30 p.m. Also available is a half-day program up to 12:30 p.m. Training is creative and developmentally appropriate for age groups.

HEALTH CARE AND WELLNESS

The quality of life in the Baton Rouge area is enhanced by excellent health care. The region is recognized as a primary care center in the Gulf South.

Baton Rouge area health centers have rapidly expanded in response to a permanent increase in population following Hurricane Katrina. In the midst of disaster, Baton Rouge hospitals proved adept in emergency response and reliability. The number of surgical and specialty hospitals has grown, and the range of options and quality of care have continued to increase. The care people receive is enhanced by the presence of three major cancer centers and an affiliate clinic of Memphis's St. Jude Children's Research Hospital. The St. Jude cancer clinic, located within Our Lady of the Lake Regional Medical Center, is one of only four St. Jude affiliate programs in the country. Baton Rouge also is home to Pennington Biomedical Research Center, world famous for its research. The growth in research and medical technology in Baton Rouge has not only created continued better care for residents but opportunities for advanced study in related fields.

This chapter highlights full-service acute-care hospitals, as well as a number of specialized hospitals and multipractice clinics. Many of the health care practitioners listed in this chapter accept major health insurance, but you should always confirm the method of payment prior to your visit. Due to space limitations it's necessary to be brief. Note that *Insider's Guides* does not endorse any of the insurers or health care practitioners listed here or the care they may or may not provide.

HOSPITALS

BATON ROUGE GENERAL/BLUEBONNET
8585 Picardy Ave.
(225) 763-4000
www.brgeneral.org
The two Baton Rouge General hospitals are community-owned, full-service hospitals. The General is the only hospital in the region with a burn unit, offering services for pediatric and adult burn patients. The hospital's special units include the Pennington Cancer Center and the Womack Heart Center. In 2007 the hospital received the Premier Quality Award for heart bypass surgery in the United States. Both hospitals have 24-hour emergency rooms.

BATON ROUGE GENERAL MEDICAL CENTER/ MID CITY
3600 Florida Blvd.
(225) 387-7000

LANE REGIONAL MEDICAL CENTER
6300 Main St., Zachary
(225) 658-4000
www.lanermc.org
This is a 137-bed primary care facility providing a full range of inpatient and outpatient services, including cardiology, rehab, and home-health services. The hospital has 24-hour emergency care.

LSU EARL K. LONG MEDICAL CENTER
5825 Airline Hwy.
(225) 358-1000
www.lsuhospitals.org
This state-run acute care medical facility serves residents in East Baton Rouge Parish and seven surrounding parishes, and it operates a 24-hour emergency room.

OCHSNER MEDICAL CENTER BATON ROUGE
17000 Medical Center Dr.
(225) 752-2470
www.ochsner.org/br

Ochsner is a 200-bed hospital offering a comprehensive array of inpatient and outpatient services, including cardiopulmonary, oncology, radiology and imaging, surgery, and 24-hour emergency care. It also has five local health centers.

OUR LADY OF THE LAKE REGIONAL MEDICAL CENTER
5000 Hennessy Blvd.
(225) 765-6565
www.ololrmc.com
Our Lady of the Lake, operated by the Franciscan Missionaries of Our Lady, provides services in more than 60 medical specialties including pediatrics, cardiology, oncology, and surgery. The newest clinics include the Lake Allergy and Immunology Clinic and the Lake Pediatric Gastroenterology Clinic, the only one of its type in Baton Rouge. The hospital operates a 24-hour emergency room.

i In spring of 2009 an East Baton Rouge Parish Emergency Medical Service team took to the streets with a computer that transmits images from a remote scene to a central scene at Our Lady of the Lake Regional Medical Center's emergency room. Using the images along with diagnostic data allows doctors to examine a patient virtually and to direct treatment to EMS specialists in the field. Baton Rouge is one of the first areas to initiate the EMS program on a citywide basis.

SUMMIT HOSPITAL
17000 Medical Center Dr.
(2225) 752-2470
www.ahssummithospital.com
Located in the eastern region of Baton Rouge just off I-12, Summit Hospital is affiliated with Ardent Health Services based in Nashville, Tennessee. The hospital maintains some 200 beds with a staff of more than 200 physicians. The hospital offers acute care services in all areas, including cardiopulmonary and oncology. The Heartburn Treatment Center of Louisiana is within the hospital complex. Same-day surgery and 24-hour emergency care are also among the services offered.

Walking for Health and Wellness

A new Medieval-style labyrinth can be found in BREC's City Brooks Community Park. It's located behind Baton Rouge Gallery at Perkins Road and Dalrymple Drive. Made with St. Joe brick and surrounded by palm trees, the labyrinth features a design inscribed in a stone slab in a church in Genainville, France, thought to date from the 14th century. It is the same walking pattern as a more familiar labyrinth found in the cathedral in Chartres, France, but it is octagonal and has four bastions. A labyrinth is intended to be a reflective experience. The walker follows the path to the center, turns around, and walks out. There is no right or wrong way to walk it. It is said to promote relaxation. It can be used as a tool for finding creative solutions, processing grief, and problem solving. The labyrinth in City Park was created as a cooperative effort between BREC and the Baton Rouge Labyrinth Project, a volunteer community effort.

WOMAN'S HOSPITAL
9050 Airline Hwy.
(225) 927-1300
www.womans.org
This is a women's specialty hospital that includes pediatric clinics, physical therapy, occupational therapy, and educational classes. Woman's Hospital is the only hospital in Louisiana to be named by *Modern Healthcare* magazine as one of the 100 Best Places to Work in Healthcare, as well as the only hospital in Baton Rouge to achieve Magnet status.

Specialty Hospitals

MARY BIRD PERKINS CANCER CENTER
4950 Essen Lane
(225) 767-0847
www.marybird.org
Mary Bird Perkins provides state-of-the-art cancer treatment to 18 parishes in southeast Louisiana. In the capital region the facility partners with Our Lady of the Lake Regional Medical Center and St. Elizabeth Hospital in Gonzales.

NEUROMEDICAL CENTER
101 Park Rowe
(225) 769-2200
www.theneuromedicalcenter.com
This physician-owned center handles cases dealing with the brain, spine, and nervous system. Twenty-five physicians are specialists in neurosurgery, neurology, neuropsychology, and neuroradiology. The center received the COLA 2009 Laboratory Excellence Award.

SURGICAL SPECIALTY CENTER
8080 Bluebonnet Blvd.
(225) 408-8080
www.sscbr.com
This specialized facility owned by physicians focuses on advanced technology and innovative procedures. Specialties include ear, nose, and throat; orthopaedics; pediatrics; podiatry; spine; and urology. The facility's design, management, and staffing are committed to patient care.

> **i** South Louisiana enjoys a long growing season. As a result groceries and produce markets offer an array of fresh produce. People especially enjoy strawberries, satsuma oranges, and Creole tomatoes when in season.

HOSPICES

In the Middle Ages, hospices were way stations (often along pilgrimage routes) for travelers, the sick, and the dying. They provided care, comfort, and solace during the journey. Today hospices strive to bring the same kind of comfort to those who are dying and their families. The first hospice in the United States was established in 1973. The concept has evolved into several types of programs including home care, separate facilities, and hospital-affiliated services. Baton Rouge is fortunate to have a number of outstanding hospices. Most hospices in the region are privately operated. When choosing a hospice, be sure to consult with your doctor to see which local hospices he or she recommends.

CANON
5700 Florida Blvd., Suite 301
(225) 926-1404
www.canon.com
Canon receives referrals from physicians, social workers, case managers, and family. Services include inpatient, home-based, and residential care. Visits by a registered nurse are available 24 hours. Patients can have visitors any time, including children and pets.

HOSPICE OF BATON ROUGE
9063 Siegen Lane
(225) 767-4673
www.hospicebr.org
In 1984 several local doctors and businessmen laid the groundwork for what is today the Hospice Foundation of Baton Rouge. Original funding came from Our Lady of the Lake Hospital and the Baton Rouge General. In 1991 Hospice of Baton Rouge became a capital-area United Way agency. It provides all the many services in providing care and spiritual support for the terminally ill and their families. Hospice can be provided in the home or any homelike setting such as a nursing home or an assisted living facility. In 2005 the hospice opened the first inpatient unit in the Baton Rouge area.

HOSPICE CARE OF LOUISIANA
8280 YMCA Plaza Dr., Bldg. 3, Suite B
(225) 768-0866
www.hospicecarela.com
This hospice provides teams of specialists in pain and symptom management, a professional

medical staff, registered nurses, and a chaplain. Team members call as often as needed to ensure a caring quality of life.

ST. JOSEPH HOSPICE
8923 Bluebonnet Blvd.
(225) 769-4810
www.st.josephhospice.com
This nonprofit hospice provides services including licensed practical nurses, social workers, and chaplains. Volunteers assist families in running errands. Profits are used to conduct educational programs and to provide care for nonfunded patients.

i The Pennington Biomedical Research Center, 6400 Perkins Rd., (225) 763-3000, is an internationally recognized research center. Established by C. B. "Doc" Pennington and his wife, Irene, in 1980, the center conducts research in many areas, including diabetes and dementia. Opened in 1988, the center houses 53 laboratories that span three programs: basic research, clinical research, and population science. It includes 19 laboratories, inpatient and outpatient clinics, a research kitchen, an administrative area, and more than $20 million in technologically advanced equipment. More than 80 faculty and over 600 physicians, scientists, and personnel focus research on 10 areas, including diabetes, obesity, epidemiology, cancer, health, dementia, and stem cell and developmental biology. Visit www.pbrc.edu.

MENTAL HEALTH AND SPECIALTY CARE

CAPITAL AREA HUMAN SERVICES DISTRICT CHILD BEHAVIORAL HEALTH SERVICES
4615 Government St. Building 1
(225) 922-0445
This public agency provides intensive individual and group child interventions that involve teams of social workers, psychologists, and psychiatrists. Fees are on a sliding scale.

CENTER FOR ADULT BEHAVIORAL HEALTH
4615 Government St. Building 2
(225) 925-1906
This public agency provides group interventions for adults involving teams of social workers, psychologists, and psychiatrists. Some individual interventions are provided. Fees are on a sliding scale.

GREATER BATON ROUGE COMMUNITY CLINIC
(225) 769-3377
P.O. Box 65373, Baton Rouge 70896
www.gbrcc.org
This community clinic provides dental, mental-health, and vision-care services to qualified uninsured, low-income working adults. Patients are assigned to nearly 500 participating providers and are seen in their private offices. Call for a screening site.

MARGARET DUMAS MENTAL HEALTH CENTER
3843 Harding Blvd.
(225) 359-9315
This community clinic treats adults residing in the North Baton Rouge area above Florida Blvd. Group and individual interventions are available. Fees are on a sliding scale.

TAU CENTER AT OUR LADY OF THE LAKE REGIONAL MEDICAL CENTER
8080 Margaret Ann Ave.
(225) 765-6005
The center offers psychiatric care, Tau Program for Chemical Dependency, and inpatient, outpatient, and day patient care.

WOODDALE MENTAL HEALTH
1335-B Wooddale Blvd.
(225) 928-4969
This clinic specializes in services for children, adults, and elders. Services include partial day program, inpatient screening, emergency, and crisis. Transportation is provided for some services. The clinic accepts Medicare, private insurance, and private pay.

RESOURCES

CATHOLIC CHARITIES CRISIS RESPITE COUNSELING
1900 South Acadian Thruway
(225) 336-8770
www.ccdiobr.org
This unit of Catholic Charities provides low-cost crisis counseling to individuals and families by licensed social workers.

EAST BATON ROUGE PUBLIC HEALTH UNIT
353 North Twelfth St.
(225) 242-4862
This agency is run by the state of Louisiana and provides immunizations and other services. Call for assistance.

FIND A DOCTOR

Usually the most valuable advice you can have for finding a new doctor is the recommendation of people you can trust. However that's not always possible when relocating to a new community. There are a few things you can do. First check with your health plan; some restrict you to certain doctors and some have tools for locating doctors within their network. A good source is "DoctorFinder" on the American Medical Association Web site: www.ama-assn.org. It contains basic professional information on virtually every licensed physician in the United States.

LOUISIANA DEPARTMENT OF HEALTH AND HOSPITALS
www.dhh.state.la.us
This Web site is packed with a tremendous amount of health information, including information on services such as adult day care, nursing home inspections, child care facilities, and hospitals. The site is easy to read and follow.

LOUISIANA FEDERATION OF FAMILIES FOR CHILDREN'S MENTAL HEALTH
5627 Superior Dr., Suite A-2
(225) 293-3510
www.laffcmh.com
This federation works with the Center for Mental Health Services, which awards grants to statewide, family-run networks to provide support and information to families of children and adolescents with serious emotional, behavioral, or mental disorders.

INDEX

THE INSIDER'S SOURCE

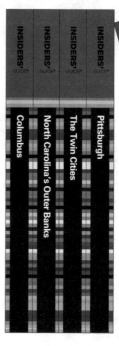